Uncommon Wisdom

Uncommon Wisdom

Fault Lines in the Foundations of Atheism

Ashish Dalela

SHABDA
PRESS

Uncommon Wisdom—Fault Lines in the Foundations of Atheism
by Ashish Dalela
www.ashishdalela.com

Copyright © 2015 by Ashish Dalela
All Rights Reserved
Cover Design: Kit Foster
Interior Design: Ciprian Begu

Published by Shabda Press
www.shabdapress.net
ISBN 978-93-85384-04-2

Dedicated to His Divine Grace A.C. Bhaktivedanta Swami Prabhupāda from whom I learnt that faith, reason, and experience were not contradictory—you learn through faith but you verify by reason and experience.

The conception of God and the conception of Absolute Truth are not on the same level. The Śrīmad-Bhāgavatam hits on the target of the Absolute Truth. The conception of God indicates the controller, whereas the conception of the Absolute Truth indicates the summum bonum or the ultimate source of all energies.

—A.C. Bhaktivedānta Swāmi

Contents

Preface

When I first thought of writing a book about the problems in atheism, I decided to seek out the most prominent (or at least the most vocal) atheists of our time and understand their arguments against religion. I had heard of the New Atheism movement championed by "The Four Horsemen of the Apocalypse" and I was interested in understanding what they had to say. So, I went online and bought books by Sam Harris, Christopher Hitches, Richard Dawkins, and Daniel Dennett to get a grip on New Atheism. As I read through some of their work, I began to discern several distinct patterns:

1. Their criticism of religion was primarily directed towards Christianity, Judaism, and Islam—the Abrahamic religions—with scant attention to Eastern religions. For instance, Christopher Hitchens devotes all of 10 pages in his 300 page book *God is Not Great* to discussing why "There is no 'Eastern' Solution." Here he devotes a few paragraphs to his prior encounter with Hinduism through "Osho", and the mix of sex, psychoanalysis, and quick-fix spirituality that he discovered. It seemed ironic to me that Hitchens thought this encounter represented Hinduism because most Hindus don't consider "Osho" as exemplifying their religion. Richard Dawkins similarly spends a few paragraphs in *The God Delusion* mocking the trinity of Hinduism after comparing it to the trinity in Christianity. Except for the word 'trinity', I could not find any similarity between the two. I found no discussions on the nature of matter, space, time, atomism and logic, and the intricate connections between these that exist in Hinduism. The level of attention to anything non-Christian was just underwhelming. I got the impression that the authors had not studied the different religions well

enough to qualify them to comment. Although Daniel Dennett acknowledges this shortcoming, it doesn't seem to prevent him from commenting anyway.

2. The critiques of religion were preoccupied with the politics, sociology, anthropology, and economics of religion, not with its philosophy. There is a great deal of attention devoted to the crimes of religion—wars, intolerance, suppression of various forms of sexuality, child abuse, and, lately, terrorism—but little attention to issues such as alternative forms of perception (even a discussion of the problems of normal perception would be welcome), the problems of religious symbolism (which are as problematic as any kind of symbolism), the role of concepts in a material world, and whether matter explains consciousness. Perhaps the author who came closest to discussing some of the philosophical issues that are crucial to understanding religion was Sam Harris in his book *Free Will*. And yet, his separation between consciousness and free will is so philosophically problematic that it would not survive a preliminary scrutiny.

3. There is absolutely no discussion on the biggest open problems in the 'hard' sciences—mathematics, physics, computing—and their implications for other areas of inquiry such as linguistics, psychology, and neuroscience. Perhaps the only area of science where the authors seemed well-versed in was the evolutionary theory of descent with modification, but even here the authors gloss over the well-known problems with the origin of life, preferring to speak only about life's evolution. The problems of atomic theory, the incompleteness of number systems and what they mean for the comprehension of meaning in machines, the problems of singularity in cosmology, all seemed to be completely overlooked. Overall, I concluded that the authors were scientifically blinkered. They give too much credence to the scientific triumphs and too little importance to the outstanding problems. As is well-known, in 1900, Lord Kelvin proclaimed the end of physics save for two

open problems—black-body radiation and the constant speed of light. We now know these problems led to quantum theory and general relativity whose puzzles are still unsolved. Underestimating serious problems, and the revisions they bring, only means that when these problems are eventually solved, history will not view you kindly.

4. There was no discussion on the philosophical issues in science. From philosophers such as Daniel Dennett I expected at least a robust analysis of the scientific method and its differences with the method in religion, culminating in why one method is superior. For instance, science is defined as the iteration of theory and experiment, but whether this iteration ever comes to an end is not known. This means that if you have a false theory you could not be sure if the theory is false because you may never encounter the contradicting phenomena. And if you have a true theory you could not be sure of its truth because you could not know for certain if contradicting phenomena would never be found. The greatest philosophers of science have acknowledged that science is an ongoing activity, always falsifiable and always tentative. Therefore, proclamations that science is in possession of a method that yields the truth is in complete contradiction to the best current understanding of the scientific method. There is an even more profound problem about scientific truth when we consider the existence of meanings. For instance, everything you read about in the newspaper or watch on TV is not necessarily true, even though it exists. Science infers existence into truth: because I can see something, it must be real and therefore true. Meanings draw a wedge here: things that exist may not be true. Empiricism is flawed in deriving truth from existence. And yet, if you claim that the religious method is inferior without examining the scientific method, you risk looking just too naïve.

To be fair, all these books are very entertaining. They are full of anecdotes, witty comments, and trifling insults, which, if we keep the seriousness of the issue aside, make for an interesting read. But, of course, the issue is rather serious, and it concerns not just the understanding of religion but also that of science and its open problems. My focus in this book is to examine both of these issues.

I would have totally ignored the New Atheism movement were it not for the evolutionary accounts on the origin of religion. They are so naïve in their premises that I became indignant upon reading them. These accounts view religion as arising from the need to find social acceptance, improve survivability, and instill collectiveness in its followers, not from the fundamental questions that begin the search of philosophical inquiry: Who am I? Why am I here? Where would I be in the future? What is death? What happens after death? Why should I fear death? Does it make sense to keep living? What is the purpose of my life? Is life in any way different from death?

There are two broad approaches to these questions. First, we can study the properties of the world surrounding us and suppose that the above questions would be answered by understanding these surroundings. Second, we might look inwards, and attempt to understand the nature of perception, thought, innate psychological tendencies and abilities, the question of happiness, etc. Whether or not either of these approaches leads us to the desired answers, it is indubitable that inquiry begins in existential questions not in pragmatic ones. In fact, even pragmatic answers are rooted in answers to existential problems. For instance, if an animal has to seek its survival, it must instinctively know that it is better to live than to die. If the animal did not care whether it lived or died, it would be pointless to crave for survival, reproduction, or social acceptance. To even attempt to survive, thus, you must have an innate sense that living is better than dying, although exactly why that is may be unclear. The philosopher attempts to ask these questions although animals may not. To treat religion as being, in essence, an attempt to delude oneself rather than to find some answers to important questions makes such a viewpoint devoid of insight about any religion.

The fundamental problems that spark any kind of inquiry stem from an existential crisis. The vast majority of the human population, however, does not care about either science or religion. The New Atheism movement seems to worry quite a bit about how most people don't care about science, but they laud those who don't care about religion. It may be worth asking: How many of those who don't care about religion do actually care about science? For that matter, how many of the people who don't care about religion even understand modern science and its problems? It seems to me that only those who understand science could care enough about it.

Unfortunately, the fact of modern times is that most people don't care enough about neither science nor religion, not because they don't know of their existence, but because there isn't an existential crisis in their lives of a large enough magnitude for them to start asking the big questions. That the Earth is round and it goes about the sun, that the universe was created by a big-bang, that life evolved through natural selection, is irrelevant to their day-to-day concerns of subsistence. Similarly, whether there is a soul or God, whether we have free will or not, how we perceive the world, are there alternate forms of perception, what is life and death, is there a purpose in life, etc., are questions that don't bother the dominant majority of people today. Even most scientists do not ask these big questions. We might have supposed that the scientists are all seeking truth, but they are not. Most scientists view science as yet another profession that provides subsistence, name, and glory.

On the other hand, there are equally many people who are neither practicing scientists nor religionists who are interested in the big questions about our origin. Clearly, their questioning is not motivated from an ideological commitment to any creed. Their questioning rather stems from existential issues about our identity, and our place in the world. To even ask such questions, one must have an existential crisis concerning one's identity and place in the world. Only the people who face this crisis even ask such questions. For the vast majority, these questions are immaterial because they seem to already have answers to them, although not well-reasoned.

Before we try to answer these questions, therefore, it is worth examining the questions themselves. Does a stone have an existential crisis? If not, why do we have such a crisis? Why are we seeking answers to our origin—regardless of whether the answers are material or divine? Why does it matter if we emerged from a big-bang or were created by God, if we will die in a few years and nothing would matter beyond that point? If the evolutionist truly believes that nature is evolving according to natural selection and there is nothing left beyond death, then why even worry about the question of origin? How does it matter how it began when you already know how it will end? What's the point of looking into the past if you already know the future? What is the origin of fear? Why do we seek to know the world around us? How did that innate need arise?

It is important to understand the questions before we try to answer them. For if we don't define the questions accurately, we won't know if we answered them. Modern materialism tries to answer the question of our origin, without addressing the issue whether that explanation can answer why we even asked that question. What kind of universe must there be to produce the kinds of objects which then begin to inquire about the origin of the universe? Unfortunately, materialism doesn't have any answers to these questions. I don't mean this lightly, in the sense of not knowing the details. The answers are not there even in an overarching sense.

Materialism is not a new idea. It can be traced to at least 600 B.C. in the writings of a philosopher named *Cārvāka* in India. In fact, theism and atheism have been studied side-by-side in Indian philosophy for a long time. Anyone who doubts this has only to pick up an introductory book on Indian philosophy[1]. So the way the contradiction between theism and atheism is treated as something novel in the Western world often surprises me. One of *Cārvāka's* verses aptly summarizes all the main conclusions of New Atheism.

There is no other world other than this;
There is no heaven and no hell;
The realm of Shiva and like regions
Are invented by stupid imposters.

Cārvāka, in fact, was so committed to materialism that he carried forward this idea into a clearer articulation of how one must lead their personal life. The following verse illustrates this well.

So long as you shall live, you shall live happily
You shall take out loans and drink clarified butter[2]

After all, once the body has been burnt,
Where is the question of coming back?

Cārvāka epitomizes the person without an existential crisis. He acknowledges the existence of matter as the only reality. As a consequence, he rejected even the use of reason (or inference) because there is no material evidence for logic or for concepts. There are only particulars in this world, and we cannot generalize them into universals. There is no need for a moral or truthful life, or for being good to others, because at the point of death, it would just not matter. *Cārvāka* did not make any serious attempts to convince others of his materialist position because trying to convince them would mean that he had a way of knowing what they believed in—which would imply that he and the others had a mind different from the body—which according to him is impossible. The world, according to him, exists only piece meal. There is no way to connect these things using concepts, logic, inference, or induction, since there is no reason to suppose any of these are true, given that only matter is real. There is hence no point in trying to formulate theories of nature, to understand the origin of the universe by generalizing particular experiences, or to form any moral theory of good and bad. *Cārvāka* exemplifies a complete and consistent materialism. If the New Atheism movement wanted to learn how atheism could be logically consistent and coherent, it would do well to study *Cārvāka*.

The problem, however, is that New Atheism is living in its own existential crisis. It could assert what *Cārvāka* earlier asserted, but that would be so out of place. Taking that position would not only deny the possibility of science, but also annul any legal or administrative system. It would convert an organized society into an anarchist dog-eat-dog world. Therefore, New Atheism advocates a new hodge-podge theory where we accept the reality of reason, logic, concepts, induction, and a host of other ideas such as space, time, continuity, causality, numbers, algebraic formulae, etc., which are all not material—at least not in the sense of tables and chairs—but denies other kinds of non-material things such as minds, souls, or God. I therefore call this view *Selective Non-Materialism* (SNM). No religious theory that I know of denies the existence of matter. The conflict between religion and science is only in the extent to which they accept the existence of certain types of non-material entities. Science too employs a wide array of non-material entities, which are used to formulate scientific theories. But New Atheism and most modern materialists deny the reality of anything beyond matter.

How convenient! Let's first decide if we are going to accept only material entities (in the sense of physical objects) or non-material entities as well. If we accept only matter, then science cannot exist, because numbers are needed to formulate science and numbers are not material things. If, however, we are going to accept some non-material things, but not others, then let's define the criteria for permitting some non-material versus other non-material. For instance, many areas of modern science depend on the notion of probabilities. Atomic objects are, for example, described as probabilities. But what is probability? Is probability an object? Then why can't we see these objects? If not, then in what form does it exist? If we formulate a scientific theory based on probabilities, then we must accept the existence of probability in some sense, even though we cannot call this existence a material object. What is that particular sense?

The problems of materialism are quite profound as they begin in the existence of concepts, numbers, logic, induction, and probability. Materialists are either ignorant of these problems or they deliberately mislead their audience into believing there is no problem. I have discussed these problems in my previous writing and will survey them in this book again for the sake of continuity. The central conclusion of that discussion is that we cannot define material objects without prior defining concepts, logic, numbers, induction, and probability. Therefore, if matter exists, and we are trying to describe these material objects by taking a conceptual world for granted, then we are victims of a serious oversight. We have committed to the pragmatic use of a non-material world to even understand the material world, but we deny all forms of non-matter. This clearly cannot be deemed logically consistent or scientifically coherent.

New Atheism wants to answer the questions arising from an existential crisis in a new way, but if the answers that New Atheism provides were indeed truly accepted by its vocal proponents, they should indicate the pointlessness of the existential crisis itself and hence of all the questions arising from that crisis. For instance, if you are truly a materialist, then why accept science, or even the goodness of organized society for material enjoyment under moral commitments? If you are truly a materialist then what is so sacrosanct about life? Why would killing, suffering, and pain be problematic? Isn't death another configuration of atoms, just like life? How can one atomic configuration be any better than another when both of these configurations are equally permitted by natural laws? What additional ideas are you trying to add or impute upon matter?

New Atheism adds a new idea to science, which is that order and structure automatically emerge in nature. This idea is drawn from Darwin's evolution, which is a theory that has never been analyzed from a physical, computational, and mathematical standpoint[3]. Its popularity, in fact, can be attributed to the fact that while other scientific theories need a lot of scientific training before their ideas are properly understood, this particular idea seems not to require any such expertise. So much has been written and presumed on the basis of this single idea that if it turned out to be false, I don't believe New Atheism would have any essential foundation. I have described the problems with Darwinism in my book *Signs of Life*—not by analyzing particular fossils, molecular mechanisms, or type of speciation—but simply by casting these ideas in a logical form similar to the problems of incompleteness in computing, physics, and mathematics. I will survey these issues again in this book, showing how the emergence theory rings completely hollow. If such an idea were true, mathematics would be consistent and complete, computing theory would be able to tell the difference between useful and malicious programs, and physics would have solved the problems of probability and indeterminism in atomic theory. What evolutionary theory supposes is thus an unattainable dream.

However, this book isn't about the intellectual poverty of New Atheism. It is rather about the origin of logic and concepts and how the material objects are constructed from concepts. I call this the *semantic view* of nature in which material objects are symbols of ideas, and the ideas precede things. Ideas exist as possibilities—which current science describes as probabilities—and they become real in time. There is also free will in observers and it appears as the possibility to explain the same phenomena in different ways—often called the underdetermination of theories by experiments. The existence of concepts and free will lead us to the question of consciousness, and, in the semantic view, there is need to distinguish between two kinds of consciousness—that which can experience one side of a distinction at one time and that which can experience the distinction itself. I will call these two types of consciousness as individual and supreme. The latter can also be called God, but it is a radically different notion of God than used in Abrahamic religions.

One of the central criticisms of New Atheists against religion is that its ideas and arguments are incoherent. I accept that criticism. They are indeed incoherent to the people who have adopted a worldview so different from the one that is commonsensically used in the everyday world that science has become the denial of commonsense. The commonsensical view, on the other hand, does not have a scientific foundation currently. The conflict between religion and science is an outcome of this departure from commonsense. For instance, the everyday idea that the world has color, taste, smell, and tone, has no place in science; all these perceptions are replaced by physical properties, although how the properties become perceptions is not known. Moving back to commonsense would require us to formulate a science in which the world could be described as taste, touch, smell, sound and sight. But that move requires many fundamental shifts that are impossible in current science. I will elaborate these shifts in the book, and how they are intimately connected to the questions of soul, God, and afterlife, in religion.

While I do not claim to clarify all possible ideas in various religions, I will try to clarify some fundamental ideas about soul, God, morality, matter, based on Vedic philosophy. It should be noted at the outset that these entail a different notion of matter, in contrast to the notions currently employed in science. I will therefore not talk about whether religion is compatible with science; we already know they are not compatible. I will rather talk about how science will change to explain religious ideas, although the revisions aren't motivated by the need to connect God and soul to science; they are necessitated by current scientific problems themselves. The conflict between science and religion, in other words, which New Atheism uses to decry religion, is also a problem of indeterminism, incompleteness and irreversibility in science and without the solution to these problems, science will itself remain incomplete.

The main thrust of this book is that the conflict between religion and science rests upon an incomplete picture of matter in modern science. This notion arises from the employment of SNM, which pragmatically uses logic, concepts, and mathematics, but denies that these have a real existence. Without a clearer understanding of how ideas interact with matter, scientific theories are themselves incomplete and the origin of the universe cannot be spoken of without the origin of ideas. The inability to understand the role of concepts in the material world leads to problems in understanding perception and conception in observers in scientific terms. Similarly, these problems also lie at the root of scientific incompleteness today. The interaction between ideas and matter requires a revision to the nature of matter itself, because without such a revision science would itself be incomplete. Once these revisions have occurred, however, the conflict between religion and science will also cease to exist. Of course, this may not entail the reinstatement of every religious idea that exists today. However, it would provide us with a clear mechanism to understand which religious notions are implied by the nature of reality and which ones are fictions.

The materialist dogma which stands at the foundations of atheism is an outcome of splitting the world of science into three different parts, and neglecting two of them: (1) the freedom to form different theories of nature rests on the possibility of free will, but free will has no role within science, (2) the use of concepts, mathematics, and logic is essential to any scientific enterprise, but these ideas are not regarded as being materially real, and (3) the world of objects which is described in science is considered the only reality. How would nature be if we acknowledged the freedom to form natural theories and the concepts used in such theories to be equally real alongside the material objects which are considered real? Such a viewpoint would not only alter the materialist dogma in unforeseen ways, but it will also change the manner in which the conflict between the materialist dogma and religion is presently seen.

1

A Definition of God

It can no longer be maintained that the properties of any one thing in the universe are independent of the existence or non-existence of everything else. It is, at last, no longer sensible to speak of a universe with only one thing in it.

—Lee Smolin

The Problem of Universals

All our knowledge must be expressed in language for it to be communicable. But what do the words of language represent? One fairly common and well-known belief is that the terms in language denote *concepts.* But what are these concepts? What is their nature? Where to they exist? Philosophers in the West have pondered these questions for millennia and there are two dominant and popular responses[4]. The *realist* claims that concepts exist in a world of ideas; Plato in Greek times was a notable proponent of this view, and the realist position therefore is also called Platonism. Of course, if concepts exist in another world of ideas, then how are they instantiated in this particular world? How does the Platonic world interact with this physical world? This problem has never been solved in philosophy, so a new school of thought called *idealism* suggested that concepts exist in our minds. This seemed to bring concepts from another world into the present world, but the position is not much better because it still raises the question of how minds interact with matter. Of course, we know that minds somehow perceive the world. While the process of perception may not be well-understood today, it seems compelling to

1

suppose that all ideas are in the mind.

And yet, for the idealist position to work, we have to explain the process of perception. If I see an apple, and call it something that is 'red,' 'round,' and 'sweet,' there must be a way by which I can classify the object into certain classes of things—such as 'red,' 'round,' and 'sweet.' For this classification to be possible, the objects themselves must be 'red,' 'round,' and 'sweet.' For otherwise, I could say that I perceive an apple but in reality there would be no apple. For my claim to be true, namely that there is an apple because I perceive something that is 'red,' 'round,' and 'sweet,' there must indeed be an apple that is correctly represented in my perception. The correctness of my knowledge requires that the world must itself be 'red,' 'round,' and 'sweet.' The concepts that originally existed in the Platonic world, and descended into the mind, must now also descend further into the world of objects, for knowledge to be true.

Philosophers have had a lot of problem with this conclusion because it seems to imply that the world of things is actually idea-like; that the world of things has taste, touch, smell, sound, and sight just the way we perceive it. The problem stems from the notion that if the world is idea-like then it would seem to have been *meant* or *designed* to be perceived by observers. It would also imply that we could not describe the world objectively, just as it would have existed prior to the presence of observers. For the world to be idea-like, the observers must have existed even prior to the existence of the world and must have dictated the properties of the world just so that they might eventually be able to perceive it. Obviously, if observers had to exist even prior to the existence of material objects, then they would have to be transcending matter. But, if we acknowledge this position, we would have to also accept that for matter to exist there must be a non-material mind prior. This mind would possess the ability to perceive taste, touch, and smell, and therefore it would create matter in just the way it can perceive it.

Clearly, if you happen to be a materialist, this is the last place you would want to go. You do not want to accept anything beyond matter, let alone a transcendent mind that existed prior to matter. So, philosophy tries to invert the process. Rather than start with a Platonic world of ideas, which then descend into the mind, which then descend into the world of things, we can as well begin in objects, then construct the mind, and then the world of ideas. This inverted process is called science; let's now explore how it works.

The Materialist Response

The inverted process asserts that there must be some objects in the world, which exist even when the observers don't. All these objects are independent of the observers and they are also independent of each other, and one object could exist even if the others did not. Nature, in this view, is unrelated to the observer and to other objects not just in the superficial sense of objects being logically prior, but in the more profound sense of lacking in all qualities that we perceive. For instance, we perceive the world in terms of color, taste, and smell. The inverted process, however, asserts that these properties are not real because color, taste, and smell, are features of our observation rather than those of matter. Matter is mass, momentum, energy, position, and time, which *somehow* become color, taste, and smell. How the physical world becomes our experiences is very hard to explain now, but scientists overlook that problem. Maybe it is a problem for the biologist; maybe qualities are just about the level of complexity in things; maybe someone else will solve it another day. Through such neglect, a profound problem of explaining how ideas—e.g., color, taste, and smell—arise from material objects is disregarded as not a serious issue, without adequate justification.

The greatest problem in modern science is the assumption with which it started. While philosophers were trying to understand perception, illusion, and how we can know the world, the materialist position began by denying the reality of all the problems that philosophers were trying to solve. Why the world has color, taste, and smell, why there are tables, chairs, and houses, is not important anymore. The materialist begins by saying that there is in fact nothing called color, taste, or smell in nature. That tables, chairs, and houses are not real. Instead, there is something in the human mind which perceives the world in terms of sensations and concepts. In other words, sensations and concepts are not properties of matter; they are rather properties of the mind. Since they cannot be applied back to the world, they are all illusions. But these illusions exist as properties of the mind, which is different from matter. Descartes formulated the now famous mind-body divide, separating the world of matter from the world of sensation and conception. These two were supposed to interact, but no one seemed to know how.

It is therefore noteworthy that when the materialist position was formulated, it rested upon the mind-body divide. It was not a completely satisfactory solution because all our perceptions were ultimately illusions. But it was still possible to say that the illusions existed. Over time, the mind-body distinction was dropped, and with that we also lost the ability to say that there is indeed a mind which thinks, perceives, and believes. Once the mind-body distinction is removed, there are two alternative paths: (1) explain the emergence of experience from matter, and (2) grant that experience is itself a delusion, not just in the sense that it doesn't give us knowledge, but in the sense that it simply doesn't exist. Of course, if you grant the latter position, then we must also give up attempts to do science: if we cannot experience and think, then how can we do science? The materialist carefully avoids this treacherous conclusion. And, so we set out on the path trying to explain the origin of concepts, sensations, beliefs, and intentions, based on matter.

Since matter is defined as independent objects, the attempts to construct a mental world from this physical world must fail for some very fundamental reasons which are inadequately understood today. The most profound reason is that concepts have three fundamental properties—*contextuality*, *intentionality*, and *abstraction*—which independent things do not. To produce a mental world from the physical world, the physical world must first explain how contextuality, intentionality, and abstraction can arise. However, if such an explanation were possible, its conclusions would contradict the premise about mutually independent objects. If such an explanation were possible, it would result in a logically inconsistent theory.

Contextuality, Intentionality, and Abstraction

Attempts at mind-body reduction don't seem to recognize the nature of the problem enough, before they carry out the reduction. The materialist claims that reports of conscious events are correlated with electrical activity in the brain, and, therefore, the mind must be the brain. Before we dive deeper into this issue, it is important first to describe what makes the mind different from objects, and why the mind's properties do not fit into current notions of matter.

Contextuality means that meanings can only be defined in relation to other meanings. For instance, whether the word 'address' denotes a noun or a verb depends on the context. Whether the color 'red' denotes passion, danger, or life, is contextual. Whether a frequency of sound denotes a high or low musical note depends on context. The value of a currency note—i.e., the currency's ability to exchange with useful things—depends upon a context. Whether the symbol 'I' denotes the English letter referring to the self or the first Roman numeral depends on the context. The meaning of the answer 'yes' depends on the question that was asked previous to the answer. And there are countless examples of similar contextuality.

Physical objects don't have contextual properties because each object is defined completely and independently by its own properties. Since a physical object's existence is independent of the other objects, addition or removal of such objects makes no difference. Contextual properties depend on the existence of other objects; hence, they cannot be described in terms of physical properties.

Philosophers of science—such as Quine—have recognized that even scientific concepts are meaningful only in relation to other concepts. For instance, the concept of mass cannot be defined independent of the concept of gravity. To measure mass, there must be a gravitational effect. And that gravitational effect cannot be defined unless mass has been defined prior. Similarly, a location in space is defined only through its metric distance from other locations. Even the physical properties of an object therefore cannot be defined unless other objects, their properties, and their effects have been defined. This problem has worsened in modern physics where objects cannot be said to *possess* physical properties because the outcome of measurements depend on the experimental setup; as the measurement is changed, different objects and properties are detected. The notion that there are real objects which exist independent of other objects is therefore physically and philosophically untenable. However, even if we grant that position, it would make such physical theories unable to describe the contextuality of concepts.

Intentionality means that some words can be used to refer to other things or words. Language's primary purpose is to describe the world of things, and language can refer not only to the world of things, but also to the other descriptions, or descriptions about descriptions about the world, and so forth. Languages call out or refer to other things and descriptions by the use of *names*. Each of us has names, physical objects are referred to by a combination tuple of numbers which represents the object's name, and when we perceive the world, we suppose that behind this perception is a reality. All these notions would be impossible without intentionality. A physical object describes its own properties, not those of other objects. My brain should therefore only be seen as physical properties of the brain and not the perception of the world. Then, why do we think that when I perceive something, there is indeed any real world 'outside' my brain? An object's properties are never a description of another object; they are simply the description of that particular object. Then, how can the brain—if it is just an object—refer to other objects? If we discard intentionality, we would also have to discard the idea of a real world discoverable through perception.

All physical measurements would now be properties of my brain rather than the properties of some external world being measured. This would also take away the ability to assert that a book on physics is a description of the nature of reality. We would have to say that the book and the world are just two distinct objects and therefore one object cannot refer to another. Newspapers would be physical things and by reading them we could not know about events elsewhere. The images on a TV screen would be properties of the TV and not descriptions of facts outside the TV.

The ability to represent knowledge of the world is an integral part of the world. There is an intentional connection between the reality and its representation. Reality and its representation are both material, but one material object points to another. By knowing the properties of the representation, we know the properties of its intended object. This is impossible in any theory of independent objects because no object—however complex—can ever describe another object. All properties of any object are always properties of that object and never a description of another object's properties. In the physical world, there can never be knowledge of the world, because knowledge requires one object to refer to another, whereas in a physical theory objects do not refer to other objects. All physical objects refer only to themselves, and they are thus things-in-themselves instead of things-about-other-things. Since intentionality is such a fundamental property of all concepts, a physical theory can never construct the conceptual world from the physical world.

Intentionality also plays a very important role in everyday notions of property ownership. Some currency notes are my money, some piece of land belongs to a country, some book is authored by a writer, some painting is painted by an artist and some composition is written by a musician. Even scientific theories are attributed to scientists. The painting and the painter are—in the physical view of nature—two distinct objects, and all such objects remain independent. Objects don't refer to other objects and hence if the world was physical then all manner of intentional relations won't exist.

Abstraction is another key property of concepts, owing to which we are able to organize concepts in a *hierarchy*. For instance, cars are instances of four-wheelers which are instances of vehicles. There is no physical notion by which we could say that one object is the *instance* of another object. After all, all physical objects are independent and we cannot posit any 'instance of' relationship between these objects. A direct consequence of this problem is that scientific theories must be otherworldly things because they are all abstract ideas underlying the present world. If the world of things is contingent properties—unique to each specific object—and scientific theories are entities that describe many such objects, then these theories cannot exist in this world. Scientists would need to accept the otherworldly existence of such theories to even do science. But if they are otherworldly, then how do we picture them in the mind? How do the otherworldly entities appear in our minds, especially since we now suppose that the mind is also a material object? How can my brain become the instance of an idea in another world?

The problem here is that when we begin in the idea of individual and independent objects, then we cannot speak about entities that span across multiple such objects, unless these properties are attributed to the *space-time* in which these objects are embedded. Only the space-time of objects is common across all the objects and if multiple objects had to have the same property, then these properties must also be space-time properties. For instance, we can speak about properties such as length, time, direction, energy, angular momentum, and momentum as being properties of physical objects, because they are properties of the object space-time[5]. Theories such as general relativity attribute the mass of an object to the curvature of space-time, making mass a property of the space-time. Similarly, it is imaginable that all physical properties are space-time properties (we would have to find such additional properties). Therefore, if some property has to exist in multiple objects, then it must be the property of the space-time that embeds these objects.

However, there are still two important problems to be addressed. First, how did the space-time with its innate structure appear? Defining material properties to be the properties of space-time solves the conceptual problem of how all objects can have these properties, but it doesn't address the problem of how the *values* of these properties are set to construct individual objects. While the theory of nature can be conceptually parsimonious by attributing all material properties to the space-time structure, the universe still needs an enormous amount of information to fix the values of these properties. Second, all these properties of space-time only make up a finite number of types, much smaller than the huge variety of concepts that exists in the everyday world. For instance, the everyday world comprises concepts such as yellow, red, and blue, which are abstractions of a concept called color, which is an abstraction of the concept called sight. Sight or seeing is elaborated into concepts of size, distance, form, besides color. Color, similarly, is elaborated into various color types, shades, and hues. While the physical properties are attributed to a *linear* space-time, the everyday concepts are *hierarchical*. If only the world of independent object is real, which exists in the linear space-time, then how could it construct the hierarchical world of everyday concepts? The materialist might claim that the everyday concepts would eventually be *reduced* to the physical concepts, but a reduction is complete only when it captures all the properties being reduced. In this case, the property to be reduced is abstraction or hierarchy. How can hierarchy be reduced to something that is essentially non-hierarchical?

The reducibility of everyday concepts to physical concepts amounts, in one particular case, to the reduction of vision to the physical properties. The problem now is that these physical properties are themselves defined in terms of perception or vision. If we could not perceive these properties, we could not say that these properties exist. In fact, science cannot be defined without the ability to empirically know the world. The materialist can argue that the properties are defined in relation to measuring instruments, but even these measuring instruments—such as meters and clocks—have to be seen before the properties can be perceived. The reduction of everyday concepts such as sight to physical properties creates a circular dependence between sight and the physical properties. Now, sight is defined in terms of physical properties and the physical properties are defined in terms of sight. This circular dependence was understood early in the history of empiricism and physical properties were defined as *objectifications* of perceptual properties. That is, the perceptual properties had to exist before the physical properties could even be defined. But this dependence implies that the observer's senses must exist even before the world of objects can exist because otherwise its physical properties can't even be defined. However, over time, this dependence of physical properties on perception has been dropped. The materialist claims that physical properties exist even when the observer doesn't. But that entails that the properties themselves cannot be defined. How can something exist when it cannot even be logically defined?

Perhaps the clearest illustration of this problem of abstraction is seen in the case of numbers, when numbers are defined as properties of sets. For instance, the number 5 can be defined as the property of a set with 5 objects. In this definition, we could say that objects are real and the number 5 is a property of object collections. The problem, however, is that if we define 5 as the property of a collection of 5 objects, then to even know that there are 5 (and not 6, 7, or 8) objects in the set, we must know how to count the objects. The number is therefore defined as the property of a set, but the set is itself defined only when the counting of numbers has been defined. This creates a circular dependence between numbers and objects[6].

Given this *problem of recursion*, there is no way to reduce everyday concepts to physical concepts, and we might be tempted to suppose that all everyday concepts are illusions. Of course, that would also imply that seeing is an illusion, which would then entail that the physical properties are also illusions, because they can never be observed. By rejecting the everyday concepts, we end up rejecting even physical concepts, defined using the everyday concepts. The materialist view that science will one day reduce the observer's perception to physical properties remains a pipe dream. While ever growing number of details about the working of the eye and the brain have been discovered, there is still no explanation of how these chemical processes become seeing, tasting, hearing, touching, or smelling. If the senses are produced from material objects, then there must have been a time when the living beings and their senses did not exist; only objects with their physical properties existed then. Since the senses did not exist, the physical properties could not have been defined because observations could not have been done. But, if the physical properties did not exist, then the world could not have existed either, since the world is defined as these properties. The fact that physical properties depend on the senses therefore precludes the existence of the material world, if the senses emerge from the combination of material parts. The materialist view states that material properties exist independent of the observation. However, *what* these properties are cannot be defined without observation. The premise that the world exists even when it cannot be observed, amounts to a metaphysical assumption. If this reasoning were extended, we might say that God exists even when no one can observe God. Clearly, that idea would be problematic.

Of course, the idea that nature exists even when no one observes it is not just problematic in regard to religious metaphysics. This assumption has also become increasingly problematic in modern physics[7] where the properties detected in an experiment depend on the experimental setup[8]. To avoid these problems, one might argue that the experimental setup is also physical, and therefore does not require the explicit presence of an observer. This argument is correct. However, remember that physical properties are supposed to exist not just independent of observers, but also independent of other objects. If an object's properties depend on the other object(s) then they cannot be said to exist in the sense that materialism supposes. It is now impossible to provide a description of a single independent object and all objects must be described only in relation to the other objects. This leads to another problem of recursion: each object is defined only in relation to the other object(s) and so no object can be defined independently. This latter problem of recursion is widely viewed as being classically unacceptable since it undermines the notion of independent objects.

The only resurrection out of this latter problem of objectivity is to go back to the original question of whether the observer's senses can be defined independently of the material objects it observes. If the senses could be defined as being logically prior to the objects, then the physical properties could be defined as objectifications of the sensations. Each object could now have objective properties but these properties would only be defined in relation to the senses and not in relation to the other objects. This doesn't necessarily imply that some sense must always observe an object for the object to have that property[9]. However, it does mean that *when* the object is observed, it must be described by the same properties as the senses can detect. For instance, the world must be described in terms of taste, touch, smell, sight, and sound. However, now we are back to the original issue about idealism: ideas have an origin in the capabilities of the observer to know the world, not in the generalizations created from a world that exists independent of the observer.

The senses of the observer, in this case, must be viewed as more abstract ideas which exist logically prior to the things they observe. For instance, if the world is yellow, red, or green, then the sense of seeing must be defined as something more abstract than these shades—it can, for instance, be defined as the idea of *color* which is more abstract than the individual shades of color. The idea of color is now the collection of various shades, although this whole is logically prior to its parts. If the parts are logically prior and the whole is defined as the part collection, then the problem of recursion between wholes and parts is simply unavoidable. However, if the whole is logically prior to the parts, then this problem of recursion does not exist. The whole, however, in the latter case, is not real in the same sense as its parts. Rather, the whole must be described using a more abstract concept than the concepts applied to the parts. For instance, if the parts were described as yellow, red, and green, then the whole must be color. Now, we have to define the whole as something that is conceptually different than the parts.

The circular dependence between parts and wholes has been encountered many times in mathematics and each time it leads to logical paradoxes. For instance, the Burali-Forti paradox[10] in number theory arises from a conflict between the cardinal and ordinal notion of numbers. Cardinal numbers are properties of collections or wholes and ordinal numbers are the properties of the individual objects within that whole. There is no consistent way to avoid this dependence if we begin the definition of concepts from objects. The natural outcome of these problems is that the fundamental properties of concepts—namely contextuality, intentionality, and abstraction—cannot be reduced to the physical world, if this world is defined as comprising independent objects. While the Platonic and idealist solutions to the problem of universals may seem problematic, the opposite solution of materialism is simply unworkable.

Problems in Platonism

The Platonic universals completely neglect all the above three properties of concepts. Since Platonic concepts exist in an eternal world of unchanging forms, there was no need for deriving concepts through elaboration. For instance, the concepts 'yellow' and 'color' are universals but 'yellow' is not derived or elaborated from 'color.' The Platonic world does not contain descriptions of anything, since this world exists independent of something that needs to be described. Concepts can refer to other concepts, but even that isn't true of the Platonic world. This means that the Platonic world has concepts but not propositions. If the Platonic world had propositions, then 'the sky is blue' and 'the sky is purple' would both be propositions and one of them would be false. The Platonic world cannot have false ideas, because it cannot have propositions. At the same time, it can have ideas like unicorn and mermaid, whose truth may be questionable. This inevitably means that the intentionality of concepts, by which concepts refer to other concepts, is simply ignored. Finally, the universals in the Platonic world exist independently of the other ideas. They exist simultaneously but their conceptual content is defined independent of the other ideas, not in relation to them. It follows that contextuality is not important.

Platonism also suffers from the problem of positing another world of pure ideas of which the present world is only an imperfect imitation. How the pure world of ideas descends into the present world is hugely problematic. Aristotle, who succeeded Plato, tried to solve this problem. His solution—called Hylomorphism—posited two kinds of entities—substance (*hyle*) and form (*morphe*). Aristotle claimed that the material world comprises both substances and forms. The substances are physical but formless, while the forms are ideas but abstract. The combination of the formless and the abstract produces objects. This idea has had a huge bearing on the subsequent development of science. For instance, modern science posits the existence of one amorphous substance—space-time—upon which various kinds of mathematical structures—forms such as homogeneity, isotropicity, and curvature—can be applied to create material objects and their properties. While space-time is real and physical, the forms (mathematical structures) are abstract and we don't speak about their existence in just the way we speak about space-time and objects. Nevertheless, these mathematical forms can be employed to describe the properties of the material world.

The problem in Aristotle's theory is that it inherits the problems of Platonism, since neither viewpoint incorporates abstraction, intentionality, and contextuality. Platonism describes the world of ideas just as classical physics describes the material world—as comprising mutually independent entities. The difference between the two worlds is only that Platonism describes the idea-world as having different *types* while classical physics describes the world only in terms of a single *type*. However, since the Platonic world does not have abstraction, intentionality, and contextuality, this difference doesn't really matter.

Classical physics reduces the type differences between Platonic ideas to the property differences between different objects. If all entities are mutually independent, then the type differences between ideas can be replaced by property differences with a single type. With this reduction, it seems imminent that both descriptions could be viewed equivalently.

Both Platonism and classical physics are, however, false. This falsity has become apparent through the subsequent development of physics, mathematics, and computing, as well as through a deeper understanding of the nature of language and scientific theories.

The properties of abstraction, intentionality, and contextuality appear in everyday language as the ability to use the same word to denote three distinct kinds of entities—*things, names,* and *concepts.* Intentionality appears in language when a word is used to call out or refer to another object or statement using a name. Contextuality appears in how the meaning of a word is given only in relation to other words in a language. And abstraction appears when words can be seen as denoting both abstract and contingent ideas, such as, for instance, the ideas of 'color' and 'yellow,' respectively. This ability to interpret a word as denoting things, names, and concepts creates many problems when languages are treated formally. How do we know when a word denotes a thing, a name, or a concept?

The unification of the idea-like Platonic world and the thing-like material world is already achieved in language because words in language are physical entities—they can be expressed as sound or written on paper—and yet they represent ideas. If we had to solve the problem of universals, therefore, we need look no farther than language and how it reconciles abstraction, intentionality, and contextuality in the material world. And yet, a profound understanding of language has been impaired by a physical treatment of objects. If objects are independent but words have intentionality, contextuality, and abstraction, then how can we correctly treat these words as material objects? Obviously, we cannot, unless our notions about matter were to be suitably revised to allow the same word—or thing—to be viewed as a name, concept, and object. This is then the central problem for a theory of matter: What is that notion about matter which can treat natural objects just like words?

A Brief Survey of Scientific Problems

Before I attempt to outline the theory that can solve this problem, it is helpful to understand how the central problem of language appears in current science. I have discussed this topic in detail in my earlier books. *Gödel's Mistake*, for instance, discusses the problem of language in the context of mathematics and computing, specifically number theory and program semantics. *Quantum Meaning* describes this problem of language in the context of atomic physics, and its struggles with trying to understand probabilities. *Signs of Life* discusses the problem of meaning in the context of biology and what it entails for the theory of evolution. *Moral Materialism* discusses this problem in the context of free will, providing a new notion of natural causality compatible with determinism. It is very difficult to recapitulate all of that content in this book, but for sake of the subsequent discussion it is important to summarize it.

In the following few paragraphs, I will attempt to provide an intuitively accessible, non-rigorous, but—I hope—a sufficiently accurate characterization of the key unsolved problems in modern science and their connection to the problem of meaning. This should prove helpful for the readers who are unfamiliar with these issues, or interested in understanding their solution. If this happens to pique your interest sufficiently to explore further, I would recommend the above books for a detailed discussion. I will successively discuss the problems of meaning in mathematics, physics, computing, and biology. One primary reason for spreading the attention wide is to illustrate why the problem of meaning is pervasive and how it appears over and over in various areas in different forms.

Let's begin with mathematics. The problem of mathematics is that numbers can be described in three different ways—as things, concepts, and names—but mathematics cannot deal with these distinctions simply because the distinction between names, concepts, and things does not exist in mathematics. The problem has been shown many times over, but perhaps its clearest articulation is Kurt Gödel's incompleteness theorem. I will not try to describe Gödel's proof here—for the obvious reason that its details may not be of interest to the readers—but only illustrate the nature of the problem through an intuitive English language example. Let's consider the following three sentences using the word 'nobody':

- Nobody has six letters

- Nobody is perfect

- I am nobody

In the first statement, the word 'nobody' is a thing, or a physical aggregation of six letters. In the second statement, the word 'nobody' is a name that refers to people. In the third statement, the word 'nobody' represents the concept of insignificance. Intuitively we understand the differences between these uses of the word 'nobody' depending on the context of the specific sentence employing them. However, it is not possible to represent this distinction in mathematics. If we use these words interchangeably, we can create some interesting conclusions such as those illustrated below.

- Nobody is perfect. I am nobody. Therefore, I am perfect.

- Nobody is perfect. Nobody has six letters. Therefore, perfect has six letters.

In the first case, we have arrived at an erroneous conclusion but it is not logically incorrect. In the second case, we have arrived at a logical contradiction because the word 'perfect' has seven letters and not six. The paradoxes above don't arise from some mysterious property of logic or linguistics. The problem stems from the fact that the symbol 'nobody' can denote things, concepts, and names. To use language correctly, we must respect these categorical distinctions, and a failure to do can result in logical contradictions.

Kurt Gödel used this type of reasoning in mathematics to arrive at contradictions that prove that mathematics is incomplete. The genesis of the contradiction lies in the fact that mathematics cannot distinguish between names, concepts, and things, although numbers can be used to describe each of these separately. For instance, the number 5 can denote the concept of fiveness. It can also represent a name, as in the 5th employee. These two are respectively called the cardinal and ordinal uses of a number. Finally, the number 5 is also a physical token distinct from its meanings. Logical systems are not devised to deal with the distinction between things, names, and meanings, and they can easily construct anomalies of the type illustrated with the English language earlier. Specifically, Gödel demonstrated that it is possible to map a statement not-P to a number P. The number P is the *name* of the statement whose *concept* is not-P. This mapping can be constructed by treating the statement not-P physically rather than semantically (in a semantic treatment, not-P cannot be called P). And once this mapping has been created, mathematics must treat it as a contradiction between P and not-P.

Gödel employed this scheme to show that mathematics can either be consistent or complete, not both. If mathematics is consistent, then it must not interpret numbers as names, concepts, and things; it must use only one interpretation at any time, although it could alternately use other interpretations at other times. But to be complete, mathematics has to treat numbers as names, concepts, and things at once, however, in this case, it could not be consistent. Numbers are treated as concepts when they denote cardinals and they are treated as names when they denote ordinals. Gödel's incompleteness is related to the existence of meanings in ordinary language because in ordinary language we can use the same word as a name, concept, and meaning, without creating logical contradictions, although not in mathematics. All such statements would be impossible in mathematics, unless mathematics treats numbers just like we treat words in ordinary languages. In this case, mathematics will now have to treat numbers as types rather than quantities.

The implication of this problem for physical theories is that when numbers are described as types, objects to which these numbers are applied would also be typed rather than typeless entities. For instance, each object at a different location in space would also be an object of a different type, simply because the number that denotes its position is in itself a different type. Since all objects in different locations are different objects, this difference can be attributed to their being a different type of object. The object is a physical thing, its location is the name by which it can be called, and its type is what distinguished the object from other objects. The solution to Gödel's incompleteness would indicate that names, concepts, and types have to be identical in a physical representation of meanings. It is impossible to map a proposition not-P to a number P now because P is the location of the proposition in space and not-P will always be located at the location not-P. This implication is relevant to quantum physics where different quanta arrive at different locations and current physics is unable to describe the significance of this arrival. The significance—when quantum phenomena are described using a typed theory of numbers—is that quanta arriving at two different locations must represent two different meanings.

In classical physics, any object can be at any location because all objects and all locations are identical types[11]. This is in turn the outcome of a physical rather than semantic treatment of objects and locations. In quantum theory, an object's position uniquely identifies the object's properties[12], so if an object had a fixed set of properties, it would also be at a fixed location in space. To explain the quantum problem, let me again illustrate it with an example.

Assume that you are drawing $100 from an ATM. When you draw this money, you don't know in advance the *denominations* of the currencies you will receive. You can, for example, receive $100 in denominations of one $50 and five $10 currency notes, or you may receive nine $10 and two $5 currency notes. In drawing the cash, you can be certain that you will receive a net worth of $100 but you don't know the denominations of individual currency notes[13]. Quantum theory similarly tells us that when we measure an ensemble of particles, there are several ways in which the whole ensemble can be divided into parts. The total energy of the ensemble is unchanged in each case, but its division into individual quanta varies. In a sense, we can know what the whole is, but there are several ways in which the whole can be divided into distinct parts.

In the classical physical view, the parts in a whole are *a priori* real and the whole is made up of the fixed parts. Quantum theory, however, indicates that the whole is more real than the parts because the same whole can be divided into many different parts. These parts become real at the point of observation although the whole is real even prior to the observation. The fact that the same whole can be divided into parts in many different ways represents a type of indeterminism in physics, where the parts are not *a priori* fixed although the whole is. Rather, the parts are created only as an outcome of our measurement procedure. The fact that the same whole can be known in terms of many parts therefore involves a role for our choices in the ordinary act of scientific measurements.

Another problem in drawing money is that when you receive the money from the ATM, you don't know the order of currency notes: you cannot be certain that the $50 notes will arrive before $10 notes or vice versa. The same amount of money can be delivered using the same denominations, in many different *orders*. Quantum theory is, similarly, unable to predict the order in which the quanta will arrive. This is yet another kind of indeterminism, where we can know the parts but we cannot predict the order in which the parts arrive. The same total whole can be delivered through the same parts, but in many different orders, and we cannot fix the order in advance. Quantum theory therefore describes the outcomes probabilistically. For instance, if we know that the denominations of the currencies are $50 and $10, then we can say that the probability of seeing a $10 note is 5/6 and that of seeing a $50 note is 1/6.

These two types of indeterminism in quantum theory can be addressed if the quantum objects were treated as symbols. The quantum ensemble will now represent a complete proposition or a sentence. The individual quantum detected would represent the words and the order in which these quanta are detected will represent a sequence of the words which constitutes a sentence. The meaning of a sentence is not reduced to a specific set of words, and the same proposition can be expressed using different words. Therefore, when a proposition is framed in different words, the order of the words will also change. When the quantum ensemble is viewed physically, it is very difficult to understand how the same ensemble can comprise different objects because we suppose that there is indeed a fixed set of *a priori* real particles. However, this problem does not exist when the ensemble is viewed as meanings, because the same meaning can be expressed in different words. While current quantum theory cannot predict the order of quanta, these can be predicted if reality is viewed as encoding meanings. The sematic treatment of nature therefore makes new predictions.

The quantum problem illustrates a central role for meanings in determining the state of a system. Now, the fact that the same meaning can be expressed using different words, and the choice of words used to express the meaning depends on the experimental setup, indicates that the meanings are more real than the words. Therefore, we do not begin in words and assume that these have to be given meanings. We rather begin with meanings and suppose that they would be expressed in words depending on the experimental setup. Thus reality is not the physical tokens of meaning. Reality is meaning which is contextually expressed as physical tokens. The measurement therefore pertains to the *expression* of meaning.

That meanings are logically prior to sentences has well-known implications in linguistics such as the fact that a semantically correct proposition is also syntactically correct but the reverse isn't necessarily true. For instance, the proposition 'colorless green ideas sleep furiously' is correct syntactically but not semantically. Therefore, if we begin with meanings and construct a sentence, and if the sentence accurately represents the intended meaning, the sentence would also be syntactically correct. However, if we begin in an arbitrary sentence and try to understand its meaning, then many syntactically correct sentences may not even have a clear meaning.

This fact has important implications for computer program semantics because programs too can be syntactically correct but semantically incorrect. An example of such a program is one that involves an infinite loop. Loops are used in computer programs to reduce the amount of actual program instructions, but whether the loop terminates or not often depends upon the input conditions to the loop. A program with a loop can therefore be syntactically correct but semantically incorrect on certain kinds of inputs. Such programs will never terminate on those specific kinds of inputs.

Before we begin executing such programs, it is worthwhile to know if the program would ever terminate. If it were possible to determine that certain programs would not stop on these inputs, then the computer could be designed to never start such programs. The question of whether a program halts on a specific input is called the Halting

Problem in computing theory and Alan Turing—a British mathematician and wartime code breaker for the British secret service—proved there is no automated solution to the Halting Problem. That is, there is no computer program that can accept an arbitrary program together with its input and determine if the program halts on the specified input. Essentially, the Halting Problem does not have a generic solution. The insolvability of this problem means that programs cannot be automatically tested; the test conditions for the program must be designed manually and the computer may automate them. Since the computer cannot understand program semantics, it cannot also automatically author programs. Both program development and testing therefore are manual tasks.

Programs that halt have a *tree* structure in which the program begins on some specific root node and traverses the branches of the tree in succession. A tree is always loop-free. So, if there was a procedure to determine if an arbitrary program represents a tree structure—without executing the program—then whether the program halts or not could also be determined. Turing's Halting Problem amounts to the statement that there is no program that can determine the geometrical structure of the program (i.e. whether the program is a tree or a loop), without traversing that program step-by-step. If the tester program traverses the tested program to decide if it halts, and if the tested program indeed has a loop, then the tester program would simply walk through that infinite loop and never terminate. The genesis of this problem is that a computer does not have the ability to 'visualize' the program as a whole. The computer must execute the program to know its properties and if the program has a loop, then the computer will never halt. Human programmers, however, can visualize the entire program and they can therefore understand whether the program is a tree or a loop.

The issue of deciding program semantics is a structural problem. The individual instructions in a program are meaningful, but the structure amongst the instructions is not necessarily meaningful. Since the program structure is defined by the language syntax, the problem of semantics amounts to the issue that all syntactically correct structures are not necessarily semantically correct. Turing's Halting problem therefore proves that there cannot be an automated procedure that identifies programs that are both syntactically and semantically correct. If such a procedure were feasible, it would also be feasible to only write semantically correct programs.

This problem of determining program semantics is particularly relevant to the discussion of whether meanings can naturally emerge in matter. The physical laws of nature are rules of syntax and they permit many syntactically correct propositions. Some of these propositions may also be semantically correct. However, Turing's Halting problem entails that there is no physical procedure to select a semantically correct proposition from amongst the syntactically correct ones. For instance, the laws of Newtonian physics can help us make semantically correct functional structures such as a clock and a bicycle (semantic correctness in this case is simply the usefulness of the objects). But the laws do not preclude arbitrary structures which would not be functionally useful in any given environment. All physical structures are equally valid according to the laws of nature, and they cannot be preferred over others.

This fact sounds the death knell for evolutionary theories of biological speciation. All molecular structures, according to the laws of physics, are syntactically correct propositions. However, only some of them are semantically correct. Evolutionists claim that the process of natural selection filters out the useful structures from the useless ones. This is in effect saying that there is a mechanical procedure that can determine if some syntactically correct program is also semantically correct. But this claim contradicts Turing's proof. If it were possible to determine semantically correct programs, then it would also be possible to weed out the infinite loop programs.

Syntactic correctness can be defined universally but semantic correctness is defined contextually. For instance, a program may halt on some inputs, but not on all inputs. Whether the program is semantically correct is defined only on the specific inputs to the program, not universally. The question of whether a living being is well-adapted in an environment is identical to the question of the semantic correctness of a program, against a given set of inputs and outputs. A semantically correct program is one that takes some inputs and produces useful outputs. A well-adapted living being is also like a program that exchanges information with its environment consistent with the 'expectations' of that environment. The problem of natural selection is to find which programs will be well-adapted in an environment: it is to weed out syntactically correct but semantically mismatched programs. A canonical example of such a program would be one that takes the available inputs but does not produce the desired output, or one that does not take the available inputs and therefore does not produce the output.

Turing's Halting proof implies that there is no physical procedure to determine if a syntactically correct structure is also semantically correct. Natural selection represents a mechanical procedure that weeds out living beings which are syntactically correct but semantically incorrect. Turing's Halting problem implies that such a procedure cannot exist, because no program has a way of determining semantic correctness. In fact, if a procedure that determines if a program is meaningful were possible, then that procedure would also be able to determine the program's meaning. And if there were a procedure to know a program's meaning, then it would be possible to determine which programs were useful or malicious. Natural selection amounts to saying that a computer can distinguish malicious programs from useful ones and eliminate the malicious ones. But if such a procedure were possible, then all the problems in computer security—e.g., viruses and trojans—could be prevented because the computer would terminate the malicious programs.

Computer programmers design complex systems comprising multiple programs—called 'processes.' A system of interacting processes can represent a biological ecosystem. All programmers know that if one of these processes misbehaves, the entire system misbehaves. No individual program can be designed to correct the other misbehaving processes, because such a program would not just have to know what it has to do but also what every other process in the system has to do. Furthermore, even if such a program—which knows both its own behaviors and the correct expected behaviors of other programs— were to exist, the other processes would still have to obey the instructions from this master program. How does one program know which other programs it has to obey? If a good program obeys a malicious one, then it is hijacked by the malice. In fact, how does a program know that a specific feedback from another program indicates instructions for program modification rather than inputs to the current program?

Finally, how does the instructing program know which instructions in the erring program to modify in order to elicit the correct behavior? It is noteworthy that the mapping between programs and outputs is indeterministic; several distinct programs can produce the same output, and the instructing program has no way of knowing the exact instructions that should be modified in the erring program to correct its erring behavior.

Of course, this is not to say that such instructing programs could not exist. It is only to say that even if these programs were to exist, they could not play the role of correcting other programs. An obvious example of a master program in a computer is the Operating System (OS), which has greater privileges than other programs. The OS can kill the other processes in the system, when they make some obvious mistakes—like trying to modify another program's data. In the context of an ecosystem, this kind of protection implies the existence of an uber being that protects other beings from attacks from malicious beings. Such an entity in the ecosystem would appear to be a "God" in the evolutionary scenario. Furthermore, while the OS can prevent some obvious kinds of mistakes, it cannot prevent all kinds of mistakes because the OS does not know the expected behavior of all the programs running on the computer. The only way the OS could ensure that all faulty programs were killed is if it knew the correct behavior for each individual program. In effect, the evolution's "God" would have to be omniscient and omnipresent (it must know what every other program in the system is doing).

As the number of programs in the system increases, the OS (if it has to play the corrective role) would become proportionately more complex. It would have to have two kinds of information about each program—the program instructions and its *expected* outputs—the latter for checking if the program is behaving correctly and the former for correcting that behavior. When the program errs, the OS would be required to find the erroneous instruction and instruct the erring program to correct it. However, this ability to map the error in the output to an actual instruction in the program is outside the ability of any program, according to Turing's Halting problem.

Finally, even if we suppose that such uber programs could exist in the system, they would forbid random mutations. To carry out a random mutation in a program, the OS must be informed prior. If there is a random mutation in a program which causes it to deviate from its specified behavior, and the OS hasn't been modified to expect this change, it would immediately consider the mutating program deviant and kill it. In such a situation, there can be a fixed system that works correctly according to the definition in the OS, but there cannot be individual mutations in any of these programs.

We are thus faced with a choice between random mutations and natural selection. There cannot be a mechanical procedure which determines if any arbitrary program is useful or malicious, and therefore natural selection in general is impossible. It is however possible to design an uber program that checks the working of some specified programs, and only those specified programs can run on this system. Such an uber program would become increasingly complex as the number of possible programs on the system grows, because the uber program must know the behaviors of all the running programs. Furthermore, such an uber program would have to have super-program privileges. If any program randomly deviates from its specified behavior, the uber program will terminate it, thereby eliminating the possibility of a random mutation. This implies that even if we try to define a natural selection mechanism to remove deviants, we would not only need an uber program, but such a mechanism would also forbid natural mutations, unless both the uber and normal programs are modified simultaneously.

The Genesis of Scientific Problems

This survey of scientific problems is by no means exhaustive. The problems of indeterminism in physics are, for example, not restricted to quantum theory; they exist even in classical mechanics, general relativity, and thermodynamics. The problems of mathematics, similarly, are not limited to Gödel's incompleteness; this is only one of the several logical paradoxes in mathematics. Likewise, Turing's Halting problem is not the only issue in computing theory; problems such as $P = NP$[14] and questions about computational complexity are other related questions. Finally, the problem of evolution is not the only one in biology; there are many other issues of information and its role in chemical reactions as well. My previous books explore a wider set of scientific problems and their relation to meaning. My aim in picking one problem in each area and connecting it to the question of meaning is to show how these problems pervade various fields of science although they arise from a common issue: science does not know how to physically describe meanings.

If we knew how meanings could be expressed in matter, then this would also entail a consistent and complete mathematics, the ability to determine if a program is useful or malicious, the ability to predict the succession of quantum events without probabilities, and the ability to explain the origin of living species. This is an important realization to have because it indicates that the problem of meaning is not just a pointless philosophical debate about the nature of universals—which has been going on since Greek times but has never been resolved—but it is also a problem that lies at the heart of all areas of modern science as their biggest unresolved questions.

Two thousand years of Western intellectual debate can be attributed to the single problem of the relation between universals, the human mind, and the material world. Since the problem was never solved in Platonism, successive generations of thinkers and philosophers have toyed with it in various ways, never completely succeeding. The idea and thing worlds were separated in Platonism; they were then brought together into material objects in Aristotle's philosophy; the ideas were evicted from matter and put into the mind by Descartes; and eventually, all ideas were evicted from science as the world was described in terms of physical properties. Neither of these solutions to the problem of universals is completely satisfactory. As we work around these problems, we find theories that seem to work for certain parts of reality, but not for others.

At the root of these problems lies a central dogma about material objects—these objects are *things* and not *ideas*. This thinking dates back to Platonism where the world is described as *substance* rather than *form*. Western philosophy has grown under the belief that the material world comprises some "stuff" called matter, which is different from the "stuff" called mind. Given the fact that various attempts to think about the "stuff" have failed, it is imperative to take a fresh look at this entire problem. This relook needs to ask some fundamental questions. What if there is no "stuff" called mind and matter? Of course, something must exist for us to be here and to perceive the world. But what if that thing that exists is not material substances— matter and mind? Then what could such a thing that makes up the universe be? Here, I will explore the idea that nature is just form without substance. Modern science reinforces this way of thinking because everything in science is described mathematically which only constitutes forms. The "stuff" view, however, continues in science because we are unable to imagine how things can just be forms. And yet, as time passes, the successes of mathematics in describing nature indicate that nature is just mathematics.

Philosophers distinguish between things and concepts. For instance, the concept of a car is different from a car. And yet, this divide between things and concepts is the primary problem in science and philosophy. Here, I will argue that the concept of car and the physical car are both concepts, although the concept of a car is an abstract concept while the thing car is a contingent concept.

The concept of a car is clearly abstract because it omits many details of any specific car. One obvious detail is that different cars appear different even from a distance and cars can be classified as sedans, sports cars, sports and utility vehicles, trucks, hatchbacks, wagons, small cars, etc. based on their appearances. Each such car has some common features such as four wheels, steering, seats, engine, chassis, transmission, headlights, storage space, head and tail lights, etc. due to which we think of these objects as an abstract car. However, each of these car features is adapted according to the manner in which the car's use is defined. For instance, the engine in the car would depend on whether it is a sports car or a hatchback. Most cars also have music systems, air conditioning, central locking, power windows, and power steering. Again, to some extent these features in a specific car may vary depending upon the car type.

As we start to define the idea of a car to greater levels of accuracy, we quickly come across a peculiar problem that there is no specific point at which the definition of a car ends, because we can incrementally refine the idea of a car by adding more details to it. As we add these details, the definition of the car ceases to be an abstract concept and begins to resemble a specific car. For instance, is the car a 4-wheel drive or a 2-wheel drive? Does the car have leather seats or fabric seats? Does the car have a stereo system or not? How many rows of seats exist in the car? What is the type of storage available? What color should the car be? What is the diameter of its wheels? Is the car stick-shift or automatic drive? What type of fuel does it use—petrol or diesel? What's the horsepower of the engine? And these are only high-level questions about the car. Each of these questions can further be refined into more specific questions.

As we try to answer more and more of these questions, we find that we are beginning to describe a specific car: it may be the car that stands in my garage and which I think is the canonical car!

Furthermore, as we add more and more accurate details to the definition of a car, we will also find that the definition starts to exclude many other things that might otherwise also be called cars. At that point, we might stop trying to refine the idea of a car to greater levels of detail. But what exactly is this point where we stop refining the idea of a car to a greater and greater level of detail? Should we just say that a car is something that has four wheels, a steering and an engine? Or should we keep providing ever more details? The problem is that too ambiguous a definition would permit even trucks and buses. Similarly, too refined a definition would leave out many things that could potentially be called cars. There is no definite point at which you can stop refining the idea of a car and be completely content that you have accurately defined a car. You can only assert that what you have is a provisional or tentative definition of a car, which can be made more abstract by omitting some details or made more concrete by adding even greater details.

A real car therefore is also a concept, although that concept has been refined by adding more and more details to the abstract idea of a car. All these details are also concepts, but they modify the abstract concept—the concept of a car. There is hence no clear divide between the concept car and a real car. The concept car can first be refined into a sedan, SUV, hatchback, sports car, wagon, etc. A specific such refinement can further be refined to include further details such as those about wheels, steering, seats, storage, engine, transmission, security, air conditioning, etc. This process has to be carried on for several iterations and each car manufacturer performs this conceptual construction process during car design.

However, there comes a point when the designer stops this design process and starts to determine the *materials* out of which the different parts of the car would be built. These include metal, wood, plastic, leather, cloth, foam, glass, etc. We generally suppose that the design of the car is idea-like but the materials from which the car is built are things or substances. But what prevents us from extending the process (by which we refined the idea of a car into the design of a specific type of car) to define the materials of the car which would make up a specific car? Can we not say that the materials that make up the car are also designed by refining abstract ideas? The problem here is that we attribute design to human beings but not to nature itself. We suppose that design involves a human mind and ideas, but nature is just idealess things. If this divide between matter and ideas were dropped, it would be possible to think of materials too as representations of ideas. For instance, we could then extend this process all the way to molecules, atoms, and sub-atomic particles and call each of these material entities as refinements of concepts. If we were able to think of atomic objects as ideas, the divide between matter and ideas would not exist. The notion that a real car is a thing but the abstract car is an idea would also not exist. Rather, all things would be refinements of ideas. The macroscopic and atomic objects would now be abstract and detailed ideas, respectively.

My claim is that this process should be continued to atomic objects. In fact, the problems of incompleteness in quantum theory can only be solved if the atomic objects were treated as ideas. This treatment requires a new number theory in which numbers are treated as types rather than as quantities. That approach would enable an understanding of semantic computing machines and thereby solve the problem of program semantics. Now evolution would not be based on random mutations followed by natural selection. It would rather be the evolution of meanings governed by the laws of meaning evolution. This evolution would represent the collective changes to ecosystems rather than to individual objects or beings.

The scientific problems related to meaning can therefore be solved, but this needs a profound shift in our understanding of matter. The shift is that objects are also ideas; they just happen to be more complex ideas produced by adding information to abstract ideas. The boundary between mind and body is not as hard and fast as is made out to be in current science. Rather, both mind and body are just forms rather than two different substances. They just appear to be different because the mind is abstract concepts and the body is contingent concepts developed by elaborating the mind. The macroscopic objects appear before the atomic objects, and therefore scientific reduction cannot begin in atoms; it must rather begin in abstract concepts. We cannot see these concepts because the senses by which we see are themselves produced by a refinement of abstract concepts. The fact that we cannot observe the abstract world with our senses is simply because the senses can perceive only those things that are more contingent than the senses. To perceive the abstract concepts, we must now employ other kinds of perceptive capabilities available within us—e.g., the mind that is capable of perceiving contextuality, intentionality and abstraction. As the concepts become more and more abstract, the senses which are even more abstract than the concepts must be used to perceive them.

This means that the development of science cannot proceed simply by developing more sophisticated measuring instruments. It also needs the development of observational faculties by which we can perceive and postulate more abstract concepts. The measuring instruments of science are more contingent than the senses by which we see them. If we had to progress in science, we must go beyond the senses and find the concepts from which the senses were developed. That in turn requires higher forms of perception.

The Platonic world of ideas and the physical world of things are not two separate worlds. There is a single world that begins in abstract ideas, which are then elaborated by adding the same ideas over and over until the abstract becomes detailed, refined and contingent. The world of ideas therefore becomes the world of things not at once, but through a repeated process of adding information. This repetition does not invalidate the existence of abstract concepts as is often believed in current science. Rather, the abstract and contingent concepts form a conceptual hierarchy of meanings in which both abstract and contingent concepts are equally real.

The World as Symbols

In this view of nature, the universe does not begin in the smallest physical particles which are then aggregated to form more and more complex things. The universe rather begins in simple (and therefore abstract) ideas which are then divided to produce more and more complex ideas. Science too professes the use of simplicity. However, even the simplest things in science require observational faculties—such as seeing, tasting, touching, smelling, and hearing—although these faculties themselves are not the simplest. Therefore, simplicity has to be conceived in a way that describes how the ability to perceive itself is being produced. The current scientific notion that senses are complex arrangements of atoms, whose properties are defined through measurements, which in turn depend on the presence of perception, is circuitous. The correct definition of simplicity is that which goes beyond the senses, and explains how the senses themselves are produced from even more abstract ideas, which can be perceived by even more subtle forms of sensation.

The smallest sub-atomic particles in the universe are the most complex ideas while everyday objects (like tables and chairs) are relatively simpler ideas. The universe as a whole—which is the idea of space—is the simplest idea, and this idea is divided over and over again to create all the locations in space. For this to be possible, the dimensions of space have to be viewed as elementary ideas which are combined to create all the individual locations in the universe. The universe is now an inverted semantic tree of ideas, which begins in an elementary idea and ends in the most complex ideas through repeated additions and refinements to the tree's root.

The fact that there is a limit to the smallest objects in the universe (indicated by Planck's constant in atomic theory) entails that there is a limit to the complexity in ideas. We cannot indefinitely divide the universe into parts because we cannot unlimitedly add information; there is a limit to this division, which is attained when the smallest sub-atomic particles have been created. The universe is, therefore, the most abstract idea and the atomic objects are the most contingent, detailed, and refined ideas. The detailed ideas are produced from the abstract idea by the addition of information.

The semantic notion of complexity overturns our approach to reduction in nature. In the physical notion of complexity, the smallest parts of nature are more primitive because we believe that small is simple. Physical reductionism therefore begins with the smallest parts and tries to build larger things by aggregation. The aggregation gives the impression that the whole is reducible to parts, although physical theories are unable to carry out this reduction, without the theory becoming indeterministic. This indeterminism, as we have seen, is a consequence of treating material objects as things, which exist independent of other things. This could be solved if the objects were also symbols, and were produced from ideas.

In the semantic approach, the world is not things whose combinations are perceived by the mind as ideas. The world is rather ideas whose combinations produce things. In the Cartesian mind-body divide, both mind and matter are substances. In the semantic approach, both mind and body are forms or ideas. There is no material substance, and there is no mental substance either. Rather, both mind and matter can be described in a single theory of forms or ideas. The mind can now be envisioned to be a simple idea relative to the meanings or other ideas it produces. Like a complex idea is produced from simple ideas, similarly, thinking or thoughts can be created from the mind. The mind therefore does not have a special position in the pantheon of ideas; the mind is just another idea. It happens to be a relatively abstract idea as compared to the ideas which can be generated from the mind. But it is not necessarily the most abstract idea; the universe as a whole is the most abstract idea.

Similarly, the senses of observation and action are ideas, too. These ideas are less abstract relative to the idea of the mind, but more abstract relative to the external objects they perceive.

A neuroscientist who studies the brain's electrical activity can conclude from this that the mind and the senses are indeed in the brain and this conclusion would not be false. However, the matter in the brain itself has to be treated semantically for the theory of senses and mind to be complete. For instance, a neuroscientist can identify a certain region of brain to be responsible for color perception. However, which specific neuron in the brain would fire to represent the color red or yellow cannot be predicted in a universal manner. In different brains different neurons will fire for the same type of color perception. Similarly, the color perception region in the brain would not be identical in all brains; the regions will vary somewhat in different brains. Likewise, the brain neurons associated with other aspects of experience such as emotion, music, language, decision making, analytic thinking, or kinesthetic activities such as painting, swimming, or cycling would also vary across the different brains.

The problem here is not that the senses and mind are not represented in the brain. All aspects of our experiences can potentially be represented in the brain and the neuroscientist can also study them. The problem is only that if we treat the brain physically then we would be unable to *accurately* predict the part of the brain responsible for different types of experiences. The specific neuronal activity—e.g., that neurons A, B, and C represent the perception of the red color—also cannot be predicted without knowing the entire brain for each specific individual brain. Neuroscience, without the semantic view of nature, would be predictively incomplete, although it would make probabilistically accurate predictions. As the brain architecture changes—for instance, when the neuroscientist studies brains in different species, or even in different individuals of the same species—the same experience would involve different parts of the brain, and different neuronal activities would be observed.

To make accurate predictions, the neuroscientist would now have to take into account the entire brain architecture, then the rest of body construction, the details about the individual's DNA, the effect of the environment on brain development, the individual's history of psychological development, their eating and exercising habits, and so forth. As we strive for more and more accuracy, more and more aspects related to the body—and its material, social, cultural, economic, and linguistic environment—have to be taken into account and woven into the predictive theory. At each point, we will find that we have increased the accuracy of prediction but the predictions are still inaccurate. The genesis of this problem lies in the fact that all these aspects about the person are present in the brain as symbols of meanings but unless we study the brain as a symbolic representation of meanings, it is impossible to know which molecule, neuron or electrical activity represents what experience.

The symbolic view also entails a radically different picture of inanimate objects. Just as the brain can represent the qualitative experiences about the world, the external objects too must be symbols of the qualities that the brain attributes to the world. In other words, if the brain sees a red apple, then the redness and the appleness of the perception could potentially also exist in the external object. The brain and the apple are both physical objects. But if the brain can denote ideas then the external world too can be ideas.

This view has historically been highly problematic. In the early days of science, empiricist philosophers—such as Descartes—drew a distinction between primary and secondary properties. Primary properties include length, mass, speed, temperature, etc. while secondary properties include color, taste, smell, sound, touch, etc. Descartes viewed the separation between primary and secondary properties as essential to the development of science because it was obviously very difficult to describe the external world if it comprised of qualities. Descartes, however, also rested the divide between primary and secondary properties on the divide between matter and mind. One distinction followed from the other and it was impossible to maintain the primary and secondary property distinction without also committing to the divide between mind and matter. While there were critics of this distinction—such as Leibniz and Berkeley—who argued that the idea of a world as primary properties can never be known because we can only know the world through sensations, the distinction stuck and has been the bedrock of modern science. Over time, however, science has dissolved the distinction between mind and matter, by showing that the brain can actually encode the properties of the senses and the mind. It should therefore follow that the distinction between primary and secondary properties must be dissolved as well. But if we commit to this dissolution then we must describe the world as apples, chairs and houses rather than mass, charge, force, fields, temperature, etc. Alternately, we must give up the idea that we perceive the world as apples, chair, colors, tastes, smells, sounds, people, houses, etc.

The ability to reduce the mind to matter is seen as a great advance in scientific reductionism. But its scientific implications are inadequately understood. The implication is that if some material arrangement in the brain can denote color, smell, taste, or touch, then similar material arrangements in the objects being observed must be able to denote these properties as well. It is important to note that the chemical activity in the brain is not directly taste, touch, smell or color; these arrangements are simply material *representations* of these perceptions. Therefore, it is not necessary for the apple to actually have the qualitative feel of redness or sweetness. The apple only needs to *represent* the ideas of redness and sweetness quite like the brain represents these ideas during perception. This ability to describe the apple as a representation of ideas rather than as physical properties (as current science does) constitutes a remarkable shift in the way we think about material objects: we would have to describe these objects as symbols instead of things.

An ordinary example can perhaps better illuminate this way of thinking. Imagine what happens when we read a book, such as a travelogue. The travelogue can be described as a collection of squiggles—shapes, sizes, etc. But, in addition, the words in the travelogue also denote meaning. Although the squiggles are not identical to the experience of meaning, they are however representations of the experienced meanings. By reading a travelogue, we *know* about an author's experiences of travel, although we don't experience the travel itself[15]. The symbols in the book thus represent *information* about the traveler's experiences, although reading the book isn't the same as traveling itself. Of course, we could imagine those experiences, but our mental reconstruction of an author's descriptions of travel may differ from the experiences of the author, and certain things in the author's experience may never be reconstructed.

Current science measures the height, weight, and speed of the travelogue, but it does not measure the meanings of the travel itself. However, even if science were to measure the meanings, there would still be a difference between the reading of the description and the experience of traveling. A neuroscientist studies the brain quite like we read the travelogue. She can infer from her knowledge of the brain what the brain's owner is experiencing, if the brain is described semantically. However, even with such a reading, there would still be a difference between understanding someone's experiences and having those experiences yourself[16]. A semantic understanding of the brain will give us insights into the person's mental state. However, the mental experience is not identical to the brain; the difference is between knowing about the travel and traveling.

The derivation of meaning from material objects is seen in the appreciation of art or music when artistically savvy people understand meanings where others may not. And yet, there are at least two ways in which we can view the perception of meaning. We might, for instance, say that the meaning of art and music only resides in the observer's mind, but not in the musical and artistic works themselves, which are nothing but physical properties. Or, we might say that the meaning really exists in art and music, although its perception depends on the observer's ability to decode it.

Which of these positions is true? By committing to the former idea, we lose the ability to assert that some object is a book, music or work of art, because the meaning is only in the observer. In this view, there is no such thing as a work of art or music; it is only our perception that makes it so. In other words, objects have no meaning because meanings are created by the mind. But if artistic or musical objects do not encode aesthetics, then how can the brain encode those experiences, since the brain is also an object? This problem is unsolvable except to say that all experience is an illusion. The notion, therefore, that music or art only exist in the mind leads to the conclusion that there is no mind and hence no art and music.

The symbolic view would instead state that meanings are objectively in the book or music. We cannot understand these meanings if we look at individual frequencies or squiggle shapes. We can, however, understand them if we view the frequencies or squiggles as representations of meaning, governed by some language which is contextually defined. The context is fixed by the object as a whole, and not by the individual objects in that context. For instance, words such as force and field have a specific meaning in a physics book, quite different from the meanings in other areas of discourse.

The comprehension of meaning therefore begins in the comprehension of the whole even before we comprehend the parts. For instance, we have to know that we are reading a book in physics before we can accurately interpret the meanings of the words in it. The comprehension of the whole prior to the comprehension of the parts fixes the *language* in terms of which the symbols are given meanings. Meanings are therefore not in the individual squiggles. They are in the relations between these squiggles and the entire context that fixes the language of comprehending meanings. We must first comprehend the whole before the parts in that whole can be given meaning. Generally, the title and subtitles of the book, the name and background of the author, the brief description of the book, the graphics of the cover and the classification of the book into hierarchically organized categories in the book stores fix this context. All this is meta-information about the book which helps the reader to determine the meanings of things within the book. The words in the book therefore do not automagically get their meanings. The meanings are rather produced from a comprehension of the context in which the book is embedded. The whole must be understood before the parts in that whole can be given meaning.

The symbolic view of nature entails some dramatic shifts in science: (1) objects are not things; they are symbols, (2) the symbols represent the same types that we can potentially perceive and conceive, (3) the symbolic meaning arises from the relations between the symbols and the overall context, (4) for the context to have a meaning, it must again be determined by its relation to a higher context, (5) the nesting of symbols inside contexts, leads to a hierarchy of meanings, (6) this hierarchy must terminate in some self-evident ideas, or the *axioms* of the theory and of the world.

Hierarchical Space-Time

The scientific counterpart of the above philosophical view is that space and time in the universe must be described as closed and hierarchical domains rather than open and linear domains as in current physical theories. To illustrate, suppose we are trying to describe a specific type of rice as the ordered hierarchical tuple of attributes: {species, plants, grasses, rice, basmati}. Each such attribute represents a set, and if the universe were symbols of ideas, it would comprise closed hierarchical conceptual domains, such as those in the case of basmati rice. Each such domain would therefore be defined through a distinction within a larger conceptual domain, and so forth, until we reach the most simple or elementary ideas.

As we saw previously, in a conceptual hierarchy, the name, concept, and thing are described using the same words. We cannot call a grain of basmati rice as a grain of soya bean. The identical description of name, concept, and thing avoids the problem of Gödel's incompleteness which arises from a contradiction between names, things, and concepts. If names, concepts, and things are described by identical words, then the contradiction between these categories can never arise even if we interpreted the name as a concept or a concept as a thing. If this grain of rice was a computer program, it would be loop-free since it has been constructed using a hierarchical tree and tree structures are loop-free. Such a program would therefore always halt, and thus avoid Turing's Halting problem. The tree structure avoids the recursion problem as well, since the higher level concept is defined before the member objects are defined. The hierarchical definition is therefore free of all logical problems.

Examples of hierarchical addressing are quite common in the everyday world. Two well-known examples include postal addresses and Internet addresses. A postal address is defined hierarchically using the name of the country, state, city, area, street, and building, with each successive entity nested inside the previous one. An Internet address is similarly described by dividing the internet as a whole into smaller subnets, each of which given a number using a dotted decimal notation such as 234.567.90.1 and/or using ordinary language hierarchical names such author.blog.company.com.

In current addressing schemes, however, there is a difference between the name of the entity (the postal or the Internet address), the conceptual meaning of the entity, and the physical entity itself. For instance, the postal address itself may not indicate whether the building in question is used as a house, a school, an office, or a shop. By knowing the Internet address we cannot always know if the computer given that name is a file server, a printer, a laptop, or a robot[17]. Even knowing the domain name is often not sufficient to know the purpose for which the individual or the institution uses the domain. It is not obvious, for instance, that www.google.com is a search engine, and companies develop 'branding' strategies to map their name to their functions, and the functions to the things.

These differences generally work in the everyday world due to our ability to distinguish between names, concepts, and things. A name is not identical to the concept (and may sometimes be opposite to the concept), and the concept doesn't uniquely identify the thing. Since we do not equate names with concepts and with things in ordinary language, the use of language does not lead to confusion. However, for the separation between names, things, and concepts to work, there must also be mapping schemes that allow us to convert names to things and things to concepts. These mappings are provided by various techniques and procedures. For instance, the mapping between Internet addresses and Internet domain names is provided using a Domain Name Service (DNS) that converts a name such as author.blog. company.com into its Internet addresses. A postal address must similarly be mapped to a property through a legal process of registering the property with the government, obtaining a legally unique name and then marking the property with that name. Mapping allows us to retain the differences between things, names and concepts while allowing us to discover one using the other.

Time is similarly described hierarchically in the everyday world. For instance, we can call the current moment 1/1/2015 10:45:23, which nests seconds inside minutes, minutes inside hours, hours inside days, days inside months, months inside years, etc. This description of time is semantic, and it exists in conjunction with physical notions of time such as the total number of seconds elapsed since January 1, 1970, which is used in computers to measure time. The physical time in the computer is mapped to the human clock time using conversion schemes similar to the ones described above. These times may further be mapped into a space-time evolution diagram for prediction of some physical phenomena in a theory.

The hierarchical notion of space-time can be semantic if the nodes in the tree were meanings. The root of the tree in this hierarchy would be the most elementary or abstract meaning, and its branches and sub-branches would be constructed by adding information to the root node. The meaning of each such subsequent addition is defined only in relation to the previous node. For instance, the meaning of blog. company.com is defined in the relation to company.com and the meaning of author.blog.company.com is defined in relation to blog.company. com. Likewise, the meaning of 12:00 is defined only in relation to the date, month, year, century, etc.

In a hierarchical space-time, locations and things are also types. Here and there, now and then, are therefore not identical locations and times. Each location denotes a unique concept, given in relation to the next hierarchically prior concept. Accordingly, when matter is described in a hierarchical space-time, then objects would be described as symbols rather than meaningless things. The neurons in my brain will then denote symbols of meaning such that a neuroscientist—who has learnt to read the language of the brain—can accurately tell what I'm thinking right now. A solution to the problems of incompleteness in science therefore requires a single shift from a linear to a hierarchical space-time. While this idea is quite simple, imbibing it would overturn nearly all conceptions about matter, perception, and concepts, widely prevalent in current science.

The Problem of Qualia

Western intellectual development has placed an inordinate amount of emphasis on thinking and reasoning while neglecting emotions and feelings. After all, it seemed that matter must be governed by logic, mathematics, and reasoning and would have no role for emotions. In fact, one of the reasons for the conflict between religion and science is their differing emphasis on reason and emotions: scientists accuse religious people of not being sufficiently rational and religionists accuse science of neglecting the emotional values. The fact that thinking is influenced by emotions is now well-known[18], and the effects of emotions on health are too numerous to list here.

But there is another aspect of conscious experience that is not emotions and yet has a strong emotional connotation. This is the subjective *feel* of not only thinking but even that of sensations such as sight, sound, taste, smell, and touch. There is a difference between the concept of yellowness and the feeling of yellowness. Hot and cold may be concepts, but knowing the concept isn't the same as feeling hot or cold. The idea of pain and pleasure can be expressed linguistically, but it is not the same as being in pain or pleasure. Of course, all feelings involve the use of concepts such as hot, cold, pain, pleasure, yellow, red, etc. But the conceptual content is clearly different from the experiential content. There is even a difference between a concept and the *understanding* of that concept, which involves the "a-ha" feeling. The explanation of conscious experience therefore does not end with the explanation of concepts. It also requires an explanation of how these concepts become feelings.

The subjective *feel* of experiences is called *qualia*. The feeling accompanies all perception, but there are several distinct ways in which a concept can be perceived. There is, for instance, a cognitive understanding of a book's content, quite different from the emotional connect with the book. A neuroscientist may understand—from the study of a subject's brain—that the subject is seeing red, and he or she would then have the feeling of understanding. But that feeling is different from the feeling of perceiving redness itself. There are many debates today in the philosophy of mind, cognitive science, and neuroscience about whether the qualitative feel of redness is identical to the physical representation of this redness, and philosophers have argued[19] that the physical representation of ideas in the brain is not even identical to the *understanding* of these ideas let alone the emotional connect to these ideas. Given that physical properties were defined to be different from their perception—by supposing a divide between primary (those which exist in matter) and secondary properties (those that exist in the mind)—the reduction of secondary to primary properties is problematic.

The semantic view brings us closer to the solution, because the problem partly germinates in thinking of matter physically rather than conceptually. The gap between physicality and feeling is obviously greater than that between concepts and feelings. The qualitative difference between sight and sound, pain and pleasure, hot and cold, is very hard to attribute to matter if these differences are reduced to physical properties. However, the qualitative difference between these experiences is more understandable when the experiences are attributed to type differences between the concepts. Of course, the concept is not identical to its understanding or feeling. However, the primacy of concepts helps us understand how there can be a subjective experience of concepts while the concept itself is objective. If we lump the concept and its understanding into a singular 'mind,' distinguishing between the two becomes impossible, leading to the question of whether the feelings are objective.

The view that concepts can be mechanized in matter is called *artificial intelligence* (AI) and the 'hard' AI proponent claims that the observer is nothing but the mechanism. The difficulty in representing concepts in matter is evident from Gödel's incompleteness and Turing's Halting Problem. However, even if matter could represent concepts, it could still not be said to 'understand' these concepts. Even if a robot measures the temperature in the environment and represents this temperature as the concept of 'hot,' we still cannot assert that the robot is *feeling* hot. The concept of hot is a representation of the worldly facts, which is different from its experience.

There is hence a need to distinguish between concepts and feelings: relative to their feelings, the concepts are more objective. This does not necessarily imply that the pleasure or pain of a person cannot be objectively known[20]. However, it does entail that concepts and experiences of these concepts are two different categories. Understanding the idea of pain is different from having the feeling of pain, and if a scientific theory has to explain experiences, it must separate the concepts from the feelings. This separation would also aid with the conceptual parsimony of the scientific theory. That is, a parsimonious theory of the mind would say that there is a concept called pain, which can be experienced in many different ways.

Conscious experiences can be classified into various categories such as doing, understanding, believing, feeling, thinking, and being. Each such category constructs a different conscious 'experience' of the same idea. For instance, understanding yellow, feeling yellow, thinking yellow, and believing yellow involve the same idea of yellowness, but the categorical distinction between understanding, thinking, feeling, and believing creates different experiences. Personality theories such as the Myers-Briggs Type Indicator (MBTI) describe a person in terms of aspects of conscious experience that predominate in a person. The categorical distinction between the above types is similar to the distinction between names, concepts, and things that I discussed earlier, although the categories of experience are much more subjective. Just as names, concepts, and things must be distinguished as three different meanings of the same thing, similarly, thinking, feeling, believing, understanding, doing, and being should be viewed as different kinds of experiences of the same meaning. Just as the thing, name, and concept are described by the same word—e.g., 'yellow'—similarly the different categories of experience also use the same words. And yet, in both cases, their meanings are different. The experiential categories are therefore different *models* of the same language—the word 'yellow' itself does not tell us whether we are feeling or thinking yellow.

The relationship between a symbol and its context defines the properties of abstraction, intentionality, and contextuality; it defines the conceptual *type* denoted by the symbol, such as the idea of yellowness. The experiential categories—such as doing, understanding, believing, feeling, thinking, and being—on the other hand define the relation between the type and the conscious observer. Like color is an abstract concept from which yellowness can be elaborated, similarly, doing, understanding, believing, feeling, thinking, and being are abstract concepts from which ideas such as color, taste, smell, touch and sound can be elaborated. There is however an important difference in that while the concepts of color, taste, smell, and sound can be defined through the interrelations between symbols, the experiences of doing, understanding, believing, feeling, thinking, and being require the postulate of an observer in relation to which these experiences are defined. The property of yellowness can be attributed to the things (as they are in everyday conversation) but the property of feeling yellowness cannot be attributed to things.

There is a sense in which a machine can represent concepts but it cannot understand them. The reason is that the understanding of concepts is different from the concepts. While concepts can be defined as the relation between things and contexts, the understanding of that concept is only defined in relation to an observer.

In fact, we might say that doing, understanding, believing, feeling, thinking, and being are elaborations of the idea of an observer. The notion of an observer is more abstract than the notion of the kinds of experiences that it can be involved in, and while each of the experiences involves an observer, the observer is more abstract that those experiences. Quite specifically, since the 'same' observer can be alternately involved in doing, understanding, believing, feeling, thinking, and being, it is impossible to reduce the observer to these experiences. We must suppose that there is some consciousness—more abstract than its qualitative experiences—and the experiences are elaborations of that consciousness. This is quite like how color is present in yellow, red, and green, but color is not any of the elaborations; rather, the elaborations are created from color. Similarly, the types of experiences of a consciousness are not themselves consciousness although they can be said to be elaborations of consciousness. The notion that qualitatively different kinds of experiences are elaborations of consciousness helps us understand how the problem of qualia could be solved in the same manner as the problem of other kinds of concepts. However, it requires us to postulate a conscious observer. This postulate raises a very fundamental question: What is consciousness an elaboration of? If consciousness is an abstract idea that elaborates into many kinds of experiences, then is consciousness itself a fundamental idea? Or is consciousness in itself an elaboration of something more basic?

The Nature of Consciousness

In physical theories, material objects are real and consciousness is an epiphenomenon. This view leads to incompleteness, recursion, and indeterminism as we have earlier seen. The opposite approach where the contingent is derived from the abstract can work but it means that objects are elaborations of concepts, concepts are elaborations of experiences, and experiences are elaborations of consciousness. The question is: Is consciousness a fundamental or derived concept? Is consciousness also an elaboration of something?

It would be necessary to think of consciousness as an elaboration if there were many individual conscious observers, because then it is necessary to elaborate them using an even more fundamental idea. Clearly, there are many individual observers, which experience different parts of the world. Are these observers elaborations of something more fundamental that their individuality? A better understanding of this idea requires the comprehension of how the different observers differ in their respective experiences.

One of the fundamental properties of all concepts—not discussed thus far—is that all concepts are defined through distinctions or oppositions. For instance, 'hot' is defined in opposition to 'cold,' 'bitter' is defined in opposition to 'sweet,' 'black' is defined in opposition to 'white,' etc. For any concept to exist, its opposite must also exist, simultaneously. The universe cannot comprise only one object; it must minimally comprise all the ideas needed to form a distinction. The smallest such distinction involves only two concepts and we can conceive of more and more complex distinctions with a prime number of concepts. All distinctions that don't have a prime number of entities can be reduced to other distinctions with a prime number of concepts. For instance, a six-way distinction can be reduced to a two-way and a three-way distinction. But distinctions with a prime number of concepts cannot be reduced in this way.

This fact helps us understand the difference between observers that experience different parts of the world: these observers must experience at least one part of an opposition. All observations are produced from the exchange of information with other objects, and to exchange information, there must actually be an informational difference between them. Since these informational differences have to be described in terms of oppositions, all observers must also be on the opposite sides of an information exchange. For instance, if an observer perceives 'hot' because some heat is being received by that observer, then, the other observer must perceive 'cold' because the heat is being transferred out of that observer's experience.

Semantic informational differences imply that no individual observer can experience both sides of a distinction because that would imply a logical contradiction. One of the basic properties of all individual experiences is that they are free of contradictions. We cannot simultaneously experience 'hot' and 'cold,' 'bitter' and 'sweet,' 'near' and 'far.' The observer must *focus* on only one part of the world and the experienced facts must be mutually *consistent*. For instance, we can experience 'red,' 'round,' and 'sweet,' but we cannot experience 'bitter' and 'sweet' at once; we could experience them alternately or experience something in between, but not simultaneously experience two distinct and opposite concepts. Each observer's consciousness is thus always logically consistent, although the universe as a whole is logically inconsistent since it must comprise mutually opposed types. Therefore, if observers describe their experiences of the universe, they would only describe it using logically consistent theories—and this would always appear to be true—even though the universe is itself not logically consistent.

To accommodate many logically consistent observers within a logically inconsistent universe, the universe must be partitioned into subsets of mutually consistent ideas or experiences, and each observer must be assigned such a consistent subset. This consistency is not perennial; for instance, it is not necessary that an observer will always experience only 'hot.' However, an observer can only experience one type of idea at one time, even though the mutually opposed types exist simultaneously. The mutually opposed types must, of course, exist in different locations in space. Therefore, the logical consistency of the observer can also be restated as the fact that an observer must always be *localized* to some part of space.

The question of what an observer is an elaboration of, therefore, can now be answered by redefining our notion of space. In this new notion, each location in space is an *elaboration* of the idea of space. The space is an idea, and the individual locations in space are the elaborations of this idea. The fact that an observer experiences only a consistent subset of the entire universe means that the observer's experience is a proper subset of all possible experiences. The space of all observers can now be defined to be a universal observer which contains all the individual observers. This inclusion does not mean that the universal observer experiences the world just like individual observers; however, it does mean that the universal observer experiences the presence of individual observers as His parts, quite like the individual observers experience their minds and bodies as their parts. Like the individual observer is more abstract than his individual experiences, similarly, the universal observer is more abstract than the individual observers. While the individual observers can be associated with only a logically consistent subset of possibilities, the universal observer must be associated with the distinctions themselves. If the universe is semantic, the existence of the universal observer is entailed by the fact that the origin of the universe cannot be traced to a single logically consistent consciousness. It must rather be traced to the origin of observers themselves which experience contradictory oppositions.

The contradiction arises because the observers themselves are in some sense logical contradictions for each other. The logically contradictory universe cannot be described in logic; it must rather be described by transcending logic to reconcile the oppositions.

One of the crucial differences between a physical and semantic universe is that the semantic universe is logically inconsistent and logically consistent subsets of that universe must be carved for individual observation. However, for such subsets to be carved, a logically inconsistent universe must exist prior. How can such a universe come into existence? Note that we traced the problem of semantics back to a consciousness, and the solution is still incomplete. To address this problem, we now have to conceptualize a consciousness whose experiences are the observers. The material world is in the consciousness of the individual observers, but the observers are in the consciousness of another observer which transcends the material experiences. We can call these two kinds of observers as perceiving *consistency* and *distinctions*; the individual observer perceives how the world is consistent, and the universal observer perceives the diversity. That universal observer is therefore the unity in the diversity. The individual observer perceives consistent subsets of the universe, and the universal observer experiences the contradictory desires of the individual observers. Therefore, we cannot speak about the universal observer within logic because that observer is the unity underlying the contradictions, although we can say that if the logically contradictory universe exists then there must be something that reconciles these contradictions.

The elaborations of a universal observer create a space-time of individual observers; elaborations of the individual observers create the phenomenal experiences; elaborations of the phenomena create concepts; and elaborations of the concepts create objects. We can now speak about four kinds of space-times: (1) the space-time of objects, (2) the space-time of concepts which are more abstract than the objects, (3) the space-time of phenomena or qualia which are more abstract than the concepts, and (4) the space-time of observers, which are more abstract than the phenomena. The universal observer can therefore be the space-time of individual observers, within which the observers exist as individual parts. Like a car can be divided into many parts, such as engine, chassis, steering, etc., the individual observers can also be functional parts of the complete whole, which is also an observer—the universal observer.

The Universal Observer

The above definition of conscious observers entails that it is not possible to define an individual experience without other experiences; only the universal experience can be defined independently of all its parts. If the universal observer's experience evolves, it would also entail the evolution of the individual observer's experiences. This raises two fundamental questions which are relevant to science. First, which particular experience in the universe is *me* and *why*? Second, how do we describe the succession of experiences?

Note that in a semantic hierarchical tree, each observer is some branch of the tree. These branches are created and destroyed by adding and removing information. If there were no conscious observer, we could describe the creation and annihilation of branches, but not their succession. Each branch would represent the *state* of matter, but the connection between these states—to form a trajectory—could not be defined. If this succession could not be defined, then the idea of an observer would also be vacuous because the observer is something that persists through the succession of experiences. And if the observer could not be defined, then which experience is *me* would be a meaningless question. This would also entail that we can describe the events in the universe but we couldn't draw trajectories connecting these experiences. It would now follow that the succession of experiences—such as the fact that we undergo birth, childhood, old age, and death—and that these events pertain to the evolution of the same *being* would be meaningless.

A cornerstone of modern science is the idea that underlying experiences are objects; in classical physics, for instance, these objects are particles and waves. The properties of objects are attributed to these objects; if the objects don't exist, then where do the properties hang? The semantic view entails that material properties are not attached to objects, but to more abstract properties. For instance, the property of yellowness is not attached to an object, but derived from (and therefore attached to) the property of color. The property of color is not a property of an object but that of a more abstract property of sight, which is attached to meanings, which are attached to phenomena, which are attached to a consciousness, which is then attached to the universal consciousness. But what is this universal consciousness attached to? The hierarchy of properties can end, if there were an *object* to which properties could be attributed. In physical theories, we measure the properties of an object but we don't ask what the object is made up of. The distinction between objects and properties is how we know and describe the world. While the object's properties can be known, the object itself cannot be known without the properties. And yet, there must be an object 'behind' the properties that binds them. Since all properties are eventually attributed to the property of consciousness, what is that object to which this property can be attributed?

The object in question is 'behind' the phenomena in the physicalist view. However, in the semantic view, the object is both in 'front' and 'behind' the phenomena; it is in front because it creates experiences, and it is behind because the content of that experience is attributed to an external world outside that observer. In this case, what lies behind the individual observer is another observer with which information can be exchanged. I am therefore the cause of the phenomena that I am seeing, but what I am seeing is not just purely my own creation; it is also due to the presence of other observers, which are in turn parts of a universal observer. Both objects—behind my experience and in front of my experience—are ultimately unknowable except through the demonstration of their properties, and the objects can therefore be said to express these properties only to know their own nature and that of the other objects[21].

The notion that there are objects underlying consciousness is therefore necessary both from scientific and philosophical standpoints although these objects can never be directly experienced or known, because they are even more abstract than the individual observer. Their existence is hence a metaphysical postulate. However, making that postulate helps us connect successive experiences into trajectories or life stories. If the succession of experiences can be predicted, then the metaphysical assumption would be true. The metaphysical postulate is also necessary for the semantic hierarchical tree to terminate because if there were no objects, then each property could be attributed to another more abstract property, and this cascading hierarchy would never end. Our knowledge, in such a case, would always be incomplete since we cannot know the most abstract entity. The hierarchy obviously ends when the properties are attributed to objects; the object terminates the hierarchy.

Of course, it is possible to terminate the hierarchy prematurely. For instance, we could say that yellowness is attached to color, and color is the fundamental object in nature. Modern science adopts such a view when it supposes that there are some fundamental properties (such as position and momentum) which are then attributed to particles. A direct consequence of a premature termination is that there would always be other properties which cannot be incorporated in such a description, and the theory would remain incomplete. For instance, if color is a fundamental object, then taste, smell, touch, sound, etc. could not exist. Similarly, if we claim that meanings are fundamental objects, then we would deny the existence of experiences—such as understanding. If we make a particular type of experience—e.g., feeling—fundamental, then we would deny the existence of other forms of experience such as understanding, doing, or believing. If we view our consciousness as fundamental, then we would deny the existence of any other consciousness. Thus, any premature termination of the semantic hierarchy comes at the expense of omitting some facts about nature from our view of nature. All such theories would be necessarily incomplete.

The correct termination of the semantic hierarchy is therefore only in the postulate of a universal observer because it allows the existence of all properties, concepts, experiences, and observers. All other things derived from this universal observer are not truly objects, but properties of the universal object. Only the universal observer is the real thing; everything else is the property of this thing. Since the universal observer expands into a space-time structure creating the experiences of all observers, space and time are also properties of the observer. The material objects are developed upon the conscious experience of the individual observers, and these experiences are created and destroyed, too. Therefore, it can be concluded that these material objects and experiences—although properties of the real thing—are not always real. It does not mean that they don't exist, although it means that they are not permanent.

Two Kinds of Natural Laws

It should be remembered that the reality which underlies the phenomena can never be known directly; it can only be known through its properties and their effects, and even then these effects only confirm the existence of the properties, not of reality. For instance, in classical physics, we can measure the effects of properties such as mass, momentum, position, etc. but we cannot measure the particle itself to which these properties are attributed. However, since multiple properties play a key role in determining the predictions, we bind these properties to an *object*. If the theory that binds the properties into an object is successful, then the object is also considered *logically* real, although not empirically real. Similarly, the notion of a universal and an individual observer—also known as God and the soul—cannot be confirmed empirically. Consciousness is a *property* of the observer and the observer is detected by its properties. But the objects underlying these properties cannot be known.

Critics of religion often ask for the proof of the existence of God and the soul. They must recognize that when consciousness is a property of an observer, then consciousness cannot know that observer itself, because the observer is logically prior to those properties. No observer can therefore completely know itself, because the mechanism of knowing (consciousness) is itself a property of the knower. Nevertheless, self-knowledge is the central goal and perennial project for all conscious beings. This project can never come to an end; however, they must keep attempting to know themselves. The attempts to know—and the variety these attempts create—constitute the evidence for their existence. While the objects underlying consciousness can never be known directly, their existence can be confirmed by the effects of those properties. The "proof" for the existence of God and the soul is thus not empirical, in the same sense that a classical particle (or wave, electron, or quark) cannot be empirically proven. The proof of God and the soul will always be theory-laden: if a theory of God and the soul makes correct predictions, then these objects would be considered logically true[22].

There are two kinds of theories in nature. First, there is the evolution of the universe as the succession of events and transactions; this evolution is governed by the space-time structure. Second, there is the evolution of the individual observer in the universe, which connects the events into trajectories. If the theory of the succession of events in the universe is found true, it would indicate the presence of an object that underlies space and time; the successes of such a theory of universal experience would imply the existence of a universal observer or God. Similarly, if the theory of the succession of individual experiences is found true, it would indicate the presence of an individual observer or the soul. Can we directly observe God and the soul? No, because objects are more abstract than properties. When the property is consciousness, the object to which this property is attributed to is more abstract than consciousness and can never be known. Nevertheless, the *order* in nature can indicate the existence of objects. In a sense, the order in experience is logically prior to experience and creates experience.

The individual and universal conscious experiences are, as already noted previously, different: the universal consciousness simultaneously becomes aware of opposites while the individual consciousness must always be logically consistent. However, for there to be an observer underlying these experiences, a sense of order must be established between the successive states. The universe as a whole is ordered if the theory that predicts this order can be formed. Since the theory will describe the universe as an experience (rather than as a set of things), the predictive successes of such a theory would indicate the existence of a universal observer. For the individual observer to be real, the observer's trajectories must be predictable. Two different kinds of natural laws can therefore provide the evidence of universal and individual observers. The question of whether these observers are real is therefore no different than any other scientific question about reality. These questions, however, depend on semantic rather than physical theories.

If the individual observer did not exist, then it would be impossible to draw trajectories connecting material states. The trajectories in turn depend on the ability to predict the succession of experiences using some natural law. If this law predicts correctly, its successes can be evidence for the reality of the individual observer. Similarly, if the universal observer did not exist, it would be impossible to unify the evolution of the observers into a universe. The existence of the soul and God are therefore scientific questions of reality. However, these questions depend on completely different kinds of theories than envisioned in current science. Current science describes the universe as material objects. The semantic view shows why this description must be incomplete, and that the solution to this incompleteness requires a four-staged understanding of the universe as objects, concepts, experiences, and consciousness.

In *Moral Materialism* I describe how the above mentioned two theories of nature can be understood through the notion of a semantic hierarchical tree, and I will not repeat that description here. I will proceed with the assumption that the universe as a whole and the individual experiences of the universe are both ordered and this order can be described in science. Materialists do not disagree with these claims, although they would assert that the order in nature and in our experiences indicates that there is no God or soul. This contention is founded upon two different visions of the universe—one in which consciousness emerges from matter and the second in which matter emerges from consciousness. When consciousness emerges from matter, there is no room for concepts, and scientific theories will always be incomplete. However, when matter emerges from consciousness, it also brings a whole swath of ideas and organizes them into a conceptual hierarchy. Which of these visions about the universe is true is an empirical question, not one of faith.

Can Theism Be Scientific?

New Atheism stands upon a single new idea—namely that order emerges in nature automatically through the self-organization of material objects. This idea takes for granted the existence of objects. As I discussed previously, the existence of objects itself requires the existence of concepts, which requires the existence of

experiences, which requires the existence of two kinds of consciousness. Any theory that attempts to construct objects independent
of concepts, experiences, and consciousness, will also be incomplete and the problems of incompleteness are pervasive in science,
although they are either neglected, ignored, or simply not well
understood.

The New Atheism movement is smarting under the partial successes
of incomplete theories. It either neglects the problems in science or
simply does not understand them very well. On one hand materialists profess the openness of the scientific enterprise in admitting their
failures and revisions to scientific theories. On the other hand, they
also act as gatekeepers on what science can and cannot be. I believe
that the problem in science is its materialist dogma, not empiricism,
rationalism, or openness. The materialist lumps this dogma with the
other useful aspects of the scientific method and presents it as rationality, often to those who don't understand it very well. Can there be
a science that is rational, empirical, and openly critical without the
materialist dogma? I certainly think so. Not just as an alternative form
of science, but even as a mainstream effort that is used to address all
outstanding scientific problems.

New Atheism is a political strategy to keep the government funds
flowing into current forms of scientific research, while keeping alternative ideas out of science. Since government funding in democratic
societies is influenced by people's opinions, New Atheism has taken
a vocal public route to influence public opinion. New Atheism propels
the materialist dogma which is an impediment to the further development of science. Under this dogma, alternative ideas about matter—even when these ideas could be potential working hypothesis for
further investigation—are shunned. Silencing alternative ideas could
be a good approach if materialism happened to be correct. But, if it
happens to be wrong, silencing alternatives is riding into the sunset of
ignominy and irrelevance.

Of course, this doesn't necessarily entail that every religious idea
is automatically true, and the marriage between theism and science
must aim to separate the truth from the chaff. The key enabler for this
marriage is a role for the mind in science where ideas are seen as objective rather than subjective and objects described as representations of

meanings rather than meaningless things. I believe that theism is also scientific, but not in the same sense that science is currently defined. Reason, experience, and open inquiry are compatible with theism but dogmatic materialism is not. In fact, dogmatic materialism is a hindrance even to the development of science. Progress in theism need not therefore begin from the recognition of God or the soul; it can also begin from the acceptance of concepts as real entities from which material objects are created.

Can we choose a path free of dogmatism? I think that is a question that only time can answer. In the meanwhile, I believe, it is important to understand which parts of science are true and which ones are rhetorical. It is important to understand where the conflict between religion and science lies. And it is necessary to explore how much of this conflict is based on established facts of science versus something that materialists add to science without adequate substantiation. I have written quite a bit about how current scientific problems invalidate many of the foundational assumptions on which New Atheism is based. These include the idea that objects are *a priori* real; that the universe is uniform in all space and time, that numbers are quantities, that the universe is logically consistent, that structures automatically emerge from random combinations followed by natural selection, and I will not revisit those topics here.

This book is about the foundations of atheism, how these foundations originated in modern scientific theories, how those theories created additional unsolved problems, and why a solution to those problems will invalidate the ideas on which atheism is founded. My aim here is not to engage in the same kinds of debates between how science is rational and religion is not. This may be a fact about certain religious practices and ideas today, but it is not necessarily the case for every such idea. My aim is to show how the essential core of religion is scientific, but this science has been lost due to the rise of materialism. Over time, when the scientific component of an ideology is lost, it is generally replaced by dogma. Since that dogma cannot be justified on the basis of anything fundamental, more dogmas are added to stilt the previously unsustainable ideas. Ultimately, the outcome is very confusing and unsustainable especially when facts and reason contrary to those ideas start to conflict with the dogmas.

A scientific understanding of religion is necessary for religions, too. It is necessary to determine which of its current beliefs are scientific and which ones are dogmatic. It is also necessary to make religion the quest of truth rather than a choice of believers. Religions have generally believed that the soul and God are transcendental to matter and therefore the study of matter cannot tell us anything about these topics. The idea therefore that the study of matter and material experiences can inform us about the nature of the soul and God may itself be new[23] from the standpoint of science. I believe that such an unconventional understanding of religion is possible, but it requires us to develop a profound understanding of nature, free will, and how nature interacts with the soul and God.

When such an understanding has been developed, the conflict between theism and science would not exist, although the conflict between materialism and theism would. The problem that this book aims to discuss is the conflict between theism and materialism; if theism can be scientific, then the conflict is between two visions of science—materialistic and semantic—not between religion and science. A different vision of science, coupled with a different understanding of material nature is therefore essential not only to solve the currently unsolved problems in science, but also to make continual progress in understand the nature of the self and beyond.

2

An Introduction to Vedic Philosophy

I am the fourth stage of consciousness, beyond wakefulness, dreaming and deep sleep. Becoming situated in Me, the soul should give up the bondage of material consciousness.
—Śrimad Bhāgavatām

Why Study the Vedas?

I deferred the discussion of Vedic philosophy until the second chapter to highlight how the questions about the soul and God can be addressed within science, and would arise naturally from theories that try to solve its current problems of incompleteness. The conflict between religion and science is not therefore one between reason and faith. It is rather between meaning and matter. Meanings appear in various ways in our everyday life. For instance, meanings appear in meaning encoding objects—books, music, art, and science. Problems of meaning are central to mathematics, computing, physics, and biology whenever they describe object *collections* rather than individual objects. Collections become necessary for numbers in mathematics, program correctness in computing theory, macroscopic objects in physics, and living entities in biology. The conflict between meaning and matter is intuitively accessible, empirically available, and its problems can be logically demonstrated. When a new view of matter compatible with the existence of meanings is developed, this view will also entail the ideas of soul and God.

However, I now also wish to describe how this understanding of soul and God already exists in Vedic philosophy. I don't believe it is

essential to know this philosophy to arrive at the truth. Nevertheless, understanding this philosophy helps us get a perspective on how
these problems have been rationally dealt with previously. One of
the unstated presumptions in modern science is that its discoveries
have brought humankind closer to truth than it has ever been; that
prior to science, there were only legends, anecdotes, and fairytales.
I hope to shake that myth by illustrating how the questions that science is trying to tackle are only a fraction of the questions that have
been answered earlier. By limiting science to study material objects,
and then conceiving matter as if the mind did not exist, science has
taken a path where it faces a dead-end. Of course, it is not necessary
to begin science in the study of the mind. However, it is necessary for
any successful scientific theory to acknowledge the mind's existence
and construct a view of matter compatible with that existence. This
has never happened in the two millennia of Western thinking, including the apologetics that used philosophical methods to justify things
beyond matter. All attempts at trying to integrate the mind and ideas
in the world have failed spectacularly.

The study of Vedic philosophy makes particular sense in this regard.
It presents a view of how the existence of the mind changes our view
of matter, and how questions of soul and God arise naturally in this
view. While Vedic philosophy is very broad and covers a wide range of
topics from matter to meditation, I will begin with a short overview of
its tenets to help connect its ideas to science.

The Four-Space Theory

One of the most succinct ways to explain Vedic philosophy—and to
highlight its differences vis-à-vis modern science—is to describe its
theory of four-spaces. All natural phenomena in modern science can
be reduced to properties of material objects in a single space. In Vedic
philosophy, this reduction cannot be carried out. Rather, there are
four broad types of entities, which exist in four different spaces. These
spaces are called *vaikhari, madhyamā, paśyanti,* and *para.*

The *vaikhari* space is the space of objects—the things that we can
see, taste, touch, smell, and hear. This space overlaps with the world

of material objects that science currently studies, although science describes these objects in terms of quantities, while Vedic philosophy describes these in terms of types in matter. The *madhyamā* space is the domain of meanings and it includes the senses by which we perceive sensations, the mind that perceives contexts and builds relations, the intelligence that perceives the order and structure in nature, the ego which perceives the intentionality and directedness in nature and a moral sense[24] which perceives values, morality, happiness, and distress. All these perceptions constitute the detection of concepts and they aren't yet experiences. The *paśyanti* space—which literally means 'seeing'—is the space of qualia or experiences. The experiences are subjective because no one else has access to anyone's experiences, although through its effects on concepts, and then on the body, it is possible to formulate *knowledge* of that experience. For instance we cannot experience someone's pain, but we can know that he or she is in pain. The *paśyanti* space represents the experiences of thinking, feeling, willing, knowing, acting, and being[25] in an observer. The concepts acquired in thinking are different from the experience of thinking. Finally, the *para* space represents the space of conscious observers that is even more abstract than its myriad kinds of experiences.

In each of these spaces, there are individual objects[26]. In the *vaikhari* space, for instance, there are material objects such as tables, chairs, houses, etc. In the *madhyamā* space there are theories, formulae, mathematical structures, intentional ownership of objects, social relationships, art, music, literature, moral values, etc. In the *paśyanti* space there are experiences of individual observers, such as their individual sensations, feelings, emotions, believing, the experience of understanding, doing and being something, etc. Finally, in the *para* space there are individual conscious observers.

The reason for separating these spaces is that the higher space can exist without the lower space. For instance, the ideas in the *madhyamā* space can exist even when their individual elaborations do not. It is possible to construct mathematical theories which have no real application. It is possible to imagine technology even when there is no use for it. Many similar examples exist in creativity, innovation, and imagination, by which the observer is able to perceive a reality even though there is no counterpart of that reality in the material objects. Vedas cite the most intuitively accessible form of this perception—dreaming. During dreams we can experience sensations, even though there is no world corresponding to the sensations. Many scientific discoveries—e.g., August Kekule's discovery[27] of the Benzene structure—have occurred in dreams. These theories are objective, although we may not see them in the physical world. The *madhyamā* state of perception is therefore also called the dreaming state. This dreaming state is higher than the waking state of object perception because objects are produced from ideas.

Similarly, the cognitive state of concepts and the experiential state of qualities are different because the cognitive state can exist even when we are unaware of it—e.g., when the senses process worldly information but the observer is not paying attention to it and thereby does not experience it. During sleepwalking, sleep-talking, and sleep-eating, the senses are active but the observer does not experience this activity. The qualities in experience cannot be reduced to the concepts, but the concepts can be derived from the qualities. The experiential abilities—thinking, feeling, willing, knowing, acting, and being—are therefore logically prior to concepts. Since the ability to experience exists even when the content of that experience doesn't, Vedas call this ability the state of *deep sleep*. If you wake up after a deep sleep, you don't remember dreams or experiences, although you remember having slept quite well. The abilities for experience are conditioned by the unconscious memory of past experiences, and the deep sleep state also therefore represents the unconscious of Western psychology. This includes our innate likes and dislikes, proclivities to certain ways of thinking, etc.

Finally, the conscious observer is even prior to the abilities for qualitative perception, and this is evidenced from the fact that we can draw our attention away from thoughts and feelings. When a particular thought or feeling disappears, we don't suppose that the conscious observer has disappeared. Rather, the *same* observer can now be said to have another type of experience. The continuity of experience therefore represents the conscious observer which transcends the individual qualitative experiences. The Vedas call this transcendent observer the *para* or *turiya* state of existence.

Aside from these individual objects in each space, we can also speak about the space itself. Beginning with *vaikhari,* each of these spaces becomes more and more personal or private to an observer. The space of objects is completely public and can be accessed by any observer. The space of sensations, thoughts, intentions, and judgments is more private, although with some effort we can understand a living being's mental states. The space of experiences is even more private; for instance, how exactly it feels to be in pain, to be humiliated, to feel the joy of solving a difficult problem, or to dislike someone, is something much more private, although if someone has been in a similar situation, he or she can relate to that feeling. Finally, the space of consciousness is completely personal and it constitutes an observer's sense of inviolable individuality and privacy.

The four spaces described above are *hierarchical.* However, they are not hierarchical in the sense of being "parallel" worlds. Rather, they are hierarchical in the sense of being a hierarchical tree structure. The universal consciousness thus divides into individual conscious observers. Each conscious observer divides to produce its faculties of experiencing—thinking, feeling, willing, judging, knowing, doing, believing, etc. Each of these experiential faculties divides to produce the methods of perception and conception— the sense of morality, ego, intelligence, mind, and the five senses. Finally, each of the senses divides to produce the "sense-data" which becomes the publicly accessible material objects. Aside from the hierarchy of the spaces, there is also a categorical hierarchy in each of the spaces.

For instance, thinking is higher than feeling, which is higher than judging or willing, which is higher than knowing, which is higher than doing or acting. Similarly, the moral sense is higher than the ego, which is higher than the intellect, which is higher than the mind, which is higher than the senses. Within the senses, hearing is higher than touching, which is higher than seeing, which is higher than tasting, which is higher than smelling. Within the material objects, there are sounds which can only be heard. The things that can be touched can also be heard. The things that can be seen can also be touched and heard. The things that can be tasted can also be seen, touched, and heard. And, finally, the things that can be smelt can also be tasted, seen, touched, and heard. The universe therefore springs from a universal consciousness and expands gradually by dividing into many parts, eventually producing material objects.

The best way to describe this universe is to think of an inverted hierarchical semantic tree whose root node is the universal observer, from which the trunks of individual observers are created, from which the branches of their individual experiences are produced, from which the twigs of perceptual and conceptual faculties are created, from which the leaves and fruits of material objects are produced. The nodes in this hierarchical tree are types—they are conceptually different, and the nodes higher up in the inverted tree (closer to the root) are experientially more abstract (that is, they are closer to consciousness) while the nodes lower in the tree are experientially more contingent (that is, they are material objects).

The closest analogue of what Abrahamic religions call "God" is in Vedic philosophy the space of all conscious observers. This entity is also the root of the hierarchical semantic tree. This root first produces the shoots of individual observers, which produce the types to experiences, which then produce the senses, mind, intellect, ego, and morality, which then produce material objects. Everything in the universe is therefore gradually produced from the root of the tree, and this conscious Being is therefore the origin of the universe. The universal Being is not identical to the universe, although the universe is an *effect* of this Being. Each node in the tree has a type and a value—the value is the node itself and the type is the node from which it is produced. For instance, a material object can exhibit redness which is a value, but whose type is color which is identified with the senses of perception. Concepts such as color, taste, smell are values, of a type—meaning—perceived by the mind. The meaning is a value whose type is a context, perceived by the intelligence. The context is a value whose type is an intention, perceived by the ego. The intention is a value, whose type is morality, perceived by a moral sense (called *mahattattva* in Vedic philosophy). The value is understood only in relation to the type. Therefore, yellowness cannot be defined unless color has been defined. Similarly, individual conscious observers cannot be defined unless God is defined.

Object and Property

All manifestations of God—beginning with individual conscious observers—are called God's properties, just as in science we distinguish between objects and their properties. An apple, for instance, has properties of redness, sweetness, and roundness. Underlying these properties are the objects called color, taste, and smell. These objects are themselves properties of another object called apple, and so forth. In Vedic philosophy, all these properties are called *śakti* or *energies* by whose presence the object can be detected. Each property requires a different kind of sense for its perception.

God's properties are also called His *śakti* or energies. The creation of the universe—which happens to be God's experience—is an outcome of the *śakti* or energy rather than of God Himself. In a sense, the universe is a property of a single undivided object—God. Every individual observer, their individual experiences, their senses, mind, intellect, ego, and all the objects produced from these faculties are all properties of God. There is, hence, only one object, but there are infinitely many properties of this object. Even the individual soul or conscious entity is not a fundamental entity; it is only a property of the supreme entity. Consequently, all individual experiences, observational faculties, and objects created by those faculties are successively "grosser" manifestations of the supreme entity. The Supreme Soul is said to divide itself first into many individual souls, which then divide into many experiences, which then create many concepts, which then create many objects. All these emanations from the Supreme Soul are properties of that Supreme Soul.

Vedic philosophy describes these properties as "rays" emanating from the Supreme Soul. All these rays are God's properties and they are therefore also called His *śakti* or energy. Once these rays have emanated from God, God does not reduce to these rays. He remains that individual entity prior to their emanation, quite in the sense that even if an object's properties were not manifest, the object would still exist. The object that exists prior to being manifested into its many properties (by which it can be known) is said to be real. In Vedic philosophy, only God is the reality and everything else that we know and experience is a property of that reality. In that sense, everything we know is ultimately knowledge of God. The properties emanated from God are not in themselves God, because equating the emanation with God would amount to confusing the object with its properties. However, in another sense, by knowing the myriad properties in the creation we can know God's nature.

The central problem of knowledge is thus defined as knowing the nature of God from which the entire universe manifests as His property. This knowledge can begin in material objects, but it would be incomplete unless the senses are understood. The knowledge can progress into an understanding of the senses, but it would remain incomplete until the mind is understood. The theory of mind would be incomplete without the understanding of intelligence, which would be incomplete without an understanding of intentions in the ego, which would be incomplete without the moral sense. All these senses would be incomplete without successively higher levels of qualia or types of experiences, which would be incomplete without an understanding of consciousness, which would be incomplete without an understanding of their original source—God. Knowledge thus remains incomplete unless the source of everything is known, and it terminates when an observer knows his own origin. To completely know anything in the universe, we must be able to trace our bodies to more and more subtle entities up a hierarchical tree.

Modern science studies material objects, and believes that these objects are the *reality*. Science attributes the measured properties to some fictitious 'objects' such as particles, waves, electrons, neutrons, quarks, etc. All these attributions are false. They create the impression that there is an external reality which exists before any observer. The outcome of this false view is that all such objective theories would always be incomplete. We have seen the evidence of this incompleteness in mathematics, computing, and physics. According to Vedic philosophy, the properties in material objects—length, weight, heat, speed, etc.—are objectifications of the senses—taste, touch, smell, sound, and sight. These senses are in turn objectifications of the mind, which is an objectification of the intellect, which is an objectification of the ego, which is objectification of the moral sense, which is an objectification of experiences, which is an objectification of consciousness, which is an objectification of God. The first step in science is therefore recognizing that material objects are created from the senses. The senses are the twigs upon which the leaves or fruits of material objects sprout. Successive developments in science would need to trace the origin of these twigs, all the way to the root origin of all manifestations.

Science would get stuck every time it supposes that anything except the root of the tree is the fundamental *object*. For instance, we might suppose that if physical properties are objectifications of taste, touch, smell, sound and sight, then the senses must be fundamental objects. This scheme would work better than supposing that length, weight, heat, speed, etc. are fundamental. But, ultimately, taste, touch, smell, sound, and sight are not fundamental because the same mean-ing—e.g., a mathematical theory—can be expressed through many different sensations—we can listen to a theory and we can see it printed in a book; if we were blind, we might even touch a theory by touching the symbols that embody its ideas. Given that the theory is present in each of these sensations, but it is not any of these sensations, it must be beyond these sensations. This problem leads to the incompleteness in the reduction of theories to sensations. A new conceptual, non-reductive understanding of theories must now be formulated, which goes beyond the sensations.

Similarly, as science progresses into ever more subtle conceptual entities, it will find phenomena that do not fit into its current understanding. To add these phenomena into science, science must be revised. In each revision, we might postulate some fundamental 'objects', but these objects would turn out to be 'properties' of an even deeper object in a deeper science. Science can terminate only when the postulated object explains all possible phenomena. Then, there is no need to search for an even deeper object, because this object explains all possible observable phenomena. Of course, in this case, these phenomena would span across different observers.

The Problem of Knowledge

The complete knowledge of reality is defined in Vedic philosophy as seeing the entire hierarchy of nodes from material objects all the way to their origin in God. Different individual observers, however, terminate this hierarchy at some arbitrarily chosen nodes on the tree, treating those nodes as the fundamental objects in nature. Such arbitrary terminations of the hierarchy are an individual's choice. Materialists, for instance, terminate the hierarchy in the gross material objects themselves. Empiricists may terminate this hierarchy in the observer's senses. Mentalists may terminate the hierarchy in the mind. Rationalists may view intellect as the basis of everything else. Psychologists may terminate this hierarchy in the ego. Universalists may terminate this hierarchy in some fundamental moral values in the universe. Existentialists may terminate the hierarchy in our experiences. Spiritualists may terminate it in our consciousness.

Every time we prematurely terminate the hierarchy, we suppose that everything else is an epiphenomenon of that reality. This thesis clearly works for things that are downstream from that node in the hierarchy, but it fails for nodes that are upstream in the tree. It also fails for nodes that are not anywhere on the selected branch. The upstream nodes become the reason that the theory eventually fails. In materialism for instance the material objects are fundamental and the observers are epiphenomena of matter. Materialism fails to account for the ability to have sensations of matter. We can describe the frequency of light, but we cannot tell why that frequency is red or yellow. We cannot explain how contextual arrangements of light lead to visual illusions, such as one color being perceived as another or why something seems bigger when it is not. After all, if vision is based on light's frequency, then the frequency is unchanged whether the other light colors are present or absent. The epiphenomenal view works for the downstream nodes but not for the upstream nodes. To solve this problem, the upstream nodes have to become more fundamental than the downstream ones.

The point at which an observer terminates the hierarchy becomes the limit of their knowledge—if that termination point is not the root of the semantic tree; anything logically prior and more fundamental than that termination point would never be understood. These choices also become the limits of the observer's knowledge. If their knowledge has to grow, then the choices must be revised. Eventually, the perfect choice is that which is reposed in God as the fundamental entity from which the observer is elaborated.

If we begin the search for perfect knowledge from the bottom of the semantic tree, and we arbitrarily terminate the search at some particular node in the tree, then anything upstream from that node would not be understood. We can revise his knowledge only if we encounter the phenomena that do not fit the current state of knowledge. For instance, if we begin in a classical physical theory of nature and suppose that nature is particles or waves, knowledge can progress if the observer encounters quantum phenomena where the wave or particle view of nature becomes inadequate. Such phenomena can be understood by incorporating the idea that material objects are phonemes— their wave-like behavior is that they are physically some vibrations, but their particle-like behavior is that these vibrations denote meanings, in relation to other particles. But how does an observer encounter such phenomena? What guarantees an encounter with such phenomena before theories can be revised and updated to incorporate deeper forms of reality?

One of the problems in the scientific method—as it is defined currently—is that it doesn't explain the *progression* of scientific knowledge. The scientific method is supposed to work through observation and theory formation, but scientific progress depends on the discovery of new phenomena that do not fit the current theories. If one has an imperfect theory of nature, but never encounters the contradicting phenomena, then the theory can never be updated. Similarly, if one has a perfect theory, he cannot know if the theory is perfect because it is not certain that contradictory phenomena would not be found in future. There are two broad approaches to the scientific method—verification and falsification—and both are problematic. The method of verification says that if a scientific theory works for a certain set of phenomena, then it is true. The problem in verification is that many theories may work equally well, and we cannot know which of these theories is real. The method of falsification says that a theory can never be verified; it can only be falsified. No extent of experimental evidence can ever indicate that the theory is perfect because the contradictory phenomena could potentially be found in the future. Similarly, even if a theory is indeed perfect, we still cannot know that the contradictory phenomena would not be seen in the future. Falsification entails that if we have a false theory we cannot know if it is false unless it fails. On the other hand, if we have a true theory we cannot know that it will not fail in future. Falsification entails that the progress in science (the changes lying in the future) cannot be predicted, because what we are missing from the theory cannot be known. We cannot know when the method will terminate or if it has already terminated. If this method was encoded as a computer program, the program could not halt.

The implication of this problem is that we can never know the nature of reality. Our knowledge must always remain tentative and imperfect. In fact, even if we did arrive at a perfect theory of nature, and nothing more needed to be done, we would not know of it.

In Vedic philosophy, this problem in the method of knowledge is addressed by the thesis of *karma* which represents the *consequences* of false theories and of incorrect actions performed under such a theory. The idea is quite simple: if you have a false theory, natural processes will arrange an encounter with phenomena that contradict the theory's predictions, and by incorporating these phenomena, you can correct the theory. If you have a wrong theory, therefore, nature guarantees the theory's correction by forcing the observer into rectifying experiences. If, however, the theory has been perfected, then the observer is not forced into naturally predetermined phenomena, because the perfect theory is compatible with all phenomena. Nature, in this view, is not just things, concepts, experiences, and observers. It is also a self-correcting system for knowledge perfection. This self-correcting system represents the moral law in nature. Under this law, false theories about nature entail a predetermined succession of experiences until the observer's view is corrected. However, when the observer has completely understood the nature of reality—and its origin in God—the observer's natural predestination towards experiences is finished.

The observer is now free to choose its experiences as it wills. This ability to choose any experience in effect entails that the observer can roam to any part of the universe, and such living beings are said to be *jivan-mukta* or free even though having a body and mind. The laws of nature do not act upon them, because they have understood the true and complete nature of reality. The goal of knowledge in Vedic philosophy is to become free of the natural laws. This entails transcending nature's morality, which arises from the perfection of knowledge beginning with God's knowledge.

The perfection of scientific knowledge is to understand how we are bound by the natural laws and the perfection of religious knowledge is to understand how we can be free of these laws. In modern science, the natural laws can never be violated. In Vedic philosophy too, the laws cannot be violated, but they can be transcended. The difference between law violation and law transcendence is crucial: it entails that the laws apply to matter, not necessarily to the conscious observer. However, if the observer has a false theory of nature, then the laws apply to the observer, too. Perfection of knowledge entails freedom from the laws of nature because the perfect theory of nature is compatible with every phenomenon. To know this perfect theory is to be able to choose any phenomenon. In each of these phenomena, the natural laws hold true. Therefore, by knowing the natural law, we can freely choose our experiences.

Is Free Will Real?

Much of the current debate in New Atheism is around whether free will is real, because if free will is real then it would seem to violate the laws of nature. Both free will proponents and opponents claim that free will *means* that everything about the individual observer is not necessarily determined by natural laws. However, both free will proponents and opponents identify the conscious observer with the mind-body. The free will proponent claims that natural laws governing the evolution of matter are incomplete and free will is the mechanism in the mind by which the material incompleteness is fixed. The free will opponent claims that the natural laws are complete (or will be complete in future), and once we know the laws of nature we would also know how free will is an illusion created by the mechanics of natural laws. Of course, if you happen to deny free will, you must also deny moral responsibility, which would entail that rewards and punishments for our actions could not be justified. After all, it is difficult to claim that rewards and punishments are being meted out due to some natural rather than societal laws.

Both proponents and opponents of free tend to equate free will with freedom. They argue that if there is free will then it should be able to change the material world. In other words, if you have free will, then its effects must be visible in matter by the choices you make. For instance, if you are driving a car, and if you have free will, then you must be able to turn the car left or right based on free will. Critics of free will argue that such an outcome would violate natural laws, because how free will interacts with matter—to turn the car left or right—is itself hugely problematic. This problem is called the mind-body duality and the difficulty in this duality is that wherever the mind interacts with the body, it must itself become the body.

The Vedic view on free will is quite different. In this view, the soul is not the driver of the car; it is only a passenger. The universe is, in this view, many cars moving deterministically (this determinism should not, however, be identified with classical physical determinism which entails continuous motion of objects; the Vedic determinism is that the events in the universe are fixed, although the actors in those events are not). The movement of these cars constitutes the deterministic evolution of the universe and the souls are passengers in these cars. If the soul gets into a particular mind-body vehicle, it is carried forward deterministically by that vehicle. The passenger cannot change the course of that vehicle, but it can change its understanding of that situation. For instance, the passenger could think that it is in fact the car, and the deterministic motion implies that there is no free will. Conversely, the passenger can believe that it is the car but the car's motion is governed by his free choices. Finally, the passenger can believe that it is different from the car, which is moving deterministically, and while he cannot change the car's course, he can still potentially change the car.

The motion of each car is deterministic, but which car is occupied next can be freely chosen, if you understand the mechanism by which the soul moves from one car to another. Those who don't understand this mechanism will see that the car moves deterministically, and therefore there is no free will. Since underlying the motion of the car are subtle material objects—such as the mind, intelligence, ego, and morality—you can also identify with the meanings in these senses and believe that the car is moving according to your mental states (which would be true) and therefore the car is under the control of your free will (which would be false). The free will opponent identifies himself with the body and interprets the deterministic motion of that body to indicate the denial of free will. The free will proponent identifies himself with the mind and interprets the mental states as controlling the bodily states and concludes that these mental states are themselves equal to free will. Both positions, in Vedic philosophy, are effectively false. Free will is a property of consciousness, not that of the body or the mind. Both body and mind are working according to the laws of nature, but these are different kinds of laws than employed in current physical science.

True free will begins in understanding how we are different from both the body and the mind. Those who do not have this understanding may propose or oppose free will, and their reasons for doing so would be false. The Vedic view is that the succession of experiences—the cars that the passenger occupies—are determined by natural laws if one's theory is false. However, if the nature's theory is perfected, by detachment from the body and the mind, then the passenger can choose the type of vehicle it wishes to travel in.

Free will is therefore always real, and it begins in the ability to choose different explanations of the same situation. Nature is a moral place because the use of false theories entails moral consequences that can correct the theories. When the theory of nature—the worldview of the observer—is perfected, morality ends. Now, the observer's choice of theories is fixed, but his choice of phenomena is free. An individual observer therefore has free will either to choose an arbitrary theory or arbitrary phenomena. These two kinds of choices are mutually exclusive. If an arbitrary theory has been chosen, then the phenomenal encounters are fixed. If, however, a specific theory has been chosen, the phenomenal encounters are free. This makes the viewpoint scientific for two reasons. First, it gives a test for the correct theory: the correct theory would reinstate the free will of phenomena. Second, if a false theory has been chosen, it leads to the formation of predictive laws about the succession of experiences. This view not only tells us which theory would be correct, but what happens if the theory isn't correct.

Where Do Theories Exist?

Morality is a natural phenomenon in Vedic philosophy, not a transcendental one. This natural phenomenon has a cause and effect: the cause is a false theory and the effect is the succession of experiences. I have described the mechanism of this cause and effect, and how it could be understood in natural terms, in *Moral Materialism*. The problem of morality—in this view—is tied to the problem of epistemology. How do we know the truth? The short answer is that if you know the truth, then the free will of choosing the theories is over, but the free will of choosing experiences begins. If you don't know the truth, then the free will of choosing theories exists, but the free will of experiences doesn't. Either way, free will always exists, although in different forms. Morality is the consequence of a natural interaction between matter and our theories about it. For this interaction to be scientifically described, theories about nature must exist materially, apart from the material phenomena they describe.

Philosophers—such as Quine—have recognized the underdetermination of theories by experiences. Often there are many plausible explanations for the same phenomena, which arise depending upon which parts of the phenomena are neglected in theory formation. For instance, the gravitational theory of planetary motion neglects the complicated structure inside the planet. If this theory were applied to much smaller objects—such as the body of a living being—the theory would fail. Obviously, the complete comprehension of any phenomenon in fullness is not always easy. To formulate theories, scientists proceed through simplifying assumptions, which often exclude many aspects of a phenomenon not directly relevant to the prediction. For instance, the color of a billiard ball may seem irrelevant to the outcome of a collision between billiard balls, and we might neglect the color in the computation of kinematic behaviors. In other contexts, color becomes more pertinent. The collision amongst the billiard balls thus underdetermines the theory by which it is explained, because it is not clear whether the explanation should include just the kinematics or even the color of the ball.

The underdetermination of theories by phenomena is an outcome of describing selective parts of the phenomena. Which parts of a phenomenon are considered relevant for theory formation is not determined by nature, but by the observer of that nature. The observer's consciousness focuses upon certain parts of the world and deems them important; the other parts are simply ignored. Ideally, a perfect theory of nature must consider all aspects of experience. But, pragmatically, science ignores most parts of experience and proceeds with several simplifying assumptions. These assumptions bring into focus some parts of experience while defocusing others. If the focus of experience were changed, some new facets of experience might be added while other facets would be dropped. The phenomena would factually remain the same, but its explanations would now differ. The phenomena would seem to underdetermine the theory, because of the ability to selectively focus upon its parts.

Do theories of nature exist in the observer? Yes, they do, not just as the outcome of scientific inquiry, but even as the observational bias of focusing on certain parts of the same phenomena. Classical physics, for instance, focused on very limited aspects of everyday experience. It started from the simplifying assumption that nature does not have color, taste, smell, touch, and sounds, although we do perceive the world through these sensations. How the world of physical properties becomes perceptual qualities was not considered relevant to physics. Then, the manner in which the brain connects successive states of an object in time, even though matter exists only right now (and not in the past or future), was not considered relevant to the physical description. The basis of our beliefs that when we see something we are seeing something that truly exists "out there" was never understood or explained. Classical physics proceeded by neglecting several aspects of the phenomena that it set out to explain. The physicist's consciousness focused its attention on certain limited parts of the world, excluding all others.

The limited successes of these theories can be attributed to the fact that we have modeled some limited parts of a phenomenon. These models are not accurate descriptions of nature. But they are sufficiently accurate models of the limited parts we aim to describe. Such models of nature are a direct outcome of perceptual filtering: we selectively discard some parts of a phenomenon and focus on others. There is nothing in nature that tells us which parts of a phenomenon we must focus upon. This focus is clearly our choice.

This filtering process is called *māya* in Vedic philosophy. It covers an observer's consciousness and focuses its attention on some limited parts of the world. *Māya* literally means "that which is not" and it acts as filters of observation: the observer is naturally drawn towards certain parts of the perceptual field and drawn away from the other parts. Modern science, in the Vedic view, is an outcome of a particular type of *māya* which compels the scientists to focus upon the material objects, while discarding the process by which the perception itself takes place. Once limited successes in such an explanation have been obtained, the scientist now attempts to extend this explanation to the perceptual process, professing that the observer is itself a material phenomenon, although failing miserably in accounting for even the most elementary aspects of experience.

Māya is also material, but it is not the material objects or phenomena. It is rather the filters applied on the phenomena to create limited experiences. When the senses, mind, and intellect are so absorbed in perception of the material objects, the process by which such a perception occurs is completely defocussed. One must stand back from the material objects to understand the perceptual process. But that standing back itself requires detachment from the objects. It also requires the development of new perceptual faculties. For instance, to understand how the senses perceive sensations, the mind must be developed to perceive the senses themselves. This in turn requires the conscious attention to be focused upon the mind rather than the senses and the objects they perceive. Similarly, to understand how the mind perceives concepts, the intellect must be developed to perceive the activities of the mind, which in turn requires the conscious attention upon the intellect. To understand how the intellect perceives order and structure, the ego must be developed to perceive the activities of the intellect, which in turn requires the conscious attention upon the ego. If the senses are completely absorbed in the material objects, higher level perceptions which require a detachment from these objects cannot arise.

By theories of nature therefore I don't mean the mathematical formulae created to explain and predict phenomena. By theories I mean the filters of perception by which limited parts of reality are understood. These filters create false theories of nature, which in turn create moral consequences which determine an observer's experiences. The living being's bondage in the material world is therefore traced, in Vedic philosophy, to an epistemological problem of not being able to perceive the whole reality and understand it. The bondage arises from the use of perceptual filters to focus upon limited parts of the phenomena, while neglecting the other parts. The goal of religion is to help remove these filters and bring the observer face-to-face with a complete understanding of reality. If you are wearing goggles that filter out certain parts of reality, you cannot expect to see the whole reality unless you remove the goggles.

This raises an important question: If we see the world through goggles then how do we know that some parts of the world are being filtered out? How can we know that certain unseen things exist if we can never see their existence? The short answer to this problem is that if you see only limited parts of reality and formulate theories of nature based on this perception, then the formulated theories would always be incomplete. They will work partially but fail in other ways. The necessity to incorporate other forms of reality therefore arises from the predictive and explanatory incompleteness of theories formed through a filtered perception. To fix this incompleteness, we must search for other forms of reality. Of course, we cannot find that reality unless we clean the googles. The problems of scientific incompleteness are therefore outcomes of the fact that we have formed theories by filtering many parts of the reality. The theories appear to work partially but they are eventually incomplete. Attempts to complete them without discarding their current assumptions lead to logical contradictions. Therefore, these theories are logically final in the sense that they cannot be improved. The improvement can come from a reformulation alone.

Ideally, such reformulations would be preceded by the ability to perceive other forms of reality within the current phenomena. But it is also possible that theories that are more complete than present scientific theories—and which incorporate additional ideas such as contextuality, abstraction, and intentionality—would compel us to seek experiences that involve such properties in nature.

The goal of science and religion in this view are identical: they involve the removal of perceptual filters by which we can see the complete reality. Present science is not the truth; it is an illusion. It is an elaborate illusion constructed by sustained focus on material objects while neglecting the manner in which these objects are perceived. Its problems have been exacerbated by a notion of matter devoid of contextuality, abstraction, and intentionality, and these problems will continuously hinder scientific progress, because these ideas cannot be retrofitted into the materialist ideology. Under this ideology, the scientists would continuously insist: Can you show me the mind? I can't see the mind; I can only see the material objects. Their dilemma is in effect that of cleaning your goggles to see what you don't see right now. Whether you clean it or not is a choice.

The Practice of Religion

The central goal for religion in Vedic philosophy is the cleansing of the goggles of perception, by which the observer attains freedom from *māya* and its free will of phenomena is reinstated. The Vedas describe four primary methods for cleansing, and they are respectively called *jñāna-yoga* or the cultivation of true knowledge, *karma-yoga* or the practice of selfless service and execution of duties, *rāja-yoga* or the practice of meditation, and *bhakti-yoga* or the practice of devotion. They all have a common goal—namely freedom from illusory knowledge—but they use different techniques to achieve it. These practices may be called the *methods* of religion, similar to the method of science. A brief discussion of these methods is helpful to illustrate how they differ, and how they achieve their goals.

Jñāna-yoga is the cultivation of knowledge, including a theoretical understanding of the nature of material reality, the process of perception, the understanding of the unconscious, and consciousness, and how this consciousness is morally implicated by its choices. By this understanding, the person becomes theoretically aware of deeper forms of reality. If this knowledge is perfected, the person can understand that nature comes into existence through a gradual process of differentiation from an undifferentiated absolute origin. With a theoretical understanding of deeper forms of reality, the person can attempt to perceive these realities. As the observer's choices shift from gross material objects to subtle and abstract forms of existence, the coverings of *māya* are also removed. This practice is said to be hard and the process is very long-drawn, especially as the philosopher delves deeper and deeper into his own experiences.

Karma-yoga traces the root of the living being's bondage to its flawed view of nature. In this view, there are two broad types of misconceptions. First, the living being can believe that there is no free will and the soul is destroyed when the body is destroyed. Second, the living being can believe that it is the mind, which is different from the body, and it therefore controls the body's functioning. The correct understanding of nature is that the living being has free will to choose the mind and body, but not to control the working of the mind or body. If you want to experience a different kind of phenomena, you would have to take on another kind of mind-body. In the Vedic view, all the minds and bodies are temporary vehicles. If you don't travel in a particular vehicle, someone else would. Once you get into a vehicle, you cannot control the course of the vehicle; however, you can get off the vehicle if you have become free of the consequences of your actions. *Karma-yoga* therefore urges the person to detach itself from the functioning of the mind-body. This detachment entails that person does not consider himself the doer of the actions being performed by the body. Neither does the person withdraw from the actions to be performed[28]. The essence of *karma-yoga* is that a person undergoes life as a *passenger*—neither attached to the results of the actions, nor averse to the actions. No consequences are produced from such observation, and the person gradually becomes free after finishing all previous consequences. Once the person has become free of the consequences, he can experience any phenomena, including those involving subtle realities. With such a direct encounter and awareness of subtle realities, the person destroys its material coverings that hid these realities.

Rāja-yoga or meditation adopts a more proactive approach to the discovery of truth. It does not wait for freedom from consequences, nor does it spend time on the philosophical understanding of subtle realities. Rather, it accepts that there are many subtle forms of reality and sets out on the path to experience them directly. To discover all these realities, the observer's consciousness must rise up the categorical hierarchy from objects to senses, from senses to the mind, from the mind to the intellect, from the intellect to the ego, from the ego to morality, and so on, in the same direction. The practice of meditation therefore withdraws the conscious attention away from the world and focuses it on more and more subtle forms of perception. The practices of *rāja-yoga* are designed to gradually raise the observer's attention and by focusing its attention to gradually more subtle forms of reality, the observer acquires a first-hand acquaintance with this reality. As the observer travels towards the root of the material tree, material coverings that blocked knowledge are destroyed and he becomes aware of the true nature of the reality. The process of raising attention involves the development of new forms of perception and its practices are often quite risky. For instance, without the guidance of an accomplished master expert in this process, such a practice can sometimes result in insanity.

Bhakti-yoga or devotion is the most widely recognized form of religion; it is also the least understood and the most criticized. Devotion involves prayer, deity worship, rituals, and myriad forms of religious symbolism, whose meanings may not always be clear even to their practitioners. Vedic philosophy, for instance, encourages the chanting of *mantras* which are sound-symbols, but their meanings and effects are either imperfectly known or not known at all. The problem of religious symbolism however is not unique to religions; it originates as the problem of conceiving any kind of meaning in matter. In physical theories, for instance, causality is in the material properties which exert 'forces' on other objects. In a semantic theory, the causality is in the meanings which the object represents. The effect of a *mantra* therefore does not depend on the frequency, phase and amplitude of its sounds. It rather depends on the meanings symbolized by that *mantra*. To understand the *mantra's* effects, therefore, we have to first view it as a symbol of meaning. This understanding can stem from within science when sounds—and indeed all physical properties—are viewed as meaning symbols. As the devotee practices acquaintance with these meanings via material symbols, he becomes aware of subtle forms of reality and the coverings of *māya* which precluded this knowledge are removed.

The foundations for religious methods are in a certain viewpoint about the nature of reality—(1) reality is hierarchical not linear, (2) the observer has the free will to form theories about this reality; different theories terminate this hierarchy at different nodes in a hierarchical tree, (3) each such termination has a consequence, unless the tree is terminated at its root, (4) arbitrary terminations stem from a perceptual covering that entails limited forms of perception, and (5) the goal of knowledge is to remove these filters. The methods of religion are designed to discover the nature of truth. To even formulate the methods, certain assumptions about the nature of reality are essential. For instance, even science presumes that nature is material objects from which the observer is created. The assumptions underlying religion are no more valid or invalid just as assumptions. Their validity only lies in the extent to which their practice reveals the existence of reality and reinstates free will.

The Problem of Religious Symbolism

In Vedic philosophy, religious symbolism is meant to help the devotees experience the meanings which transcend matter by representing them in matter. While the meaning is transcendent, its expression is sensually accessible. The problem of any symbolism involves an understanding of how meanings can be encoded in matter, but it goes beyond the problem of material symbolism. The difference between material and religious symbols is that their meanings are dual and non-dual respectively. Let's understand this difference.

As we saw earlier, all material meanings are defined through a distinction from the opposite type of meaning. Thus, for instance, 'hot' is defined in opposition to 'cold,' 'sweet' is defined in opposition to 'bitter,' etc. These distinctions are created as the opposite branches of a semantic tree, but the root of this tree is non-dual. Since the root of the semantic tree is non-dual, to represent this root in matter, the meaning in the symbol must also be understood non-dually. This means, for instance, that if the symbol represents the root of the semantic tree, then this representation cannot be defined through material oppositions since the root is itself not defined via oppositions. All material meanings are defined contextually[29], but the root of the semantic tree is defined prior to all contexts because it originates them. The symbol that represents the transcendent meanings must therefore be defined independent of contexts.

The problem of religious symbolism can be resolved only if the meaning of such symbols—e.g., sounds, sights, colors, forms, movements, etc.—are universal and not contextual. Contextual meanings abound in our everyday world. The color red, for instance, can contextually denote the material meanings of 'danger,' 'passion,' or 'stop,' and these contextual interpretations entail that the meaning of red is not fixed independent of contexts. If religious symbols were treated just as the material ones, then their meanings would be defined in relation and opposition to other symbols. The oppositions would mean that a single meaning cannot be defined, and the relation would mean that meanings have to be defined in contexts. As the context changes, the same physical object would denote different meanings, and each such meaning would be opposed to other meanings. While such symbols could denote material meanings, they would not represent any non-dual or universal meaning. If some symbols have to denote religious meanings, then these meanings must also be context-independent and therefore non-dual.

The resolution of this problem requires an important distinction between an *instantiation* and an *elaboration* of a concept. Let's consider elaboration first. If we take the idea of a car, its elaboration involves adding details to this idea by which the abstract concept becomes a contingent concept. The abstract concept, in this case, is an object and its elaboration is the parts that make up that object. For example, the elaboration of a car can comprise details about the engine, chassis, steering, wheels, etc. The car as a whole is an object, but the parts of the car are functionally different entities, and their functions are defined contextually in relation to the whole. Contrast this fact with the instantiation of the idea of a car. Through instantiation, we can create many individual cars, but these cars are not functionally related to the other cars. If the car is treated as a collection, its parts would not be different parts of a single car; rather they would each be individual cars. In an instantiation, each member of a collection is also a car. In an elaboration, no member of the collection is a car; rather all members together make up a car.

This distinction is important because the contextual meanings of the parts within a collection exist in the case of elaboration but not in the case of instantiation. As we have discussed previously, the parts of a functional system get their functional properties in relation to the whole, and therefore the whole is logically prior to the parts. In the case of instantiation, too, the whole is logically prior to the parts. In both elaboration and instantiation, therefore, the whole is logically prior to the parts and the parts are defined in relation to the whole. Nevertheless, in the case of elaboration the parts together make up a single whole, while, in the case of instantiation, each of the parts separately represents the whole. While, in elaboration, different parts of the whole must be described in terms of opposites—such as head and tail, front and back, top and bottom—in instantiation, the different parts of the whole don't need opposites.

The difference between material and religious symbolism can therefore be attributed to two distinct ways of expanding a concept by elaboration and instantiation. Material symbols are elaborations of the semantic root, while religious symbols are instantiations of the semantic root. A material symbol is a part of a whole—like a steering is part of a car—and it represents only a part of the meaning of the whole. In contrast, a religious symbol is also a part of the whole, but it represents the complete meaning of the whole. The material universe is created by elaborating the root node in the semantic tree. The religious symbols, however, must be created by instantiating the root node itself within the universe. The processes for constructing material and religious symbols are therefore different. Quite specifically, even though the religious symbols also appear to be material objects, semantically they are quite different.

In Vedic philosophy, certain material objects—such as the sound of God's name, pictures, and deities of His form—are viewed as instantiations of the whole within the whole rather than elaborations of the whole into parts. While they certainly appear to be material objects, their meanings are not parts of the meaning of the bigger material context that surrounds them. Rather, the meanings of such symbols are directly the meanings of the whole from which other parts—the symbols with material meanings—are created.

The simplest scientific analogue of this phenomena is the use of words such as 'space,' 'time,' and 'universe' within the space, time and universe. The meanings of the words 'space,' 'time,' and 'universe' are not defined in relation to the other symbols such as temperature, mass, speed, energy, etc. Rather, temperature, mass, speed, energy, etc., are themselves defined in relation to space, time and universe[30]. The words 'space,' 'time,' and 'universe,' therefore, refer not to specific objects within space, time and universe, but to the entire space, time, and universe as a whole. They are symbols of the whole within the whole. While individual locations in space, time and universe are *elaborations* of the idea of space, time, and universe, the words 'space,' 'time,' and 'universe' are *instantiations* of space, time, and universe within the space, time, and universe.

Of course, the words 'space,' 'time,' and 'universe' (which instantiate these ideas semantically) also exist at some specific location in space, time, and universe, and these words thus appear to be material objects. Therefore, the objects have to be looked at semantically rather than physically. In the semantic description, we will find that the meanings of some objects go beyond the meanings of the entire context that contains them materially. Such objects cannot be treated like other material symbols; they have to be seen not as elaborations of the containing context, but as instantiations.

Meaning, Choice, and Pleasure

The ability to represent the whole within the whole entails that the whole has a form. If space, time, and universe can be spoken of in words and described in scientific theories, then they must also have forms. If these were formless, it would be impossible to represent them or speak about them—the question would simply be: What word, sentence, or mathematical theory accurately describes something that cannot be described? This raises the question: What is the nature of the whole from which the individual parts are created? Vedic philosophy describes that the Supreme Being has three aspects: *sat* or existence, *chit* or choice, and *ananda* or pleasure. Each of these three aspects has a six-fold division—there are six kinds of existence, six kinds of choices, and six kinds of pleasure. The Supreme Being's form is the collection of these eighteen aspects.

God's existence is the combination of six original ideas: knowledge, beauty, objectivity, fame, wealth, and power. These represent the essential meanings from which all other meanings are constructed and they constitute the existence of God, also known as *sat*. Everything expanded from God is also some combination of the above six meanings; everything is some knowledge, beauty, objectivity, fame, wealth, and power. All such expansions of God are also meanings, and they can be viewed as symbols of meaning. These symbols have myriad interpretations, which are constructed from six fundamental kinds of abilities to interpret—thinking, feeling, willing, knowing, acting, and being. The manner in which a symbol is interpreted represents the *models* of language, or the ways in which the meanings can be experienced. The thinking, feeling, willing, knowing, acting, and being of a symbol are different ways to experience a symbol—e.g., the word 'clean' can be interpreted in different ways as thinking clean, feeling clean, willing clean, knowing clean, acting clean, and being clean. Common manifestations of such interpretations are available in language when the same word is interpreted as an adjective, noun, and verb. The world 'clean,' for instance, can denote a noun (the house needs a clean), a verb (he is cleaning the house), and an adjective (she is a very clean person). These interpretations of the word are called *chit* which means the ability to choose, and represents the *activity* of the soul. As these interpretations are experienced by consciousness, they also become *ananda* or pleasure. The Vedas describe six ways of enjoying the interpretations forming different kinds of relationships—self, appreciative, servitor, friend, parent, and amorous. The relationships result in different activities, which act upon different meanings.

God is therefore said to be the *form* of six kinds of meanings, activities, and pleasures. Each of these six categories begins in God's self— God is an object or individual, He has the choice of being or interpreting the meaning of His own existence, and He bears a relationship to Himself, namely, the relationship of self-awareness. Everything else is said to be expanded from these three categories.

Thus, all knowledge is expanded from the idea of knowledge, all beauty is expanded from the idea of beauty, all wealth is created from the idea of wealth, and all objects are created from the idea of objectivity. God is therefore also an idea, although God is the origin of all other ideas. Philosophers in the Western world have had a problem with this notion; they believe that ideas and things are distinct; that the things exist in this world and ideas exist in another Platonic world of ideas. But this separation between ideas and things is problematic not just in understanding God, but even in understanding material objects; as we have seen, science can be completed only by treating material objects as symbols of ideas. These symbols don't combine idea and matter (as Aristotle thought). Rather, even matter is an idea, and it exists in a hierarchy of material categories, which are all different ideas. There is hence, in Vedic philosophy, no material substance; there are only material ideas.

The creation of the universe is creation of material ideas. When the universe is dissolved, the material ideas disappear. The origin of all ideas is some fundamental ideas—knowledge, beauty, objectivity, fame, power, and wealth—and these ideas are themselves not material. However, they can have a material manifestation. Vedic philosophy distinguishes between material and spiritual ideas: this distinction is based on the manner in which these ideas are constructed. The material ideas are constructed through oppositions (such as between hot and cold) while spiritual ideas are constructed without oppositions. Therefore, when knowledge, beauty, objectivity, fame, power, and wealth are refined to produce mutually opposite ideas (such as hot and cold), the ideas are material. When hot and cold are not mutually opposed, the ideas are spiritual.

Whether 'hot' and 'cold' are mutually opposed ideas depends on the type of logic used, and all refined ideas are produced from abstract ideas by the use of logic (I will further elaborate this point in the next section). The logic of the material universe involves three principles: *identity, mutual-exclusion,* and *excluded-middle.* For instance, if we speak about the weather, it can be either hot or cold (mutual exclusion) and it cannot be both hot and cold (excluded-middle)[31]. The logic of the material universe is not the only possible logic; other kinds of logic can be constructed by dropping either the principles of mutual-exclusion and excluded-middle, or both[32].

The Vedas describe four kinds of realms constructed from different logics which use or drop one or more of the principles of mutual-exclusion and excluded-middle—(a) the material world uses both principles, (b) the *brahmān* realm drops non-contradiction but retains mutual-exclusion, (c) the *vaikuntha* realm retains non-contradiction but drops mutual-exclusion, and (d) the *goloka* realm drops both mutual-exclusion and non-contradiction. In the *brahmān* realm, the choice between hot and cold exists (mutual-exclusion), although there are no real objects that are hot and cold (non-contradiction). While the preferences for one of the opposites exist, these choices are not actually enacted, and the living beings in this realm can fall into matter, when this choice is exposed to reality. In the *vaikuntha* realm, the choice between hot and cold (mutual-exclusion) is dropped, although mutually opposed objects (non-contradiction) exist. The living beings are free of these contradicting choices, and they are equal to both hot and cold, although in reality these choices can be made[33]. Living beings in this realm can fall into matter if the existence of opposites develops into choices for one of the opposites. In the *goloka* realm, both the choices between opposites and the opposites themselves are dropped. Living beings in this realm never fall into matter, because there is neither the desire to pick opposites, nor is there any exposure to opposites in reality.

The three principles of material logic—namely, identity, mutual-exclusion, and non-contradiction—are therefore not themselves fundamental because there can be other kinds of logic. The various kinds of logics are modifications of a more fundamental principle of truth, choice, and pleasure denoted by the terms *sat, chit,* and *ananda*. In the material world, the term *ananda* or pleasure denotes the identity principle and it signifies the individual observer which underlies all kinds of individuality. *Chit* or choice is the principle of mutual-exclusion due to which we are inclined to pick one of the opposites. *Sat* or existence is the principle of non-contradiction by which opposite meanings are created. Thus, in matter, objects are opposed, we choose between the opposites, and we enjoy (or suffer) either of the opposites. In *brahmān* the choice between opposites exists but the opposites don't exist, and hence the experience of opposites is never created. In *vaikuntha* the opposites exist but they are never chosen, and the living beings hence never enjoy or suffer them. Finally, in *goloka* neither the opposites nor their choices exist, and hence the experiences of these opposites are never generated[34]. In each of the realms (*brahmān, vaikuntha,* and *goloka*) the duality of the material world is not experienced, either due to lack of choice or due to the lack of reality or both, and they are thus non-dual. Only the material world creates the conscious experience of duality.

Since the universe is produced from *sat, chit,* and *ananda,* which is also the complete form of God, the understanding of *sat, chit,* and *ananda* further simplifies our view of God: God is logic! The current study of logic, however, makes several simplifying assumptions about the nature of logic. First, logic is defined as consistency in nature which precludes the existence of opposites, and hence the existence of meanings. Second, the choices of a living being—which exist as mutual-exclusion in logic—are denied because only one of the choices could be true: If choices were to exist, then we could potentially choose false things, and that would violate the consistency of nature. A universe, in which both true and false things could exist, could not be described using consistent logic, and therefore the choices of truth and falsities must not exist. Finally, the notion of identity is transformed from the individuality of observers to the individuality of material particles; only material particles exist, and all other identities are fictitious. Modern thinking has thus transformed the principles of *sat, chit,* and *ananda*—which begin in the nature of God—into a logic of the material world that comprises material particles, which are devoid of choices and meanings.

The subsequent debates about the conflict between religion and science are the outcomes of a very fundamental flaw in construing the nature of logic. The flaw in current material logic is the idea of *consistency.* Logicians suppose that the universe must be consistent: that is, there are no conflicts, no wars, no disagreements, and no semantic oppositions; that there is only one logical law, which governs everything deterministically. Clearly, if the universe is logically consistent, then even the disagreement between religion and science must be an illusion! We must suppose that even this contradiction is created from a deeper level of logical consistency! If the universe is logically consistent, and our theories about nature are only manifestations of nature, then nothing could be false. Even the so-called evolution of science is just the same laws of nature producing newer ideas in our heads, and these ideas are epiphenomena of the real laws of nature, which produce the theories. How, then, can the same law produce two contradicting theories? Would it not entail a logical contradiction within the laws themselves?

To actually progress in the study of nature, we must allow the existence of false things, which require the existence of opposites, and thereby reinstate the existence of meanings. Once opposite meanings can exist, there must also be a room for choices. Logicians in effect are trying to construct a material universe that is devoid of meanings and choices. Clearly, the problems of this view of nature and logic begin in the problem of meaning and choice. If nature has meanings, then opposites would exist. Those opposites would enable choices, and those choices would require a new kind of identity—the individual observer that can experience the consequences of these choices. The problem of meaning therefore not only impacts how the world is understood, but also changes how logic itself is understood. While the most fundamental thing in the universe is logic, this logic is a variation upon *sat, chit,* and *ananda.* Therefore, when we speak about logic being the most fundamental entity in nature, we can be speaking about God, provided logic is defined as meaning, choice, and individuality. The idea that God is the origin of the universe will not be illogical if God is understood as logic.

Logic and Time

One of key problems in understanding the rational behavior of nature is: How is this logic *computed*? Science, for instance, describes nature in terms of mathematical laws, which have to be computed to determine the evolution of the universe. If an object is at state X and its next state Y is determined by a formula F, then F must be computed with X as its input to determine the next state Y. How are these computations being carried out? Where is the computer that computes the natural laws? Note that when all of nature is described mathematically, then if such a computer were to materially exist then it would also be governed by the same (or some other) mathematical laws. Before this computer can compute the laws for the rest of the universe, it must be functional as a computer, which would require the computer itself to be computed by some yet another computer, and so forth, *ad infinitum*. The idea that nature is logical and mathematical is therefore not as straightforward a thesis as it seems at first sight, because the laws themselves have to be computed, which require some machine to compute them, which would in turn have to be computed by another machine, etc.

The only way this problem can be avoided is if there is a machine that computes its own behavior and does not depend on another machine outside of it. No such machine can be conceived materially because matter needs to be driven to compute, and if that drive is determined by a mathematical law, then there must be another driver to drive the machine that first computes those laws.

In Vedic philosophy, there is a driver—a form of God—who self-computes. While the form of logic in each realm is called *Vasudeva*, the self-computing form of this logic is called *Saṅkarṣaṇa*. This latter form of God appears in the material world as *time* and He is a form of consciousness that converts logic into computation. The material universe is said to be a manifestation of this self-driven computer who computes and controls the entire universe. The computer in the universe is therefore not another material object; it is rather time. Time drives the creation, conservation, and annihilation of the universe. During creation, two opposite ideas are created simultaneously thereby manifesting a distinction. During annihilation, the distinction between the opposite ideas is destroyed. During conservation, the opposite ideas may be used to modify other ideas. Whether two ideas are created, destroyed, or modified is determined by the nature of time. While the semantic properties of nature can be understood by the theory of *sat*, *chit*, and *ananda*, how these properties produce an evolving universe requires an understanding of how the logic of nature is being computed by time.

Time is said to be consciousness because it is self-driven, and its choices are beyond the material objects. While the material objects

are defined as opposites, time is the creation, annihilation, and mutation of these opposites[35]. The creation, conservation, and annihilation
of opposites form a cycle of change, and time is therefore said to be
cyclic; the life of the universe is quite like our lives—we are born, we
grow and sustain, and eventually we die. The cycles in the universe are
more sophisticated because they operate at several levels of abstraction: the abstract levels of matter undergo a slower evolution relative
to the contingent levels of matter. Atomic objects too are cyclic, and
they are called "sound," in analogy to a vibrating membrane which
vibrates cyclically[36]. The periodic oscillatory pattern of atomic objects
makes them phonemes or sound-symbols whose meaning content is
given in relation to other phonemes.

While *sat*, *chit*, and *ananda* represent meaning, choice, and pleasure which are eternal, their expansion through time—which follows
a cyclic pattern of creation, conservation, and destruction—makes this
eternality temporary. There is hence a profound connection between
the fact that meanings are defined through oppositions in material
logic, and the temporariness of the material world. The oppositions
between meanings define the structure of universal space—namely,
that locations in space represent types. The oppositions between creation and destruction define the structure of universal time—namely,
that instances in time also represent types. The duality of the spatial
structure entails the duality of the temporal structure, and vice versa.
The structure of space represents all that can *exist*, while the structure
of time *constructs* these things. The construction represents computation, and these computations select the possibilities to create the
existents. This selection of actuality from possibility is time; it is a type
of choice and it evolves cyclically: the same possibilities become real
(appear) and unreal (disappear) at different times. They are, therefore, logically possible always, but they are *created* and *destroyed*
(manifest and unmanifest) in time. None of these possibilities is, however, *disproved*.

Any empirical theory of nature can therefore unprove ideas if they
are not discovered in nature, but it cannot disprove them; those ideas
would be proved at another time when time manifests them as realities. In classical logic, if X is true, then not-X must be false. In semantic
logic, X and not-X are always simultaneously defined by their mutual

opposition. Of course, if we find X and don't find not-X, we can con-clude that X is true and not-X is false, but that would be a mistake of using classical logic which relies on consistency. In a semantic sys-tem, if we can prove X then we can also prove not-X because both are defined simultaneously. The focus now cannot be whether X or not-X is true; the focus must be how the pair of opposites (X and not-X) are simultaneously created[37].

The semantic view alters not just our view of matter, the notions about space-time, the nature of cognition and perception, the ideas about soul and God, but ultimately, the nature of logic itself. The con-flict between religion and science is a consequence of this profound difference between these two views. However, this difference can be rationally understood and empirically confirmed. Those who have argued that religion has nothing to say about the nature of the mate-rial world need to take a closer look at Vedic philosophy. The religious ideas cannot be reconciled with those in modern science because they involve different presuppositions about matter, perception, con-sciousness and ultimately logic. However, the religious ideas can be expressed using a new kind of *semantic logic*, which will significantly differ from the logic of modern science. The semantic logic will also make predictions although these predictions will differ from those made by modern science. The confirmation of the new predictions of semantic logic represents a new science in which soul, God, and morality, will be essential scientific ideas.

3

Epistemological Issues

A little philosophy inclineth man's mind to atheism, but depth in philosophy bringeth men's minds about to religion.
—Francis Bacon

The Problem of Illusion

In the previous chapter I briefly discussed one of the problems in the scientific method, namely that the method doesn't tell us if a scientific theory is true because all theories are always potentially revisable depending on the phenomena they encounter. I also alluded to the fact that all scientific theories set out to describe limited parts of a phenomenon to simplify theory construction; all physical theories, for instance, ignore the manner in which sensations occur, how the mind creates and perceives ideas, and why these ideas and sensations are applied back to the world. One of the biggest unstated assumptions in all current scientific theories is that they proceed with simplifying assumptions, and aim to describe limited aspects of any phenomena. As more aspects of a phenomenon are incorporated into a theory, those simplifying assumptions must be dropped, leading to profound revisions in the theory. Classical physics is for instance an approximation of quantum mechanics, relativity theory and thermodynamics, and it fails in different scenarios when it has to deal with very small, very large, or even everyday collections[38].

There is, however, an even more profound problem in the scientific method which arises when we incorporate the existence of meanings in nature. In the physical view of nature, if a thing exists, it is also true; there is no difference between existence and truth. For instance, I can say that the sun exists because the observations indicate some facts which can be interpreted to be true. However, this line of reasoning cannot be applied to semantic objects—e.g., a newspaper or TV. Everything we see on TV or read in the newspaper is not necessarily true, even though it exists. The distribution of squiggles on a newspaper and the pixels on the TV screen are facts of nature. However, these facts are not necessarily true. The assumption that since these pixels and squiggles can be observed, their existence must also indicate their truth is false. The fact that the squiggles and pixels could have represented the truth, but they do not necessarily, entails that when matter describes other material objects, then the existence of matter does not indicate truth.

Scientific theories are now required to explain both truths and falsities, and we cannot conclude the truth of a proposition from its existence. Physical objects don't refer to other objects; they don't have any representational capability and they do not denote anything other than themselves. The physical property of an object is the truth about that object, and that's all the truth that science needs to know. Semantic objects differ in this sense. A semantic object refers to other objects and it represents their properties. The physical properties of such an object can indicate the existence of that object, but the representational and intentional properties of that object indicate whether the object in fact represents truth. If we only look at the physical properties, and don't understand or decode their meanings, we would infer the object's existence into its truth.

The problem for a scientific theory is now two-fold: (1) it must explain the observations, and (2) it must tell us whether that observation is true or false. Just because I can see something (and confirm its existence through repeated observation) does not imply its truth. The problem is similar to the observation of the TV or newspapers. We can be sure that they exist through repeated observations. But whether their existence itself tells us something true is not certain. When an object is only a thing, then its existence is the truth. When an object is a message, then its existence is not always the truth.

The flaw in empiricism is that it equates existence with truth, because empiricism is defined as the measurement of physical properties. If empiricism were defined as the measurement of meanings, then the existence of things would not be a complete empiricism. Rather, one would also need to know if that existence indicates truth or falsities. For instance, in the case of relativity, a moving observer detects time dilation and length contraction, and these are treated as physical facts about nature. Since experiments are defined as measuring physical facts rather than meanings, different moving observers will measure different lengths and times, and we cannot assert which of these measurements is in fact true. If measurements were defined as the detection of meanings, some measurements would be deemed false: they would be akin to visual illusions. The illusion exists, but its existence doesn't indicate the truth. It follows that my conclusion that lengths are contracted and time is dilated is a fact about my perception rather than a fact of reality.

The problem of illusion was considered early in the history of empiricism: If our experiences can be illusions, how do we know that we actually perceive reality? Empiricists postulated that the solution to this problem was *induction*: if we observe the same thing many times over, and each time the result is the same, we can conclude that the observation is true. This conclusion is false because everyone sees the tracks of a train converge at a distance, but we never conclude that the tracks actually converge. We have learnt to discard such perceptions as illusions[39]. No matter how many times we see certain things, we don't believe them to be true. The idea of induction is therefore flawed because the problem of illusion is never solved by repeated experimentation. Instead, it is solved by attributing the perception to the observer rather than to reality. In this case, we must suppose that the apparent track convergence is not due to the tracks but due to quirks in our perception. In relativity, similarly, we must suppose that the lengths and times do not actually shrink, although we will perceive these as contraction and dilation if we have been moving. We might also say that the length contractions and time dilations are a property of the meters and clocks we are carrying (which are analogues of our perceptual apparatus) rather than a change in the length and time itself.

This conclusion, however, raises a serious problem for empiricism: How do we know which experiences are properties of the observer (and could therefore be illusions) and which ones are facts of nature? After all, we only have access to our experiences to know the world. How do we know whether these experiences themselves are true or false? Remember that repeated experimentation doesn't solve the problem because we can be repeatedly deluded. This idea is of course not new when taken in its most generalized form. Empiricists, for instance, have relegated qualitative properties—taste, touch, smell, sound, and sight—to the observer's mind (and thus treated them as illusions), but maintained an object's physical properties—such as length, time, speed, mass, etc.—as facts about nature. This distinction between primary and secondary properties was supposed to solve the problem of illusion, but it doesn't. As clearly seen in the case of converging tracks, we know that even the length measurement can be illusory. Similarly, as confirmed by relativity theory, different observers will see the same object to have different lengths. Removing secondary properties from science and using repeated experiments are both inadequate for illusions.

The solution to the problem of illusion is semantics: first there must be a theoretical room for allowing the possibility for some experiences to be illusions, which in turn requires a distinction between existence and truth. The experience exists in the observer, and the facts exist independent of the observer. It is not sufficient to observe the world, and not sufficient to observe it repeatedly. We must rather learn to see the state of the observer itself, because only when the observer's state is known can the observer know whether it perceives facts or sees illusions. Perception itself is therefore not true or false unless we know the state of the observer. Clearly, we cannot know this state through sensual perceptions, when it is the problems with this perception that we are trying to resolve. The problem of illusion drives a wedge between meaning and truth; what I perceive is the meanings I have, but they may not be true, because these meanings are conditioned by my current state. To know if my perception is true, I must first know my own state.

Western philosophers have had a lot of problem with this conclusion because it seems to imply that the knowledge of my own state is *a priori* knowledge (that which cannot be gained by the senses) and to gain such *a priori* knowledge I would have to adopt methods beyond empiricism. The above analysis implies that empiricism only gives us meanings (experiences) but does not tell us if these meanings are also true, because experience can potentially be an illusion. The problem in empiricism is that the facts obtained in experience have to be interpreted before they become truth. Is the converging track due to my senses or due to reality? That interpretation is foregone in empiricism. We suppose that we can observe the world as it exists, and once we observe it, we know that the observation indicates truth. If, however, we have to acknowledge an explicit role of interpretation in determining truth, then there is a far greater role for the observer in science than conceded so far.

Two Failed Solutions to Illusion

In lieu of an actual solution that determines the observer's state *a priori*, philosophers have offered two alternative solutions. These are respectively called *Coherentism* and *Foundationalism*. Coherentism says that we cannot know the truth of any single fact in isolation. Rather, as we go on collecting many facts, and if these seem to fit together very well, we can believe in their truth. For instance, we can say that all length measurements must be performed by taking the scale of measurement to the place of the measurement. As we aggregate these facts about the track distance at different locations, we would find that the tracks remain equidistant. At that point, the perceived track convergence would be deemed a visual illusion.

The flaw in Coherentism is that it depends on the facts we have checked so far. In the track convergence case, a visual illusion would be detected only if we checked the track distances at many locations along the track. What if we hadn't carried out these measurements? What if our fact checking involved repeated measurements from a single point on the track? Naturally, we would have concluded that the world becomes smaller at a distance. The problem here is that if we widen the observation, some facts may turn out to be illusions. If we read a newspaper but then validate it against the facts, the newspaper may turn out to be false. On the other hand, we might read many newspapers which print the same false story, and the news would then appear to be confirmed by many different instances. So, how wide must our observations be before we can be convinced of *any* truth? Isn't it possible that many things we consider true currently could become illusions[40] by the addition of new facts? Unless we know all the facts, can we even be convinced of the truth of any specific fact? Furthermore, can we even know all the facts?

Foundationalism says that we must know the truth before it is used to interpret the facts about the world. That is, you must have a theory of reality *a priori* before you use this theory to interpret the observed facts. For instance, if you are reading a newspaper, the only way you can know the truth of the stories in it, is if you already knew the truth before reading the newspaper. If you are observing the converging tracks, the only way you can know if this perception is false is if you knew that the tracks were designed to be parallel. Our knowledge—in a sense—does not begin in perceptions. It rather begins in some theories and beliefs about the world, which are then used to interpret the *truth* of what we see in the world. If you begin with the supposition that matter is length, mass, momentum, energy, etc., then you would interpret your perceptions of taste, color, smell, touch, and sound to be illusions. If, however, you begin in the supposition that your perceptions are true, then your interpretations of the world as physical properties would be false. Depending on your theory of nature, the same experience would be true or false. In Foundationalism, therefore, the basis of knowledge is not in experience; it is rather in our assumptions about the reality.

The problem with Foundationalism is underdetermination. We can begin in many different assumptions and they would in turn treat different facts about nature as being true or false. Which assumptions should we adopt? What should be the axioms of our view of nature? The problem is further exacerbated by the fact that science proceeds with simplifications; in science, we model limited parts of any phenomena, ignoring the other parts, and thereby the assumptions that would be necessary to be explain all parts. The premise that some parts of the phenomena are epiphenomenal illusions of some other fundamental facts is often a problem whose solution is left for the future. Whether this problem would eventually be solved is not known when those assumptions are made, and therefore whether the ignored parts are actually fundamental or epiphenomenal is a postulate in our current view of nature, which could be falsified in future. If all parts of the phenomena had to be explained right now, a different foundation would be necessary.

Geometrically speaking, Coherentism represents knowledge in a circle: ideas are circularly justified by each other. Foundationalism represents knowledge in a tree: there are some fundamental ideas whose truth must be known *a priori* before the truth of the facts can be understood. The practical problem in Coherentism is that its truth depends on the collection of all possible facts, but such a collection is never complete. The addition of a single new fact can change the entire approach to coherence and that has happened many times in science when a single new fact—such as the constant speed of light, or black-body radiation, or the irreversibility of thermal phenomena—have dramatically changed the scientific view. The theoretical problem in Coherentism is that it assumes that nature is logically consistent. That is, as we go on broadening the known set of facts, we must find a greater degree of consistency between them. However, if the universe is logically consistent, then how can false things even arise in the universe? How can false ideas exist in my mind, if both the ideas and the world are supposed to be logically consistent? Coherentism fails theoretically because nature is logically inconsistent. The existence of falsities, illusions, misperceptions, and deceits entails that nature is logically inconsistent.

Once nature is known to be logically inconsistent, there can never be consistency. There will always be some things that are 'hot' while other things are 'cold.' In fact, in the semantic view, both types of opposites must be equinumerous—every time we find an instance of 'hot,' there must also be an instance of 'cold.' It follows that if we were hoping to judge the truth of a proposition by finding a greater number of propositions which happen to be mutually consistent, then we will never find that consistency because there are always an equal number of anti-propositions in nature. The only way we could arrive at consistency is if we focused upon limited parts of the world, ignoring the other observations. However, this clearly entails incompleteness in our theory of nature, and the theory could potentially be falsified by a single contrarian instance.

Coherentism thus works only if the world is without meanings—which are defined by mutual opposites. If the world is without meanings then there is no distinction between existence and truth. The problem of truth therefore does not arise because every observation is in fact true. If you claim that the sky is purple while others say that the sky is blue, both ideas would have to be true, since clearly both are based on your perception or belief and there is no way to judge a truth beyond those perception and beliefs. The judgment of truth involves a distinction between existence and truth, and that distinction rests on the possibility of meaning, which in turn depends on the existence of mutual opposites, which in turn deny the possibility that nature is ultimately logically consistent.

Foundationalism, too, as it is defined currently, requires logical consistency because we derive conclusions from axioms using logical deduction. To correctly use the axioms for deduction, the axioms themselves must be consistent, and such consistent axioms would never produce the oppositions in meanings. Furthermore, if the axioms are consistent, then the universe of facts must also always be consistent and such a view cannot explain the emergence of lies and falsities. This is not a practical problem of checking all the facts. It is rather a theoretical constrain on any logically consistent system.

Practically, the number of axioms you incorporate into an axiomatic system depends on which phenomena are being explained. When limited parts of a phenomenon are being explained, the axiom set is also limited. When the phenomena are expanded or more parts of a single phenomenon are considered, the axioms themselves must be revised. This revision is not always obvious: How do we know which axioms to drop and which ones to add? For instance, if we had to explain sensations, should we try to derive them from physical properties, or should we replace physical properties with sensations? Foundationalism practically struggles because as new phenomena (or newer parts of a phenomenon) are added to a theory, it can cause a dramatic rejig to the axioms, which entails that the phenomena that were previously explained using one set of axioms must now be explained using newer axioms. This, however, entails that a newer explanation of all the phenomena must be found if even one part of one phenomenon was left unexplained.

This obviously means that doing science is easy in the beginning when there are many plausible explanations for any phenomena; all these explanations would appear to explain the facts equally well. However, as science progresses, explaining the phenomena that were so far unexplained become harder and harder because the newer explanation must not only explain the new facts, but also the old facts in a newer way. Finding explanations that fit both new and old phenomena can be very tricky because now there is a greater resistance to throwing away the ideas that worked so well for so many of the facts, even when they don't seem to fit the new facts. Furthermore, if there is a distinction between truth and existence, then it should be possible to construct false statements in a logical system, and that would in turn violate the assumptions about logic. How can a foundation of thinking have logical inconsistencies?

Coherentism and Foundationalism are therefore problematic for both theoretical and practical reasons. The theoretical problem is logical consistency which precludes the ability to explain falsities and distinguish them from truths. If you change the axioms, things which were true earlier become false, and vice versa. Similarly, if you encounter a true fact, but it doesn't fit with the known set of facts, should we reject the truth of all the known facts or just the truth of the new one? There are no *a priori* methods of deciding these questions and therefore these solutions to the problem of illusion are inadequate. The problem began in the quest for an observer's own state before the world state can be interpreted to be fact or illusion. However, both these methods leave the observer out of the picture, even though the problem of illusion begins in the observer. The problem lies not in reason and experience *per se*, but in how these are used by the observer. If I cannot decide the truth of a single fact independently, then I cannot decide which facts in a collection of facts are true or false. If I cannot determine which axioms are *a priori* true, then I cannot decide which axioms in a set of axioms must or must not be used. Therefore, the idea that collecting larger sets of facts solves the problem of the truth of a single fact, or the logical consistency between a large set of axioms makes each axiom true are both problematic: (1) the universe is not a consistent place, and (2) because it is inconsistent, we don't know which of the inconsistent facts or ideas are true, unless we know the truth *a priori*.

Decoding the Epistemological Problem

The central problem of epistemology is that of the proverbial five blind men and the elephant. The blind men see different parts of the elephant and think that the entire elephant must be like a tail, trunk, ear, stomach, or legs. They would like to see the entire elephant but they cannot see that elephant if they happen to *be* the tail, trunk, ear, stomach, or legs. To see the entire elephant, the perceiver must stand apart from the elephant and this is impossible if the observer happens to be a part of the universe. How can we step outside the universe and observe it from that "universal observer" perspective? No matter where you stand inside the universe, you will always see certain limited parts of that universe and you would *be* a limited part of the universe. Being a limited part of the universe would give you an understanding of the whole universe if all the parts of the universe were essentially identical. Modern science assumes that the universe is *uniform*; that the same laws of nature hold everywhere and the same reality exists everywhere in the same way.

The assumption of uniformity stems from a physical construal of nature, when there is only one *type* of thing in the universe, which can be described by the same kind of law. However, if the entire universe is only one type, then how do we construct the various types in perception? The problems of incompleteness, indeterminism, uncertainty, and irreversibility arise when a typed universe is reduced to a typeless physical world. Science will remain incomplete unless the types are restored. However, when we restore the types, then the universe is no longer uniform. Now, seeing what we see on Earth (or anywhere else in the universe) would not suffice to know the rest of the universe, because in a typed universe, we become one of the types. When you see the world being a certain type, then your perception is 'colored' by that type. Moreover, types similar to or consistent with our type would be considered true while all other types would be considered illusions. The typed vision modifies the world according to our type, and limits our recognition of other types. At the very least, the opposite types cannot fit into the same theory of nature without creating logical inconsistencies.

If you happen to be the tail of the elephant, you can never understand the elephant's belly, unless both the tail and the belly are seen as *parts* of the complete elephant. This in turn means that we must know the whole even before we determine the nature of the parts. If you observe the tail and model it like a rope, then that model would never explain the belly, because these are different types of entities. To understand these types, we must know that there is a type—the elephant—which reconciles the differences between the parts. The problem, however, is that arriving at the conception of the whole seems to require us to stand apart from the elephant; we cannot know the complete elephant if we are only a part of it.

The central problem of epistemology is therefore two-fold: (1) the universe has to be described as comprising many types, and (2) there has to be a type that reconciles the diverse types of the parts of the universe. If we drop (1) and treat the universe physically, then all descriptions are incomplete. If we assume (1) but don't use (2) then all descriptions would be inconsistent. All present theories of nature oscillate between these two extremes: either the theory is incomplete, but if we try to make it complete, it becomes inconsistent[41]. The consistency cannot be arrived at by taking a single type and applying it to the entire universe; the consistency can only be obtained by *deriving* the types in the parts from the whole type.

In the semantic universe, therefore, Coherentism cannot hold true because the trunk and the tail will never be the same type. Coherentism can only hold when the elephant as a whole is understood as a different type, of which the tail and the trunk are parts. Similarly, Foundationalism cannot be true, unless the elephant as a whole is fundamental and its parts are derived from this whole. Once the elephant has been understood, then the parts in the whole naturally become coherent. With such an understanding, the elephant becomes the foundation from which its parts are derived. Therefore, both Coherentism and Foundationalism become valid philosophical positions when the whole is understood, but they both remain false otherwise. The whole in this case is conceptually more abstract and logically prior to the parts in it. And that problem brings us back to the issue we started out with: How do we gain this abstract *a priori* knowledge? How do we know that we are the tails and legs of an elephant such that the perceived differences are not classified as truth and illusion, but rather reconciled as being relatively true from the standpoint of our current *perspectives*?[42]

The semantic hierarchical view helps us address this problem. Each observer in this view is a particular branch of the tree. The end-nodes of this branch are material objects—our body. Deeper than these end nodes are higher nodes—senses, mind, intelligence, ego, etc. Deeper than these nodes are qualitative experiences, and deeper than that is the individual consciousness. Even more subtle than the individual consciousness is God's consciousness. The higher types are therefore available in every single object and phenomena, provided we study that object or phenomena completely. For instance, the elephant's tail requires an understanding of the whole elephant. Similarly, the objects require an understanding of the senses, mind, intelligence, ego, etc. It is possible to trace the root of the tree from any branch of the tree, and a study of all the branches (the entire universe) is not necessary. The higher nodes in the tree define the types of the lower nodes, and to know the higher nodes, higher forms of perception are necessary. All branches of the tree exist, although they could be semantically opposed to the other branches. We cannot logically reconcile the end-nodes on the tree themselves, although we can reconcile the end-nodes to the root. In simple terms, we cannot have a common theory of the tail and the trunk of the elephant, if these are compared to each other. However, there can be a single theory if they are compared to the elephant.

To observe the deeper nodes in the tree, deeper forms of perception are needed. This perception is not the perception of the world; it is rather the perception of the self. To know that our perception may not be a fact about the world but a byproduct of our senses we must discover the nature of the senses. This perception is possible if senses themselves were derived from something more abstract, quite like the senses are more abstract than the objects they perceive. In Vedic philosophy, the mind is more abstract than the senses, and can therefore observe the senses. This means that before we can know the truth of sensations, we must a have theory about sensations—the theory would explain how the different senses are like the tail, leg, stomach, ear, and trunk of the elephant—in this case, the mind. The mind itself may be flawed, and its imperfections have to be observed by the intelligence which is more abstract than the mind. The intelligence too can be flawed, and it must be observed and corrected by the ego. The ego itself may be flawed and it must be corrected by a moral sense. This hierarchy continues into deeper forms of perception, up to the supreme consciousness.

The epistemological premise in modern science—that we already have the required methods of acquiring knowledge, namely, sensation and reason—is flawed because both methods produce theories of the tail and the trunk, not that of the elephant. The elephant itself cannot be observed if you happen to be the tail or the trunk. In fact, if you happen to be the tail of the elephant, you would try to model the trunk as a tail, and thereby fail to explain its behavior. Therefore it is impossible to understand the different parts of the world by modeling it after one part. The modeling problem can only be solved if we see the parts as products of a more abstract whole. Thus, for instance, in the semantic hierarchical view, the conflict between the tail and the trunk can be reconciled if we travel up the hierarchical tree of abstractions. This understanding in turn requires going beyond sensations into deeper forms of perception. Without such deeper kinds of abstractions, all theories will remain incomplete. Their incompleteness can be shown through predictive shortcomings; e.g., in the above case, attempts to model the trunk like a tail may work in some cases, but not in others. When the modeling doesn't work, we might be tempted to suppose that nature is random; sometimes it behaves like a tail but not always. This indeterminism prevents scientific progress. The correction of the theory needs deeper kinds of realities, which can perceive the fault in the theory rather than attribute the fault to randomness in nature.

Most scientists today don't adopt this view; they attribute the incompleteness in science to probability and randomness in nature, because the deeper forms of perception do not exist in them. In effect, the theories based on physical properties are incomplete, but they cannot be completed unless these objects are related to the senses and their perception of qualities. The theory of senses cannot be completed without relating these qualities to meanings, and so forth. Science is faced with a choice: it can view its inability to predict as an outcome of randomness in nature, or it can formulate deeper kinds of entities which will bridge this shortfall in prediction. Whether or not science makes this leap remains to be seen.

The Question of Faith

While an epistemology based on the development of deeper forms of perception can be stated quite easily and understood based on the semantic hierarchical view, there are clearly practical problems in developing such perception. How do we develop our mind to perceive the senses, and then develop the intelligence to perceive the mind, etc.? How do we even know that mind and intelligence are separate realities which exist in nature? In other words, how do we know what we don't know because we cannot experience it?

This problem amounts to the question of how we know the elephant if we can only see parts of that elephant. This is where it is important to see the elephant not as a collection of the parts, but as a more abstract entity from which the parts are derived. The elephant cannot be understood from the parts, because the parts are mutually contradicting. However, the parts can be understood if the elephant was understood. To understand the elephant we must see it as an abstract idea logically prior to the parts from which the contingent ideas are derived. Just as the idea of color is present in the idea of yellowness or greenness, and yet transcends it, the elephant is present within its leg and tail, even though it transcends it[43].

The key problem in looking at the tail and trunk of the elephant to derive the elephant is that as our knowledge progresses, it must attain a greater amount of unity. As we move up the hierarchical tree, we generalize and abstract. The problem in generalizing and abstracting is that you posit new kinds of conceptual entities, although you may not know how to measure or detect these entities. How then do we accept that these entities are real? How can we even make the generalizing step if we cannot suppose that these entities could potentially be real? The problem here is not that such generalizations cannot be logically shown to be true. The problem is that we cannot even *think* of such generalizations unless we have some experiences that correspond to these generalizations. As Einstein once said, all science is the refinement of experience; we first experience billiard balls and water waves before we generalize them into point particles and infinitely extended fields. If newer abstract entities have to be generalized from the contingent phenomena, then the corresponding experiences must already exist. But if the experiences don't exist, how can we even find such entities?

The only resolution to this problem is faith. Both science and religion adopt this approach to knowledge: they put their faith in some assumptions and use those assumptions to interpret the truth of the facts. Science, for instance, begins in the assumption that nature is physical properties, and some sensations (e.g., detector clicks and pointer movements) are interpreted as the measurement of physical properties. We don't have direct access to the physical properties themselves except through sensations, but we suppose that the world is objectively real physical properties. Religion similarly begins in the assumption that consciousness transcends matter, and the material world is then described as being produced from this consciousness. These are assumptions that we believe in; we don't know for sure that these would eventually be held true.

Faith is thus an unavoidable preliminary step in knowledge, unless the observer can develop advanced forms of perception by which he can perceive the *a priori* abstract realities from which the contingent facts are constructed. If such an advanced form of perception is absent, there is no alternative path to knowledge of reality, other than to put you faith in something—either your own thinking, the truth of the facts that you are perceiving, or the words of someone else who you suppose indeed knows the truth. If you perceive a tail and believe that the world must be tail-like, then that interpretation would hold true in some cases, but not in others. If you perceive a tail, and believe that it must belong to a tiger, again, it might work in some more cases (e.g., legs, belly and ears), but it would fail in the case of the elephant's trunk. If you trust the words of someone else (and use it to interpret the truth of the observed facts) but that person is misleading you because he is himself ignorant, the ideas may work partially but fail in other situations.

The above three methods of knowledge are respectively called rationalism, empiricism, and authority and they correspondingly put their faith into reasoning, observation, and specialists. Each of these three methods is potentially flawed, but the first two methods are *logically* flawed. Sensation is logically flawed because we can perceive illusions but we cannot know if they are illusions. When we observe something, we cannot be sure if that observation is a property of the world or of our perception. Which perceptions must be attributed to the world and which ones must be attributed to our senses? Unless we know how to attribute the perception to the senses or the world, we cannot know if it is true or false. And since this attribution cannot be determined from sensation itself, sensations are logically flawed methods of determining the truth.

Reason is logically flawed because the concepts used in a theory must be generalizations of the world of objects, the process of perception, the qualities of experiences, and the observer, but each of these are *per se* outside reason. They are only facts about our experiences and depend on those experiences. To generalize, therefore, we must have deeper kinds of experiences before we can even know what that generic entity is; reasoning follows the postulate of such generalized concepts, but they cannot arise without experiences. So, the problem of rationality reduces to the problem of experiences: if we were indeed under illusions, then we might postulate the wrong kind of concepts—e.g., believe in the visual illusions.

Authority is also potentially flawed if we happen to depend upon uninformed consultants, but it is not *logically* flawed. Science distributes the informed authority into a society of partially informed scientists, which evolve a consensus via discussion and debate. But this distributed authority also suffers from the problem of experience and rationality if the authorities derive their knowledge from these methods. The distributed authority system also suffers from the problem of Coherentism—if the world was actually coherent, the meanings and falsities themselves could not have existed. The notion that a set of scientists would eventually arrive at a coherent worldview is in itself false; such coherence can only be achieved by ignoring some experiences, ideas or authorities, which would appear true, consistent and relevant to other scientists.

While knowledge from authority can potentially be suspected, this is the only method that does not suffer from any logical problem.

This means that while knowledge from authority could potentially be false—if the authority is not trustworthy—the other two methods of empiricism and rationalism are certainly not reliable (especially when they are limited to object sensation and reasoning). This conclusion can set us on the path to a clearer understanding why the methods in religion—which are ostensibly based on reference to authority—may potentially be worth looking at. But at present there is a deep misunderstanding about how knowledge is acquired from authority and the role reason and experience play in this acquisition. When a student learns about a scientific theory from a qualified teacher, he trusts the teacher to acquire this knowledge, but he can also independently verify this understanding. For instance, the student can subject this theory to experiment and reason, and the theory would be accepted only if it succeeds in this test. Authority itself therefore is not a problem *per se.* The problem lies in how the knowledge from authority is tested against reason and experience. This *testing*, however, is different from *discovery.*

Discovery vs. Verification

There is an important distinction between *solving* a problem and *verifying* a solution. Both seem to necessitate the use of reason and experience, but there is a big difference between using reason and experience to formulate a theory and using them to test the theory.

In computer science, this is called the P=NP problem and it refers to the question of whether the methods of solving a problem and verifying a solution are identical. It seems from practical experience that there are a wide variety of problems that can be quickly verified but cannot be quickly solved. For instance, when you log into your computer using the correct password, the computer quickly verifies the password. However, if you did not know the password, then figuring it out through repeated trial and error can be very time consuming. The password verification requires linear[44] time, but the password cracking requires exponential time. If science is defined as the verification of theories, then it only requires linear time. But if it is defined as the discovery of theories, it requires exponential time. As the password complexity grows, the time taken to verify the password only grows linearly, but the time taken to crack the password grows exponentially. Similarly, as nature's complexity grows, the time required to discover the complete theory of nature grows exponentially, but the verification of such a theory—if the theory was known—would only need linear time.

Of course, even this exponential time depends on you remembering the passwords that have previously failed authentication. If you happen to forget the passwords that you have tried earlier, the problem is not just exponentially hard; it is impossible. For instance, now, you would be trying the same passwords over and over, even though they have previously failed authentication. This repeated trial of the same passwords makes the solution infinitely long.

The problem of not remembering (or even knowing) the previous mistakes is frequently encountered in current academia. For example, many physicists make elementary philosophical mistakes because they are simply unaware of what philosophers have discovered in the past to be pitfalls in thinking. Many philosophers similarly make elementary physics mistakes because they are unaware of what physicists have discovered in the past to be pitfalls of thinking. Physics and philosophy just happen to be just two of the many fields in academia, but the learnings from their history themselves present too much information to be digested by the practitioners of the other craft. It is hard enough to keep up with the knowledge in one area of inquiry, let alone understand the inquiries in many fields. In effect, each of these fields of inquiry are trying to independently crack the password, repeating the same passwords that previously failed authentication in another field of inquiry, simply because they have no ability to share all the previously attempted passwords. Occasional improvements in ideas occurs when diverse fields are joined together in inter-disciplinary studies, because then the password crackers share the list of failed attempts. But such inter-disciplinary studies suffer from a different problem: their practitioners must acquire a lot more information (learning about the failures) before they can even propose a new attempt.

The problem of science is not just that the methods of reason and sensation are independently flawed (when these methods are defined as the observation and reasoning about the world of objects), and that science must iterate over and over to search for new theories, but also that it is impossible for any individual scientist to know about all the failed attempts, to preempt his using them.

In effect, the computer program that is trying to crack the password is memory constrained: it is forced to recycle the memory of failed passwords, thereby overwriting the passwords which earlier failed, which makes the process potentially infinite. The problem is further nuanced by the fact that in the case of password cracking, the computer unlocks, and that's how you know the password is correct. In the case of nature, you can get partial successes which unlock some parts of nature but not others. This partial unlocking corresponds to successes in modeling limited parts of nature. We might feel satisfied that we found a password that unlocks the computer, but after some time we may find that we do not have permissions to access all the data in the computer; our permissions may be limited to certain files. We would have to lock the computer again, and initiate a fresh search for the password that unlocks other kinds of data that were previously invisible. Note that, ideally, we would like to find a single password by which we can see all the files on the computer, not separate passwords for different files. The single password for all files corresponds to the universal theory of nature, while individual passwords would be partially useful but otherwise disparate theories. The challenge in hacking the password in such a scenario is that different passwords unlock different files, and we neither know the number of files to be unlocked nor how many such passwords exist, nor the particular kinds of files that each password protects. And, as we already noted previously, we cannot store all the failed attempts at password cracking.

The process of password cracking described above assumes that the computer has no intelligent way of guessing the password. That it must use random combinations of letters to arrive at a string that unlocks the computer. This may not always be the case. For instance, if the computer was fed personal information such as name, relatives, pets, date of birth, etc., the cracking process may be simplified in some cases. In the case of scientific discovery, this is tantamount to *intuitions* about the nature of reality, which come from some deeper forms of perception, although the perception may be so fleeting that one might not be able to understand its origin. Science often makes progress through such intuitions, but the role that these intuitions play in science has never been understood, because the nature of creativity and innovation itself requires a deep understanding of the nature of the mind, which currently doesn't exist. The premise, therefore, that science relies purely on reason and experience is flawed; it involves a key role for intuitive apperception of reality, but how this perception occurs is not currently known. Even so, the process of scientific discovery is very convoluted, because such intuitions and apperceptions about reality are quite rare.

However, all these problems pertain to the *discovery* of the password, but not its *verification*. If you had the correct password that allowed you to see all the computer data, its verification would be easy. You would only need to acquire that password and test it against various kinds of files to check if it actually unlocks all of them. Similarly, if we had the correct theory of nature, testing it against the various phenomena that the theory predicts would be easy[45]. Can we now redefine knowledge to be the *verification* of a solution rather its *discovery*? This would be possible if there were a theory that could be obtained from authority and it described a solution that could potentially be verified. You are no longer trying to crack the password; you simply ask the person who knows it.

This is pretty much how religion has been treated in the Vedic tradition. The goal has never been to discover the truth, but to learn it from those who know this truth. Does it entail that this solution could not be understood rationally or its implications could not be described empirically? Certainly not; the religious theories have been described rationally, and they have been practiced for millennia, not just for spiritual advancement, but even for material betterment. However, these theories are distinct from modern science in two respects. First, they provide a radically different view of nature than prevalent in current science; the Vedic view of matter is semantic rather than physical. Second, the theories themselves were not formulated from experiment and speculation; as we have seen, if the universe is semantic, then the methods of reasoning and experience work only if we are able to go beyond sensations; to go beyond sensations you must either have advanced perceptual abilities or a faith in the possibility of such forms of perception that you invest a substantial part of your life developing such perception.

Vedic "science" therefore differs from modern science in that it is not the *discovery* of the truth but the *verification* of truth. They are different in the sense of a trying to crack the password to the secrets of nature versus verifying that the password is indeed correct. The search for truth in Vedic "science" does not begin in the analysis of experiments and mental speculation to formulate theories of nature; this method of knowledge began in the Western world from Greek times, and Greeks are therefore rightfully the owners of the scientific method. It was refined in modern ages during Renaissance and Enlightenment, as the combination of rationalism and empiricism, but as we saw above, the method is forever incomplete.

The search for truth in Vedic philosophy begins in the search for the person who knows the truth. Once such a qualified authority has been found, the seeker of truth learns the truth from the authority, practices its tenets, verifies the truth of what he has learnt, and becomes an authority on the subject matter to pass it to others. This process of knowledge transmission is called the disciplic succession, and the epistemological process is called *śabda* or hearing from authority. While the knowledge learnt through *śabda* can be understood and verified rationally and empirically, it is not discovered rationally and empirically, because you don't know what you don't know. If your theory of nature is incomplete, you can believe that nature behaves randomly and the theoretical incompleteness is due to that randomness. Alternately, you may also believe that nature is complete but the current theory is incomplete and therefore there must be something beyond the theory. Even the second conclusion is not intuitively straightforward, especially if we are dealing in problems of meaning because it seems that there is nothing beyond sensations. However, even if we arrived at this conclusion, the experiences necessary to formulate such a theory may be missing.

The reliance on faith therefore stems from a very fundamental premise that truth is hierarchical and involves several deeper forms of perception. If I don't have those forms of perception, then how can I know that truth? I can only approach a teacher who knows the truth and who can teach me how to develop its perception. Science opposes faith because it supposes that everything that exists can be seen through the five senses and theorized rationally. If this premise turns out to be false, as we have seen, faith is not just a useful method to obtain knowledge; it is also the only method to know. Of course, you still have to repose your faith in those who truly know. Putting your faith in those who don't know, or whose knowledge cannot be explained rationally or verified empirically, obviously leads to frustration. But the answer to that frustration is not returning back to a faith in your own powers of reason and experience, because these methods will always remain incomplete. The answer lies in reinvigorating the search for the teacher who truly knows. One of the basic qualities of this teacher is that he too must have acquired the knowledge from another teacher, and so forth, because the teacher who knows through reason and experience is equally flawed in his knowledge as the others in the discovery mode.

New Atheism opposes the faith based methods of religion and argues that they are inferior to the reason and experience based method of science. This accusation is false on two counts. First, it assumes that reason and experience will deliver a complete understanding of nature, which is true only if advanced forms of perception and reasoning based on increasingly subtle concepts can be developed, but false in the current notions about perception and reasoning as sensation and objects. Second, it assumes that reason and experience are employed only in the discovery of knowledge, not its verification. The fact is that a student learns science from his or her teachers based on faith, but verifies it based on reason and experience. Faith enters the picture when the process of knowledge acquisition is very hard, or if the knowledge already exists and it is far easier to just ask someone about it, than to find it yourself. Faith is therefore not opposed to reason and experience. In fact, reason and experience can act as great aids to knowledge from authority.

The role of reason now lies in validating that the ideas gained from authority are rationally consistent and the role of experience lies in validating these ideas through practical involvement in developing new forms of perception based on these ideas. This role of reason and experience is a far cry from the role attributed to them in current science, and they differ in being verification and discovery, respectively.

The idea that science is rational and empirical while religion is based on faith (and thereby irrational and dogmatic) is therefore misunderstanding the two kinds of roles that reason and experience play even in modern science. The process of rational and empirical discovery is very difficult if nature is hierarchical. The use of faith based methods to knowledge aid in its simplification. A theory developed based on such ideas can be described rationally and tested empirically, even though it would not be discovered using reason and experience; it would only be verified by these methods. Do we really care how we arrive at the truth as long as we arrive at the truth? The process of scientific discovery is no doubt very exciting, but the time taken in this process is hugely expensive[46].

In a semantic universe, the cost of not knowing the truth is not just epistemological; it is also moral. Those who believe that the excitement of scientific discovery is more important than the truth of this discovery are obviously welcome to keep trying that method. For everyone else more interested in the truth, the faith based method—if it can be understood rationally and verified empirically—presents the shortcut to an otherwise very arduous journey.

The Knowledge of Soul and God

The use of faith doesn't by itself solve the problem of knowing God because even if you accept something on faith, you must eventually experience it. Can we experience God to validate the faith? In the semantic hierarchy, abstract ideas are higher nodes in the tree and the parent nodes in the tree are necessary to define the child nodes because the child nodes aren't defined by themselves. The higher nodes are also the instruments or methods of knowing the child nodes; the method of knowing is defined before the object of that knowing is defined. It follows that the objects of knowledge cannot be defined unless the methods of knowing them are defined.

The individual soul is a child node of the parent node—God. This child is not like the birth from the womb of a mother, as we generally understand parents and children. Rather, the soul is the child of God in the sense that God is more abstract than the soul, and the soul is derived from the parent, quite like yellow is derived from color. Color must exist before yellowness can exist, and child nodes cannot directly perceive the parent because the contingent cannot know the abstract, even though the abstract is necessary for the contingent to exist. For instance, the observer's sense of color can perceive yellow, but yellow cannot perceive color, because the senses are more abstract than the properties in the objects themselves.

The search for an abstraction begins from the realization that a particular concept is not the most fundamental idea. In the semantic view, contingent ideas are produced from the abstract ideas. Therefore, if an idea is the most fundamental, then it must be the source of all other ideas. If any idea is not completely defined by its own existence, then this idea also cannot be fundamental. For instance, if yellowness can only be defined through its distinction from redness, blueness, greenness, etc., then yellowness cannot be fundamental; there must be another idea more fundamental than the idea of yellowness. Similarly, if I am not the only being in the universe, and I am not the origin of all the other beings, then there must be another being logically more fundamental than me; this being must also be necessarily a more abstract idea than the idea of my existence.

This conclusion, however, only represents a theoretical argument for the existence of something more abstract than our own existence. We are rationally required to postulate a more fundamental existence because we don't happen to be the origin of everything. The thing more fundamental than our existence would also be a more abstract idea than our existence and this idea cannot be understood by the conventional methods of knowledge where the contingent is perceived by the abstract. Several problems in epistemology arise when we attempt to go beyond the individual observer. We can know the objects using the senses, the senses using the mind, the mind using the intellect, the intellect using the ego, the ego using morality, and the morality using consciousness, because the instrument of knowing is more abstract than the object known. But if the instrument of knowing (the individual observer) is more contingent than the object of knowing (the supreme observer), then this method of knowing can no longer be used. It is now essential to define a new method of knowing the abstract by the contingent.

Vedic philosophy defines three modes of knowledge. First, the abstract knows the contingent and the knower is necessarily more abstract than the known; this mode of knowledge exists as the material senses and their respective objects, and is called *bahiranga śakti* or 'external' knowledge. Second, the knower and the known are equally abstract, and by this knowledge the knower knows his own existence, thereby creating self-knowledge; this type of knowledge is called *tatastha śakti* or 'self' knowledge. Third, the known is more abstract (and logically prior) than the knower, and this mode of knowledge exists as an observer being able to know its own source; it is called *antaranga śakti* or 'internal' knowledge.

Atheists often question the possibility of knowing the existence of soul and God, in the same sense that we know the existence of material objects using our senses. In Vedic philosophy, the knowledge of soul and God are possible, but they require different methods of knowing or epistemologies, because they respectively involve an entity knowing an equally abstract entity, and an entity knowing an even more abstract entity than itself, quite different from material knowledge where the abstract knows the contingent. The methodology of knowing soul and God cannot therefore be understood in terms of material methods because the process by which material knowledge is acquired is itself not well-understood in current philosophy and science. Before we can understand the method of knowing soul and God, we must understand that sensual, mental, intellectual, intentional, and moral knowledge involves successively deeper forms of perception using senses that are necessarily more abstract than the objects that they perceive. Only when the relation between abstract and contingent is understood in the case of material perception, can the problem of self-perception and God-perception (as more abstract than the self) be discussed.

The knowledge of material objects, the self, and God, involves the use of three different kinds of consciousness because they deal in different relations between abstract and contingent. Accordingly, they also require three different kinds of epistemologies. An epistemology is nothing other than the type of consciousness which creates a particular type of knowledge. Matter, too, is therefore a type of consciousness, although it is a consciousness that knows more contingent things than itself; the successively more contingent categories become the objects for the previous categories. The observer is a consciousness that knows itself, and when this consciousness is combined with the material consciousness, the experience of the world is created. Similarly, when the observer is combined with the consciousness of God, the experience of God is created. The soul and God can be known, but they need different kinds of consciousness. The knowledge of matter, self, and God constitute three separate classes and we cannot acquire the knowledge in one class using the methods of another. Specifically, knowing soul and God requires a different method than the knowledge of material objects via senses.

Knowledge via Theory Formation

Epistemology is not merely the definition of a method of knowledge, but also a deeper question about what knowledge is. There are two broad approaches to this question. First, we can think of knowledge as individual experiences. Second, we can think of knowledge as the law or theory by which these experiences are produced. To form theories, we must have multiple experiences; but to have those experiences, the theory of experience must exist prior. Experiences help us discover that theory, and while the theory can be seen in each experience, the theory itself is beyond the individual experiences. It is thus necessary to distinguish between the knowledge of individual experiences and that of the theory that explains all the experiences. The theory defines and controls the experiences.

Material knowledge is obtained when the knower is controlled by matter; self-knowledge is attained when knower and known distinction is dropped and the knower controls himself through his free will; God knowledge is manifest when the knower is controlled by the will of God. In each of the above cases, the knower is controlled by the known; however, the known can either be less abstract, equally abstract, or more abstract than the knower. The known is the theory and the knower is the individual observer whose experiences are controlled by that theory. In the case of external knowledge, time is the law of nature which produces, destroys, and conserves this knowledge. In the case of self-knowledge, the existence, choices, and the consciousness of living entities represent the theory by which their experiences are produced. In the case of internal knowledge, God is the theory of control. The self-control and God-control are therefore different from material control, and they pertain to different forms of knowledge: in material control, the known is less abstract than the knower; in self-control, the knower is equally abstract as the known; in God-control, the known is more abstract than the knower. Accordingly, the theory will be less, equally, and more abstract than the knower itself.

Depending on which environment the observer is in, it forms a theory about itself, by discovering the order in its own experiences. If the observer is in matter (and controlled by material laws) he forms a materialistic picture of his own existence, considering free will, self-awareness, and consciousness to be epiphenomena of material laws. Of course, the observer has free will by which he can choose the correct theory of nature after gradually removing his filters of perception. If the observer accepts this free will (even theoretically) and attempts to become free of the material laws, he eventually comes to the point of self-knowledge, where he is controlled only by his own will. In this state, the observer again forms a theory about his existence based on how his free will works—i.e. the kinds of choices that he prefers to make, which eventually define his non-material personality. The observer, in this state, has a good understanding of his innate nature, but still does not know the nature of reality beyond his own existence. The observer is part of reality but does not know the nature of the complete reality; the observer only knows the nature of his own existence. To understand this nature of the whole reality, the observer can choose to become subordinate to God whereby God becomes the law that governs the observer's experience. In this case, the law of experience is not *made* by God; rather, God *is* the law. Even though God is more subtle than the observer, the observer can know God by understanding the order in his own experience in pretty much the same way that the observer orders his experience in matter and under free will.

In every kind of theory, the reality is represented or symbolized. When we know such a theory, we don't become the reality, although we *represent* that reality within us. To know matter, we must represent matter in our consciousness; to know the self, we must represent the self; and to know God, we must represent God. The three forms of knowledge described above involve three different kinds of representations—less abstract, equally abstract, and more abstract—than the observer. Consciousness thus is defined as the possibility for acquiring the three kinds of knowledge[47].

Ultimately, self-knowledge and God-knowledge are produced from the order amongst experiences, which also happens to be the method by which material laws are formulated[48]. However, the outcome of experiential analysis is different in the three cases: it respectively produces theories about the God, matter, and the self. The three forms of knowledge—internal, external, and marginal—are therefore outcomes of experiential analysis, although they emerge from different presumptions about the nature of causality. If the observer believes that his experiences are produced due to matter which exists even when the observer doesn't experience it, the law of nature is material. If the observer believes that his experiences are produced due to his own free will, then the law of experience is the observer's personality. Finally, if the observer believes that his experiences are controlled by God, then the law is in fact God.

The fundamental question in arriving at a law that governs experiences is: What do we suppose governs our experiences—matter, the self, or God? Even in the material world, for instance, we can attribute our experiences to the laws of matter, to our free will and personality, and to the nature of God. In that specific sense, there is no particular "world" called "material world" different from "observer world" or "God's world." They are the same world; the difference is merely in how we understand the world by using different assumptions about the nature of the world that controls us. The materialist believes that he is controlled by material laws; the spiritualist believes that he is controlled by his own personality and free will; the transcendentalist believes that he is controlled by God. The law governing experiences uncovered from the analysis of experiences therefore depends on the choice of whether we believe we are controlled by matter, by our free will, or by God. This choice, however, is not without consequences. Whichever assumption we begin with, the law of experiences changes, too. The law of nature is therefore not simply an interpretation of our experience; rather, the assumptions underlying the law formation change the lawfulness.

That is, if we believe that we are controlled by matter and we don't have free will, then we are indeed controlled by material laws. If we believe we have free will and can control our destiny, we can indeed control our destiny. Finally, if we believe that God controls our destiny, then indeed God controls that destiny. These three forms of our knowledge are choices, and the choice of knowledge changes the nature of the law that controls our consciousness.

Materialists often argue that there is only one law of nature, and that law is material. In Vedic philosophy, however, the law is unique per observer; as you change your assumptions about reality, the law itself becomes different. Even in the material world, therefore, the law of nature is not identical for everyone. Rather, as one deepens one's understanding of the nature of self, he becomes liberated from the control of material laws and gains free will of choosing the phenomena. This free will includes the choices of our own personality: we can choose to be a different *kind* of person and depending on the kind of person you are determines the order in your experiences. As one experiments with various kinds of personalities, he finds that this free will is itself a problem: the choice of personality is arbitrary. How does one define one's true nature if he can be anything that he wants to be? This is a more profound problem than not being able to define what one wants to be, if indeed the person is controlled by material laws. The solution for this problem is the selection of a reference in relation to which the observer has to choose his innate personality. In other words, free will leads to arbitrariness and it requires the observer to go beyond itself in search of his true nature. To define one's own real nature, the observer has to go beyond free will, and search for the relationship between his self and the rest of reality. The observer has to now choose a reference—reality—beyond itself. This reference has to be more abstract than the observer, and the observer (to know his true nature) must define his persona in the relation to the reality beyond himself.

The solution to the problem of determinism in matter is free will, and the solution to the problem of arbitrariness arising from free will is God, when God is defined as reality. From the standpoint of the individual observer, his self-knowledge, free will, and choice of personality are higher than the knowledge of material objects; furthermore, the subordination of free will, choice, and self-knowledge to the nature of God is even higher. Why? This is because ultimately the living being has the power of self-determination but matter doesn't; however, even this power of self-determination does not make all of his choices true: we can choose to be whatever we want, but who are we *beyond* these abilities of choices? The living being's choice is not absolute because he is a part of the whole. If the individual observer were the whole truth, then his free will would also be the absolute truth; the observer could choose whatever he wants to be (i.e. his personality) and that personality would be the absolute truth. But the observer isn't the whole truth; he is only part of the truth. Only God is the original truth and therefore His will is also the absolute truth. In that respect, our free will needs an anchor in God's will, but God's will doesn't need an anchor.

Atheists resent this preeminent position of God. They ask: Why does God have to be that autocrat who gets to decide everything? Why do we have to surrender to Him? The short answer to this question is: we have to surrender to something—to material laws, to our personality, or to God. We can choose the object that we surrender to, but we cannot avoid surrender. The surrender to material laws is problematic because the soul is more abstract than matter; the abstract must be independent of the contingent, but if it comes under the control of the contingent, then that is unnatural. In this case, it means that the soul loses his free will to define himself. The surrender to a freely chosen personality is not as problematic as surrender to matter, but it is ultimately incomplete because the choice of personality doesn't indicate what the real personality is. Free choices lead to arbitrariness in self-knowledge which defies the answer to the original existential question: Who am I? In surrendering to a freely chosen personality, the living becomes his own autocrat—he has complete control over himself but nothing else. When the living being realizes that this free will is a hindrance to the knowledge of truth about his self, he surrenders to God, and defines his personality in relation to Him. This is a progression in knowledge, although a reversal of free will. God becomes essential to a person because of the conflict between truth and free will.

All philosophical inquiry begins in a fundamental existential question: Who am I? The materialist answers this question by reducing himself to matter. The spiritualist answers this question by freely choosing a personality. The transcendentalist seeks to know his nature by defining it in relation to the primordial truth. Which approach you take is a choice; however, the choice comes with its consequences. We are free to deny our free will, accept our free will, or surrender our free will, thus creating three kinds of knowledge. The surrender of free will appears to be the denial of free will, but it is not. The surrender of free will is voluntary; it acknowledges the existence of free will but considers it inadequate. The root of all knowledge therefore lies in our free will, and how we choose to embrace it in answering the questions of our existential reality.

There is an absolute reality from which other realities emerge as different kinds of knowledge; this emergence includes the individual living being. The internal knowledge of the absolute reality is that reality trying to know itself. The living beings produced from that reality should therefore be mechanisms to serve the purpose of creation—i.e. self-knowledge of the absolute reality—and constitute internal knowledge of that absolute reality. However, since this creation is also capable of self-knowledge, it has the free will to define its personality independently, and create self-knowledge. As this need for independence becomes defiance or opposition to the absolute reality, the living being becomes external knowledge. The material knowledge is thus not the end of knowing because there are other forms of self-knowledge even higher. The higher forms of knowledge stem from the realization that knowledge is about the self. The knowledge has to be consistent with what the self is (i.e. free will) as well as complete (i.e. it should not be arbitrary).

4

Problems in Atheism

When two opposite points of view are expressed with equal intensity, the truth does not necessarily lie exactly halfway between them. It is possible for one side to be simply wrong.
—Richard Dawkins

Material Reductionism

I opened this book with the problem of universals and showed how it has never been solved in Western philosophy, although attempts to derive universals from material objects have led to many problems of incompleteness in science. Atheists either don't understand these problems—and why they are logically unsolvable—or they deny the existence of ideas beyond individual things. *Charvāka*, for instance, denied the existence of universals. New Atheism, however, doesn't. In fact, New Atheism claims that we can derive universals from material objects, and science with its mathematical theories of nature would eventually explain how the world can be rational without necessitating God. This position is logically inconsistent. There is no consistent and complete theory of nature if universals are derived from objects; incompleteness manifests in the idea of randomness in nature, leaving theories predictively incomplete.

However, if we try to solve the problem of universals in a way that it can be solved, we end up not just with universals in another world of ideas, but a hierarchy of concepts that include many subtle forms of existence that cannot be sensed as sensations because they are more abstract than the senses. Such forms of existence cannot be seen, tasted, touched, smelt, and heard, although they must exist if the world of sensations has to exist. This categorical hierarchy ends in a supreme consciousness which becomes the root of the hierarchical tree of the universe. The root stands independent of the universe, and yet the universe is an expansion from that root. The root can be understood rationally, spoken of in science, but cannot be perceived by the senses, because it is far more abstract that the senses by which we perceive sensations. In that respect, God and the soul can never be seen, tasted, touched, smelt, or heard. But this is also the manner in which meanings cannot be perceived by the senses, even though they exist. God and the soul are not the only things to transcend material objects; senses, mind, intellect, ego, morality, and qualia, too, transcend material objects. In so far as the latter constitute scientific problems, they are outside current science. They don't have to be outside science forever; but a science that incorporates these abstract concepts would have to contend with the question: How can I perceive such realities? The answer would necessitate the development of new forms of perception.

However, the problem of meaning is not just in the study of our perception and mind. It also appears in the study of material objects themselves, when we describe object *collections* rather than *individual* objects. The reason for this is profound: meanings are defined collectively rather than individually. If you look at an individual object, you can imagine that it exists independent of the other objects, and this description of nature appears to work in some cases. The notion of independent objects, however, fails dramatically when it is used to construct macroscopic objects and to define properties of such objects. Problems of such collections are well-known in modern physics (e.g., quantum theory, thermodynamics, and general relativity), mathematics (e.g., numbers are properties of collections), computing theory (e.g., program semantics is a property of a collection of computer instructions), and biology (e.g., the functional properties of living beings are attributes of the whole system).

And yet, the reductionist claims that collections are nothing but the aggregations of independent parts. It is certainly true that a collection is an aggregation of parts. However, the parts are not mutually *independent*. If we try to change one part, we must also change the other parts in a way that we can no longer speak about the parts as being independent. We must rather speak about collections as being logically prior to the parts and the parts as being derived from the collection. In the case of a physical system, the collection represents a more abstract meaning; in mathematics, the collection denotes a number; in computing theory, the collection represents a program concept; and in biology, it denotes a living being. There is simply no other logically consistent and complete way of describing such systems in scientific theories, and reductionism therefore fails not because the whole is not made up of parts, but because the parts in the collection are not mutually independent. The parts are defined to exist only when the whole has been defined even prior.

What this whole represents conceptually can vary depending upon which parts we are speaking about; for instance, the whole can represent sensations, meanings, structure, intentions, etc. However, the pattern of the whole-part relation is always the same: the whole precedes the parts, and parts must be created from the whole, if this description has to be consistent and complete. The whole cannot be described to be a *physical* collection anymore. Rather, it has to be defined as a more *abstract* concept than the concepts which are applied to the parts in that collection. For instance, the collection of parts in a car—chassis, wheels, steering, engine, etc.—has to be described using a more abstract concept—car.

The reductionist claims that the car is an epiphenomenon of the parts in the car. The correct position, however, is that the parts in the car are an epiphenomenon of the idea of the car. Even if the parts of the car do not exist, the idea of the car still does, although we cannot perceive that idea by the senses. The idea of the car always existed even before any particular car was created. However, someone had to perceive this idea using their mind and then refine it with details over time, before actual cars could be produced. Every human creativity, innovation, or invention is therefore an act of perception. We don't own ideas, and the modern notions about intellectual property (and misappropriation of such property) are misplaced. All ideas are actually perceived by the mind, and since they are perceived, they must have existed prior to their discovery. Time manifests these ideas through a natural process that science currently doesn't understand because both space and time are described as typeless entities. The manifestation of an idea is therefore not our creativity, nor is it a byproduct of the molecular combinations in the brain. It is rather an effect of semantic space-time.

All problems of modern science are outcomes of a single difficulty— the inability to incorporate concepts into matter. In Platonism, ideas existed in another world. In Hylomorphism, Aristotle brought ideas into the present world but maintained the divide between form and substance, never clearly illustrating how form and substance combine. Then, Descartes separated ideas from matter as mind and body and the empiricists argued that all these ideas are different from how the world natively exists as physical properties, although the interaction of mind and body, and the problem of perception as the conversion of physical properties into qualities, was never solved. Finally, with the advancement of science, the mind itself has been reduced to the body although how the body creates the mind has never been understood. Science and philosophy in the West have been toying with the problem of concepts in the material world for two thousand years, and there is no solution so far.

And yet, the widespread belief these days is that the problem is not important. That we will eventually prove that concepts are illusions of human perception and that the world existed even before humans. The late arrival of humans into the universe is supposed to affirm the view that matter exists independent of the mind.

Perhaps the last nail in this idea's coffin is the myriad problems of indeterminism in purely physical theories of nature. The more science has tried to avoid the existence of concepts, the more it has faced the consequences of this avoidance. The breaking news (if we can even call it breaking, since some of the problems are now a century old) is that every theory of material phenomena is incomplete: physics, mathematics, computing, and biology, included. We might not see the connection between the problems of incompleteness and the problem of meaning and concepts, and that would only delay their solution. But if we recognize that connection, there is only one way to proceed, which is to acknowledge the reality of concepts and work upon their integration in the world of material objects.

Given that all previous attempts to integrate mind and body have failed, and given that all attempts to reduce the mind to body have failed, we are left with only one choice: reduce the body to the mind. In other words, the body is an idea, too; it just happens to be more refined and contingent idea, relative to the ideas in the mind. The mind-body divide is now false; there aren't two different substances, and there aren't two separate worlds. Rather, the present world is idea-like, and material bodies are more concrete ideas while the mind is an abstract idea. The body is simply a refinement of the mind; the body is developed from the mind, and the mind must therefore exist even prior to the existence of the body.

We still maintain reductionism, but now reduction is defined to be the reduction of complex ideas to simple ideas rather than the reduction of complex things to simple things. A macroscopic object is a complex thing and an atom is a simple thing. However, a macroscopic object is a simple idea and the atom is a complex idea. When we reduce complex things to simple things we run into problems of collections, but these problems do not arise when a complex idea is reduced to a simple idea. Scientific reductionism therefore works very well when it is defined as the reduction of ideas rather than the reduction of things. Now, the universe begins in simple ideas.

Atheism rests upon the thesis that ideas are unreal. If this were true, then science itself could not exist, because science depends upon a host of ideas—number, logic, probability, and space-time—which have no material manifestation. If the existence of ideas is acknowledged—and it must be acknowledged to solve the scientific problems—then it would also logically entail the soul and God. The soul would now be the idea of free will and self-determination, by which a living being wishes to know itself as a certain kind of knowledge, beauty, individual, power, fame, and wealth. Similarly, God would be the knower of more abstract ideas—namely, beauty, knowledge, individuality, power, fame, and wealth, themselves.

Scientific Determinism

Many atheists believe that science is deterministic and that determinism in nature entails there is no free will. If free will is unreal, then there cannot be morality, or at least no moral judgment. And if there is no moral judgment then a God who performs such a judgment would be unnecessary. This argument is flawed in so many ways, that I would first list the flaws here, before describing them in detail in the below paragraphs. First, current science is not deterministic; if someone isn't convinced then then he or she ought to study the problems of indeterminism in science before moving further[49]. Second, we should aim for determinism but that goal is unattainable without incorporating meanings. Third, free will is not the same as freedom; the latter means we can change the functioning of our body and mind while the former means that we can change the body and the mind. Fourth, moral judgments are not connected to God; rather morality is a natural process of discovering the truth necessitated by an encounter with phenomena which are required to improve the theory. If morality did not exist, then there would be no test for scientific completeness: we could not know if a true theory is true and that it would never be falsified in the future.

Let's begin with the belief in determinism. This belief was accurate in classical physics, which described individual objects, but it has failed every time physics has attempted to describe object collections. The problem of object collections can be illustrated by the following example. Suppose you have a bottle of ink which you want to spread on paper. As you can imagine, there are infinitely many different ways to distribute any given amount of ink, if indeed there is more than one ink particle. If there is only one ink particle in the universe then wherever you place it, the universe looks identical. But as the number of ink particles grows, the different particle distributions begin to look different; for instance, you could produce different books with the same amount of ink. It turns out that in physical theories there is no good way to describe such distributions because the theories deal in physical *invariants*—mass, charge, energy, momentum, angular momentum, etc. Just as there are infinitely many ways to distribute the total amount of ink on paper, similarly, there are infinite ways to distribute the total amount of physical invariants on space-time. All these distributions are *equivalent* but not *identical*. They are equivalent from the standpoint of the physical invariants, but they are not identical from the standpoint of meanings. Each such distribution represents a different universe. Which one these possible universes happen to be *our* universe?

The first step in solving this problem is to be able to distinguish the different matter distributions based on some objective facts. Clearly the current physical invariants are inadequate to solve this problem. But if such matter distributions were distinguished by the meanings that they encode, then it would be possible to distinguish between them objectively. The distributions that appear physically equivalent would now be seen as different *texts* encoding meaning. Each text will have the same total amount of ink (physical properties), but the ink's distribution on paper would be indeterministic. However, now, the distribution has to be attributed to an act of encoding meaning. If causality is described based on such meanings, then the causal effects would obviously make new predictions. With such predictions, we can know which amongst the universes is made possible by redistributing matter is our particular universe.

But we will still need to ask: Which of the various possible objects in this universe is *me*? Potentially, I could be any one of the objects in the universe, so, how do we decide which object is which individual? You might say that individuality is an imaginary idea; there are no personalities; there are only material objects. However, that view doesn't address the problem because we can speak about individuality even in the context of objects. For instance, object individuality comes into play when we draw object trajectories: the same object is supposed to have different physical properties. If only physical properties were real and individuality was not, then we could not have drawn trajectories connecting these properties.

The ability to draw such trajectories is itself non-material because the 'object' underlying the measurable states cannot be measured. In classical physics, the continuity of states in a trajectory was postulated on the basis of infinitesimals; this postulate has since been proven incorrect by the discreteness of matter. We can no longer say that a particle moves from one place to another; we can only say that one state disappears and another one appears. Such a universe is clearly deterministic in the events, but not deterministic in the trajectories. That is, there are several possible ways to connect the events into trajectories, and these cannot be predicted. This is a point that arguments for determinism must understand carefully: there can be complete determinism of events, and yet there can be complete indeterminism of the trajectories. All the events in the universe can be fixed, but the lines joining these events (and which we suppose are individual observers) are not necessarily fixed.

The ability to change the events in the universe is freedom, but the ability to change the lines joining these events is free will. Free will does not entail a new or different set of events. It only entails being able to take a different path in the universe. This distinction helps us understand the trouble with the debates on free will: the trouble is that we are not truly talking about free will; we are actually talking about freedom. We suppose that if we have free will then the effect of this free will would manifest in a new event which could not have been predicted by a deterministic theory. If we find such an event, we would know if free will is real. What if free will is not about producing new events, but about connecting them? What if my free will is the path I follow through the sea of events?

The conflict between free will and determinism is based on a material conception of freedom and cause-effect relationships: if you have free will then you must be able to show it to others by causing new events; if we don't see the power of change in you then you don't have free will. This notion about free will is naïve because events don't change by free will; only trajectories change. Such changes in trajectories can be detected by other observers if only they knew how to predict their own trajectories. However, to even predict such trajectories, they would have to suppose that they are objects that persist even when all material states have changed. Free will is entirely non-material because trajectories are non-material. Underlying the idea of a trajectory is the notion that there is something that remains 'unchanged' even when physical states change. The thing that remains unchanged cannot be a physical state. Therefore, trajectory predictions based on physical states must eventually fail, and they have failed even in current science.

To predict trajectories, we first need the notion of something that remains unchanged through the change. Such object conceptions don't exist in current science; they existed in classical physics, but they have now been invalidated. If nature is discrete, there can never be any notion of continuity, unless the continuity is defined in a new way different from matter. To define this continuity we need a non-material entity which can remain unchanged through state changes. Once such an entity has been postulated, then the evolution of the observer becomes distinct from the changes in events; even when the events are fixed, the observers can change their experiences by moving over to different events. In effect, we are now distributing trajectories over events. The laws of such predictions can be formulated—as I have shown earlier—but even before we attempt to formulate these laws, we must recognize that these laws are laws of free will and its implications, and their existence does not contradict the determinism of events. It must be recognized that even if all the events in the universe were determined, the universe would still be underdetermined without the trajectory definitions.

Classical determinism worked because it supposed the determinism of individual parts, which in turn caused the determinism of the whole. When the whole-part relationship (as construed in classical physics) is inverted, then the wholes are logically prior to the parts. However, now, the determinism of the whole still leaves room open for the choices of the parts, and this is the reason that current physical theories become incomplete when dealing with collections. The indeterminism takes many forms: (1) dividing matter into individual object types, (2) distributing these types in space-time, and (3) connecting the succession of these types into trajectories. The first two can be addressed using material concepts, but the last one needs a non-material observer. The free will of the observer has empirical effects—namely the trajectories that connect events—but these effects cannot be traced to anything material. The conflict between free will and determinism is thus based on classical determinism. This notion is two steps removed from what we know today: (1) the theories are not deterministic in the sense they were in classical physics, (2) when we recover the determinism, it would be the determinism of events, which will still be open for choices.

Biological Evolution

Evolution has exerted a greater influence on New Atheism than materialism (opposed to the notion that ideas are real) and determinism (opposed to the claim that we have free will). Evolution depends on the ideas of random mutation and natural selection, both of which are independently problematic. Random mutation is problematic because it undermines scientific completeness; we believe that things are random only if we are unable to predict them. But if things were truly that random, then this theory would be unable to predict them, too. What is the true value of such a theory that makes no predictions? For me, this is not a rhetorical issue, because I believe that the randomness is a shortcoming of the current physical description and it would be overcome in a semantic description. Furthermore, the idea of natural selection cannot be defined unless the *boundary* between an organism and its environment is defined, and the physical basis for assuming such boundaries does not exist. The physical basis of boundaries exists only at the level of individual objects in current physics, and not at the level of object collections; collection boundaries are assumed without a physical basis.

The difference between physical and semantic views of nature is that in the semantic view boundaries have real effects, whereas in the physical view they are imaginary demarcations with no real effects. If boundaries were real, then it would be possible to draw many such boundaries in nature making everyday objects—such as tables, chairs, houses, and cars—also real in the same sense as living beings. Such boundaries must now also have physical effects. In the semantic view, the boundaries are real, and therefore there is a real demarcation between the living being and the environment. However, the boundaries also have real physical effects: the boundaries 'entangle' the objects within the boundary such that they are only defined in relation to the boundary; the boundary represents the abstract object and its members represent the contingent parts of that abstraction. The boundaries therefore have to be defined conceptually rather than physically. They can exist in space and time, but they cannot be understood as material properties of objects.

If the boundary between an organism and the environment is imaginary, then the point at which the organism ends and the environment begins cannot be defined, and natural selection—which is supposed to operate at this boundary—cannot be defined. If the boundary is imaginary, then the organism and the environment are a single system; but now, there is no physical theory upon which the ideas of adaptation, natural selection, or fitness can be based. Those who believe that evolution is a physical theory must closely examine the problem that if molecules in a gas chamber do not evolve and adapt into more sophisticated structures (no matter how densely we pack them) then why do living beings evolve and adapt? What physical principles are we adding to model a living being and its environment any different from molecules in a gas chamber?

Natural selection is the simple thesis that square pegs fit well in square holes, while round pegs fit well in round holes. The questions underlying this thesis are however quite profound: (1) how does the ecosystem divide into pegs and holes, and (2) why are there specific peg and hole shapes? For instance, we could carve the same block of wood into many different peg and hole shapes—oval, hexagonal, octagonal, triangular, etc. Why is a particular peg-hole combination real? How we divide the block of wood into a peg and a hole itself needs a deeper understanding of nature, because if we cannot explain how the block of wood is divided into peg and hole, then we also cannot speak about their mutual compatibility. Conversely, if we can speak about the boundary between the peg and the hole, then this boundary would also be responsible for structure and form in nature, even though the boundary is not material.

There are several other issues in evolutionary theory that I have discussed in *Signs of Life*, which I will briefly mention here. The key point of these discussions is simply that evolution is not a logically consistent theory. It postulates randomness which is a sign of incompleteness, and then completes it with natural selection which requires meanings. If meanings indeed existed, then nature would be complete and randomness would not be needed. If on the other hand nature is random then natural selection cannot be postulated because randomness arises from a rejection of real boundaries but natural selection depends on the existence of natural boundaries. Without both natural selection and random mutation, the theory is incomplete. With both of them in place, the theory is inconsistent. One only needs a closer look at the logical form of the theory to see what it is really saying, and its problems become too obvious.

The semantic view shows that order and structure in matter are not random; each such structure encodes some meaning. The structures are byproducts of concretizing the abstract meanings. The species therefore has to be defined not as a type of body, but as a type of mind, from which the type of body is produced. It should be remembered that in the semantic view the mind is not free will; it is not even experience; it is simply concepts that are more abstract than sensations. For instance, the concept 'car' is the mind when the concept has not been elaborated into taste, touch, smell, sound, and sight. When it is thus elaborated, then it becomes a macroscopic object. As the elaborations continue, the car is concretized into atomic objects. The mind, therefore, is an objective level of reality, different from free will or experience, which cannot be perceived because it is more abstract than the five senses of perception. Nevertheless, once it has been concretized as objects, its presence can be known simply by the coherent functioning of the whole.

The semantic view illustrates that species are never created and destroyed. Rather, as ideas, all species are always possible. Nevertheless, these possibilities are *realized* occasionally by time which transforms them from abstract concepts to contingent objects making them available for observation. Furthermore, the species are fixed by the context or ecosystem; no single species can emerge in isolation without the evolution of the entire ecosystem. The macroscopic evolution of the ecosystem is the true cause of the microscopic mutations. A living being does not randomly mutate to adapt to the environmental changes. Rather, the environment and the living being co-evolve through a new kind of material process that can only be described when matter is treated semantically. This co-evolution of the whole and part can be predicted in a new kind of evolutionary theory that models living beings as minds rather than bodies. Unlike current evolutionary theory, which makes no predictions, and can make none, the sematic evolution would be predictive. In fact, this evolution would be cyclic, and hierarchical. That is, the model of evolution would apply not just to living beings, but to higher abstractions such as ecosystems, societies, and cultures.

The same species, in this evolution, would appear and disappear at different times and places. Paleontologists who see such reappearances may postulate migratory patterns, but actually migrations are not needed, because nature does not build a type of body; it only manifests a type of mind into a type of body. This type of body need not have genetic similarities to its parents. Instead, in the emergence of new species, completely new genetic patterns would be produced even without any similarities to the parental genes.

One of the key reasons that evolutionary theory triggers so much debate is because the Abrahamic religions claim that God created all the species as they are today. The idea therefore that the species arrived gradually through evolution would deny that God had any role in creating life, and would therefore entail that these created beings have to follow the commandments of God. The Vedic philosophical view of creation is quite different. The Vedic view is that God is primordial ideas from which more complex ideas are generated. Different living bodies are different kinds of ideas or minds. All these ideas are eternal as possibilities but they become reality under the influence of time. Essentially, time converts the possibilities into realities. This generation, annihilation, and preservation of species is therefore a consequence of time, and these species appear and disappear over and over again. The creation and destruction of species is a natural process and not a divine process. However, the soul or living being transcends the mind and body and remains unchanged even when the body and mind are changed.

Are all the species eternal? Yes, they are, but only as possibilities. Did God create all the species? No, God only created the elementary ideas but the structure of time produced the rest. Do species remain invariant over time? Certainly not; the species appear and disappear; in fact what we call 'human' itself changes with time. Is the complexity in the living being an indication of God's design? No, the complexity is a representation of a material mind; we cannot see this mind, but it exists as ideas more abstract than sensations. To perceive the ideas, one is required to develop newer forms of perception beyond sensations. From the Vedic perspective, both Darwinian evolution and Christian creationism are false ideas. The real evolution in nature—which includes biological evolution—is governed by the semantic space-time structure, and this process is natural. However, the mechanism of evolution is not random mutation and natural selection; rather it is the evolution of meanings.

Nearly every idea in the modern *theory* of chemical evolution is false, although evolution itself is not false. The evolution is neither random nor is it individual. Instead, the universe as a whole evolves, as do smaller and smaller parts of it. All these evolutions are evolutions of meaning, and they follow a cyclic pattern of emergence, growth, decay, and death. The order in this evolution can be predicted in a formal theory of hierarchical space-time, although the theory would predict not just species, but even the evolution of societies, cultures, economies, ideologies, civilizations, and ecologies.

Cognitive Relativism

Religions have greatly aided the rise of Atheism by being unable to recognize that what matters in the end is the truth rather than belief. While it may often be necessary to believe in some ideas at the start, and most knowledge begins in belief in the authority of the teacher, eventually you must find ways to validate that knowledge. How do we validate the beliefs? Religions don't seem to make the transition from belief to truth. If two religions disagree on something—for instance whether the soul transmigrates or not—the disagreement is never put to a test of truth. Perhaps some of these questions are not easy to verify—can we then verify other truths which are logically connected to those claims? As Quine has argued, knowledge is an interconnected web of ideas that touches experiences only at the periphery; it may not be easy to verify every possible belief, although it should be possible to validate at least the periphery of that belief system. This periphery corresponds to the leaves of the semantic tree, and the inability to verify the core corresponds to the difficulty in perceiving the roots. The onus lies on the believer that if the core of the belief system cannot be validated, at least its edges must be. Conflict at the edges is not an innocuous problem; it points to difficulties in the truth of the core itself. And yet, the various religions haven't rigorously pursued the truth, not only in the sense of discovery but also in the sense of validation.

The modern world provides tacit support for the separation between truth and belief. The democratic societies profess the freedom to practice any kind of religion, in as much as they permit the choice of sexuality, the car you drive, or the partner you marry. Secularism has convinced everyone that religion is a personal matter. So personal, in fact, that no one has a right to challenge your convictions. There is hence a public life and a private life; the public life is controlled by the state and subject to scientific inquiry, but the private life is not. We can ask questions about truth in the public sphere but we cannot in the private sphere. There is only one truth in the public world and we are all supposed to accept that, but there are as many truths in the private world as there are people, and it is not a crime to not justify the truth of what you actually believe in. This separation between truth and belief is so entrenched that attempts to unseat them would be viewed as violating personal freedom, contradictory to the democratic principles of society.

When religious ideas become personal, they lose objectivity, and eventually the concern with truth. You may have a strong faith in your beliefs and you may think that everyone else who doesn't believe in these same ideas must be either ignorant or an idiot. However, you cannot say that openly. After all, we are not supposed to discuss personal matters publicly. The separation between the private and public is very convenient, but it is also very insidious—it indicates that there are many possible 'truths,' and each person is free to choose their truth, as they find convenient. That religious differences are not a question of true or false, that what you believe about religion is a matter of personal choice, and that we are all free to interpret things as we like them, are all deeply problematic if we treat religious knowledge also as knowledge of reality. But treating religious knowledge as pertaining to reality also subjects it to the uncomfortable fact that some of these beliefs may be untrue. Would we be ready to evaluate our beliefs against the nature of truth?

Privately everyone believes their particular faith is the right one, but publicly we acknowledge that everyone's faith is equally good; or, at least, everyone has the freedom to pursue their faith without interference from the other faiths. The Western world arrived at this conclusion after many long religious wars. It led to the separation between faith and truth, and this separation—while a useful arrangement to prevent wars—is ultimately detrimental to the cause of all religious thought in so far as they claim to be true. If scientific ideas can be debated and criticized openly, but religious ideas cannot be discussed in this manner, there is something profoundly wrong with the way we have approached this belief.

New Atheism benefits from the relativism of religious beliefs. They can ask: If the different religions cannot agree on the nature of God, soul, afterlife, and morality, then how do we know *which* religion should we follow? Might we not just discard *all* religions because there is actually no consensus even amongst religious people on the nature of their beliefs? Part of the problem in debating an atheist is that it is not clear which particular religion he is fighting against. Since the atheists don't understand the religious differences very well, they pretend that the differences are not relevant or important to the debate. I have often encountered atheists who seem to deny the existence of soul and God, but they don't actually have a very good definition or understanding of what they are denying.

The relativism of religious beliefs is not a problem of atheism *per se*; it is more a problem about religious belief itself. The origin of this problem lies in the fact that every contingent fact has a number of abstract facts behind it. All differences of opinion arise from one of the following assumptions: (1) terminating the categorical hierarchy prematurely, (2) omitting some parts of the hierarchy in a leap of faith, (3) connecting parts of different branches, even though they are not connected, and (4) inverting the process of constructing the contingent from the abstract to the abstract from the contingent. The reason that religious theories are not so open to discussion is because they deal in more abstract topics such as the nature of the mind, morality, happiness, and desire, whose existence cannot be measured by sight, sound, taste, touch, and smell. Their existence rather requires deeper forms of perception and involves more abstract kinds of categories, which do not fit the public world of material objects. Without developing deeper forms of perception and rationality, it is impossible to debate the truth of these beliefs.

I believe that the development of a semantic theory of nature will aid the resolution of religious conflicts. It will establish the nature of God as an entity which is neither identical to the world, not separate from it. It will establish a definition of consciousness that can know itself, and distinguish between two kinds of consciousness that respectively know one part of a distinction and the distinction itself. It will distinguish the nature of consciousness from various types of subtle material categories such as the mind, intelligence, ego, the unconscious, etc.; one primary reason for disagreements between religious ideologies is that many material categories are confused with spirituality. It will establish a clear understanding of morality as a natural rather than divine causation. The problem of theodicy—or why there is evil and suffering in the world—would be understood as an outcome of mistaken theories and actions rather than the will of God. Notions about accountability and responsibility, whether one person's sins can be transferred to another, whether sins can be pardoned or modified by prayer, the connection between actions and consequences, will all emerge from a natural moral theory. Finally, much of what is today considered miracle and divine causation would simply turn out to be a subtle level of material reality which requires advanced perceptual development, not necessarily religious beliefs. If nature is hierarchical, with the subtle levels controlling gross matter, it is possible to manipulate matter at the subtle level and while the effects of such control would be visible at the level of the five senses, their causes would remain invisible. These so-called 'miracles' need a new kind of scientific explanation, rather than beliefs that natural laws of causation are violated.

The relativism of religious theories is a problem arising from a shallow understanding of reality. Different religious outlooks either don't see the complete scope of matter and spirit, or confuse something material with spiritual, or simply don't understand the complex relationships between matter, mind, beliefs, and consequences. They don't fully grasp the nature of free will and how it differs from the determinism of nature, and how God interacts with the world. I believe that these problems will disappear when a true understanding of reality is developed. The conflict between religious and scientific thinking, or the conflict between various forms of religious thinking are not fundamentally different; they both stem from an incorrect understanding of the nature of reality. This incorrect view of nature can either be inconsistent or incomplete or both. But the manner in which we deal with such problems is not unique to either science or religion. The cognitive relativism of modern secularism is certainly false; it is an escape route to avoid the difficult problems.

Notions of Causality

Modern science operates under a notion of causality in which objects push or pull each other by forces. The cause of an effect is therefore *farther* from the effect, and science establishes a connection between the cause and effect only if the cause can be measured prior to the effect. In the semantic causal model described earlier, the cause is *deeper* from the effect, and we can never measure the real cause using a material object (in the same way that we measure the object), because the cause is more abstract than the effect. The current scientific notion of cause-effect relation rests between the leaves of the semantic tree. The semantic notion of nature instead views causality as a relation between the branches and the leaves of the tree. If something has already become visible to sensation, then it has crossed many levels of manifestation, each of which exists materially but cannot be perceived because these forms of matter are more abstract than the senses by which we try to perceive them.

The atheists often ask: If there are senses, mind, intelligence, ego, personality, unconscious, soul, and God, then can we measure them? This notion about reality assumes that everything in nature can be observed by the senses, because it must exist as an observable object. This view of reality is mistaken even for perception itself. Consider, for instance, the perception of color. The material objects are various shades of colors—red, blue, green, etc.—and by their observation we can know the shades of color. However, can we measure the property of *color* itself? The problem here is that while we can sense redness, yellowness, blueness, etc., we cannot sense color. The instrument of sensing—the eyes—themselves have to be defined as the concept of color, and this instrument is necessarily more abstract than the shades it perceives. For instance, if we have to distinguish between red and blue, then we must compare them along some *color axis*. We can see the points on the color axis but we cannot see the axis itself from within the space. To see the color axis, we must step outside the color space, and observe this space from an even more abstract space. For instance, the color space can be observed from the *sight* space which contains other aspects of vision such as form, size, distance, and direction, besides color.

The point is quite simply that we cannot see the color of the ability of seeing color, because they are two different levels of conceptual abstractions. The ability of seeing represents the concept of color, but the objects seen through this ability represent yellow, red, blue, etc. Color is the dimension and yellow, blue, and red, are objects on this dimension. Similarly, color, form, size, distance, and direction are objects in an even more abstract space called sight. Sound, sight, taste, touch, and smell are objects in a further more abstract space of meanings—this space is called the mind or *manas* in Vedic philosophy. These meanings are objects in a deeper space of order and structure—called intelligence or *buddhi*. Order and structure are objects in a deeper space of intentions called ego or *ahaṃkāra*, which are objects in a deeper space of moral values called *mahattattva*. The semantic tree comprises of nodes, such that the parent node is the dimension (or space) of the child nodes and the child nodes are the objects within that dimension (or space).

The dimensions of a space cannot be understood from within the space, although we can measure the values of objects against that dimension. To know the dimension, we must enter another deeper space in which this dimension is an object. Accordingly, if objects in the deeper space are not manifested in the shallower space, their presence cannot be detected from the shallower space. The problem of physical causality is that we try to measure everything in terms of sensations, even though we cannot describe the senses in terms of sensations, because the senses are the dimensions using which the sensations are differentiated. These dimensions can be perceived through a deeper form of perception in a more abstract space where the senses will become objects. The semantic causal view essentially states that there are interactions not just between objects in a fixed space, but even between the dimensions of various spaces, which become objects in a deeper space. The interaction between dimensions will have effects on the objects which can be measured, but the cause of these effects is not in that space. In that specific sense, there can be effects whose causes lie outside the specific type of space that we are using to measure.

Such cause-effect relationships cannot be modeled in current science. They will appear as miracles, even though they are not miracles; they just happen to be effected by deeper forms of material reality which requires deeper forms of perception. In Vedic philosophy, the states of the mind (and other subtle matter) can be used to control and change the bodily states. To effect such changes, the experimenter must have developed advanced forms of perception in which he can perceive abstract objects such as color, taste, touch, smell, and sound. By manipulating these objects, the experimenter would modify the form of the space-time 'container' in which experiment is being carried out and the changes would be detected by the measurement, but the causal origin of these changes cannot be understood. To understand that origin, one must step into deeper spaces. What many religions call miracles, therefore, are deeper forms of causality in Vedic philosophy. These causal effects appear as miracles because matter is structured into a hierarchy of types. The subtle forms can affect the gross forms, and the effect can be measured using gross measurement but the cause cannot be detected by such measurement. These effects therefore appear as miracles, the demystification of which needs a different science.

Atheism works under the premise that there is only one space which universally extends everywhere. This is an outcome of thinking of space linearly rather than hierarchically. When space is treated linearly, higher dimensions cannot be accessed from within the space. However, when space is treated hierarchically, then some locations in space are also higher locations than others. They will physically appear to be the same as the other locations, but they are actually higher dimensions. In fact, semantic locations are also dimensions, although a new notion of space and time is needed to explicate this notion. The locations which represent abstract types would appear to be "empty" because we cannot perceive any objects in those locations. But, actually, these locations are not empty; they have a form and represent a type more abstract than the sensations, which can be perceived by the mind, intellect, ego, morality, etc. When such an "empty" location appears to cause effects, we cannot model them in current science, and they will appear as miracles. But these miracles can be understood via deeper kinds of perceptions.

Modern science recognizes that about 95% of the universe is 'dark-energy' and 'dark-matter' which exist although they cannot be perceived. In Vedic philosophy, these forms of matter are not dark, although they cannot be perceived by the gross senses, because they represent more abstract information than what the senses can see. These invisible forms of matter have an effect on the visible matter, but these effects cannot be causally modeled and understood unless the space and time are described using a hierarchical theory. In the semantic theory, black-holes, worm-holes, dark-energy, and all such exotic concepts will become different types of material locations. Furthermore, they will abound all over the universe—at both small and large scales—and will not remain exotic objects anymore. If we happen to enter these locations, we would have new kinds of experiences—for instance, direct perceptual encounter with concepts, order, structure, intentions, and morals; we would be able to perceive and understand the nature of these subtle types of entities.

The Universe Is Flat

Suppose an Indian travels to America on a US visa. He carries with him his Indian attire, his food habits, his language and accent, his thought patterns, his mannerisms and his cultural identity. Even though the person enters America, he still remains an Indian. At the gross material level, the person's body is in America but at the subtle material level, his mind, intellect, ego, and consciousness are still Indian. As he moves around in the US, he may be physically close to some American people but he does not become similar to them, because he is—at a deeper level—connected to a different heritage. If we described this person's location physically, he is in America, and if the properties of the object were defined by the location, he would also be called an American. But even though physically in America, the person is not an American, because his location is defined not physically but hierarchically and at the subtle level, the person is still in India. As people live in other countries, their thinking patterns may change over time and they may become more naturally American, detaching themselves from their previous identity.

This example helps us illustrate two ways in which we can travel in the universe. First, we can travel to a different part of the universe quite like the Indian travels to America without changing his subtle body of thoughts, beliefs, sensations, and habits. Even though he enters America, he is still not an American; he may see some new things in the new place, but by and large he continues to have the same thoughts, feelings, emotions, desires, etc. Second, we can travel to a different part of the universe like an American returning to America after a travel abroad. This person is natively accustomed to the culture and traditions of that country and when he enters the country, he is both physical and mentally in there. If we define the locations physically, then the Indian and American standing at the same spot in space would have the same perspective about the world. But if we define the locations semantically, then the Indian and American standing at the same physical location in space are actually not at the same semantic location in space.

This issue is very important to the understanding of life in other parts of the universe. For instance, if we travel in a space ship to outer space, what is our real location? Physically we are in outer space. But semantically we are still in the Earth's atmosphere, carrying it around in our space-suit, and living in the human world comprising language, ideas, beliefs, and outlook about the world. If we had to compute our semantic location, we would still be earthlings and not truly outer space beings. Being in a different part of the universe is not just a physical change in the location in the space of objects or sensations. It also requires a change in the location in deeper forms of space underlying the space of the sensations. If the gross location has changed but deeper locations haven't, only a very minor change has occurred, and the major changes are yet to occur.

Let's illustrate this with an example of a hierarchical naming convention. Assume that I'm a blogger who blogs at the location indian. blogs.acme.com. All the information about these blogs would be stored in the blog.acme.com database, regardless of what I happen to call myself. If, for instance, I change my blog location to american.blogs. acme.com, my absolute location has changed a bit, but relative to the blogs.acme.com, my location is still the same. If I had to truly change the blogging experience, I would have to join a different blogging website altogether. While changing the name of my particular blog does change the location, semantically speaking, this name is still attached to the previous domain provider's domain.

Going to America without giving up the Indian identity is like changing the blog name from indian.blogs.acme.com to american. blogs.acme.com. There is indeed a change in this renaming of the blog location, but it is not substantial. Similarly, going to outer space in the semantic universe while retaining the human identity is not a change in the location; we have only shifted to another part of Earth, where the Earth is defined as the human identity, mindset, and culture on the Earth. It is important to note that in a hierarchical space (e.g., using dotted-decimal notation), there is a full space of numbers or names available at each level of the hierarchy (e.g., after each dot). For instance, if your address is defined hierarchically as 10.24.87.92, and you happen to change the location in the least significant space (i.e., change the last digits of the address), you will still remain attached to the hierarchical 'subnet'. Truly changing the network entails a change in the successive hierarchical digits of the address, not just the last digits of the current subnetwork.

At each level of the hierarchy, the entire set of names or numbers are available for naming an object, but their meanings are not quite the same. Thus if we go to the moon in the space shuttle, our address has become moon at the physical level, but it remains Earth at the mental level. If we find this part of the universe barren, it means that there is an address space range which is not occupied because it comprises of earthlings traveling to the moon. It appears barren because it is an unused part of the address space. If we truly wanted to experience the moon, we would also have to change the other parts of the address space in the deeper spaces as well. For instance, an earthling can travel to the moon by becoming the address e.e.e.m, although the moon dweller has an address m.m.m.m. By changing the last digit of our address, we may claim to have entered the moon, although we have only entered a certain part of the Earth's address space. This address space is unused, as there are no earthlings going to the moon, and the moon appears to be barren. If we happen to colonize the moon and start living there we would still not meet any true lunar beings, because we haven't truly entered the lunar space; we are still in the Earth's address space.

The universe that astronomers observe through the telescope is actually not the real universe. It is rather the universe mapped into the Earth's address space, specifically the part of the address space that can be accessed by the senses and the telescope. We are in effect observing the leaves of the semantic tree, without understand the deeper structure of where these leaves are joined into the twigs, branches, trunks, and eventually the root. Some objects that appear very close to us may be semantically quite different, because they are actually leaves from a different branch. Likewise, two leaves that appear very far may actually be quite close because they are just leaves off the same branch. This distortion of distance is quite like cartographic projections of the earth's surface on a plane whereby the points at the equator appear closer while the points the pole appear farther. The distortion is caused by projecting the universe into a particular observer's address space. The true nature of the universe can only be understood if we understand the deep semantic structure of the tree rather than just its visible leaves.

In Vedic philosophy, different locations in the universe represent different types. They are inhabited by living beings that have different kinds of bodies, senses, minds, intellects, egos, and moralities. The livings beings can be described by a hierarchical naming convention and to truly know these beings one must know the entire hierarchical address. These living beings cannot be understood from our current perceptual address space because the reality is distorted in the process of representation. To even understand what we are seeing we would have to transform the observations into a new form which would be perceived if our senses were different.

The Vedas describe that the universe comprises many different types of locations. Some of these locations are more abstract than our experience, and they are said to be 'higher' living beings. Other locations are more contingent than our experiences, and they are said to be 'lower' living beings. The Vedas describe millions of such higher and lower living beings whose bodies, senses, and minds are different because they predominate in different concepts. The living beings who reside in the semantically higher locations are called *devata* or demigods and those beings who reside in semantically lower locations are said to be *daitya* or demons. The higher and lower locations can be given a precise definition in a semantic theory. Essentially, those beings who are engrossed in the material objects and sensuality are said to be lower, and those beings who are engrossed more in the mental functions such as intellect, ego, and morality are said to be higher. The demons enjoy the control of the atomic world and their senses are so refined that they can perceive miniscule details in taste, touch, sound, smell, and sight; the world is very high-definition for them, because they can perceive the very small details about material objects. The demigods enjoy the control of the universe at the large scale and they experience the universe in the abstract through mind, intellect, ego, and morality. Their world is also high-definition but in that world are abstract entities like numbers, music, art, love, dance, knowledge, and mystical powers.

The world that we live in is said to be in between these two worlds. We cannot experience matter at great levels of detail because our senses cannot perceive atomic objects; our experiences are said to involve macroscopic objects. Our minds and intellects are also not highly developed and we cannot perceive abstract forms of reality very easily; there is hence a limited understanding of the subtle world: very few advanced personalities accept the reality of such a world, while others think that ideas are simply illusions. By contrast, the demigods have a far greater intellectual enjoyment than us and the demons have a far greater sensual pleasure than us. Both kinds of living beings are material; they are neither divine nor are they evil (as often pictured in Abrahamic religions). They just happen to have different kinds of minds and bodies more suited to perceive and enjoy the sensations from atoms and molecules much more than us, or perceive the world of abstractions much better than us. We have such abilities, too, but they are limited in us.

Atheists naturally scoff at these ideas; for them, there is no high and low in the universe, and there is probably no life on any other planet and even it does exist it must be quite like our existence. Atheists must recognize that our existence is quite mediocre from a material standpoint. We have neither great sensual pleasure, nor do we have very well developed minds and intellects. Imagine if you had the eyes which could separately analyze each photon while looking at a vast grassland, the nose that could smell each molecule emanating from a garden of flowers, the tongue that could taste every atom of mineral in fresh sparking water, ears that could listen to every individual note played by each musician in an orchestra, and skin that could feel every atom of smoothly blowing wind, what great sensual pleasure that would be! Or, imagine that you could see the world of all mathematical theorems, with numbers combining and splitting to produce immensely magnificent forms; imagine that you could see the structure and order created by forms in music and art, imagine that you could comprehend the structure of space-time, and look into the enormous past and the farthest future, how great would the intellectual pleasure be! By comparison, our sensual, mental and intellectual faculties are quite pitiable. Demigods and demons in Vedic philosophy are not divine and evil. They are just living beings with far greater intellectual and sensual capabilities.

To the extent that greater intellect brings us closer to the understanding of reality, and thereby reinstates our free will (which is divine), greater intellect is closer to divine, although still material. Similarly, to the extent that sensual pleasure absorbs the consciousness into the material objects and takes us away from a true understanding of reality, sensual pleasure is evil, although material.

The universe is not flat in the sense of being the same everywhere. The universe is hierarchical, but this hierarchy is not physical as the top and bottom of a house. The hierarchy is conceptual as being more abstract at the top and more contingent at the bottom. The conflict between the religious postulate about other kinds of living beings in the universe and the scientific inability to find them so far can be resolved if nature were viewed hierarchically and living beings primarily focused upon different parts of this hierarchy. Demigods and demons would now not be illusions of religious theories; they may even be the life that we aspire to have, provided we understand how to develop the senses, mind, and intellect to enjoy different facets of matter. The Vedas don't encourage this enjoyment, but they provide the information if someone needs it. Any material enjoyment is temporary in Vedic philosophy. No living being can therefore permanently have a certain type of material body. Rather, nature subjects the living being to different bodies to acquaint him with different facets of reality. This knowledge can help the living being become detached from material enjoyment.

Morality Is Belief

While you can measure the velocity of the bullet emerging from the barrel of a gun, you cannot measure whether the shooting is good or bad. Are wars good? Or are they bad? Is death penalty good or bad? Are abortions right or wrong? The problem in answering these questions is that you must have something to measure any claim against (to check if it was true or false) but we don't know what we can even measure to determine such claims. It is not even clear if the question of good or bad is the same as the question of true or false. For instance, if someone said that sex education was wrong, how would you measure this claim against some facts to confirm or deny its truth? Liberty, justice, equality, and beauty, are just some of the many areas which suffer from the same problem: we don't know if they are true or false. For instance, is hurting some people good or bad? If good, then hopefully you won't mind if someone hurt you? If bad, then what would you say to hurting their religious sentiments by criticizing their religious beliefs? Is it right to look into people's private data for national security? Is vegetarianism better than meat-eating? How about polygamy? Of course, my intention here is not to take any sides in the above debates; I only wish to highlight that the problem in answering them stems from a single fact: we don't know the facts we must measure to confirm or deny them.

The natural outcome of this predicament is that many people would often term these claims as beliefs. The world has fought too many battles and killed too many people because they thought that it was alright to kill other people if they did not agree with you. So, modern societies now "agree to disagree" to continue living. Every culture, society, community, or nation has its own views about right and wrong, which might be false in other cultures, societies, communities, or nations. We have stopped (in most cases) trying to find out if any of these things are indeed facts, because we don't know what we will measure to decide if those claims are indeed facts.

Morality just happens to be one of these things that we don't know how to measure. Therefore, we call it belief, not necessarily true or false. If you take the claim made by Protagoras (a Greek philosopher)—man is the measure of all things—seriously, then you might be tempted to also assume that morals can never be true or false; beauty lies in the eyes of the beholder and so do the morals. Of course, there are many ethical naturalists today who claim that morality is in fact an objective question. Some beliefs are also true, but not all. That the sky is blue is a true belief; that the Earth is flat is not, even if you happen to believe it. The ethical naturalist holds that one day questions of right or wrong would also be answered by the measurement of their natural outcomes. The naturalist however does not say exactly how we will *define* the nature of the good. Is good what makes me happy? Then clearly man is the measure of all things, and everyone is free to decide what is good for them and there is not basis on which we call morality a true or false judgment. If, however, good is which makes a large number of people happy, how large must the set of people be to determine the goodness? If some people became unhappy, would we neglect them? Then would we not violate the goodness principles of equality and justice?

If this discussion seems hopeless, let me try to simplify it. Current science measures the facts of the world, but it cannot measure the truth of the claims because it cannot measure meanings. There is an important difference between facts and truths, which is generally not understood, unless you analyze the nature of falsity. For instance, suppose that I believe that the sky is purple. The thought exists in my brain and can be measured, and science can detect that there is something that exists. But it is impossible to determine that the thing that exists in the brain actually signifies the belief that the sky is purple. The only way we can arrive at this conclusion is if we asked the person what he felt at the same time that someone observed his brain, and he or she told us about the experience of their belief. However, let's suppose for the moment that the brain process is actually the meaning of the belief. Since the brain is material, the brain process is created by some natural law which must be true in all cases, although this law seems to produce contradictory beliefs—some people believe that the sky is blue while others might believe that it is purple. How can the same law of nature produce contradictory beliefs? And if it does produce contradictions, then how can some of these beliefs be false? After all, if the premise (the natural laws) is true, then the conclusions derived from these premises (i.e., that the sky is blue or that the sky is purple) must be true as well, even though some of these conclusions are self-contradicting.

The problem in science is that we cannot interpret physical facts into meanings. And if we actually interpreted them into meanings, it would lead to a logical contradiction. If we cannot interpret facts into meanings, we cannot make claims about true or false, and that is clearly problematic: it makes nature incomplete. But if we interpret the facts into meanings, then nature is logically inconsistent. We encountered this problem earlier in the context of mathematics—it is called Gödel's incompleteness theorem—which concludes that any logical system can be either inconsistent or incomplete. If it is incomplete, we cannot decide the truth of claims, when they are treated as concepts, representing some other facts besides their own existence. Mathematics can derive some theorems from axioms—essentially tokens from tokens—but these tokens cannot be considered *representations* or *descriptions* of facts. If we happen to treat the tokens as concepts, then mathematics is inconsistent.

Physical theories of nature can measure the *existence* of things, but not their *truth*, because to decide if they are true, we must first give them meanings, and that makes the system logically inconsistent. The problem for a physical theory is—how can false things exist? If nature is logical, then it must only permit true things because we assume that it begins in true axioms which are converted into true conclusions by the application of logic. If nature were indeed logical then everything that exists must also be true. Since the belief that the sky is purple exists in my brain, it must also be true.

The problem of morality stems from the fact that we separate *existence* from *truth*: ideas about morality exist in my head, but they may not be true. Judgments of right and wrong exist as beliefs but they may be incorrect. How can something false exist in nature if nature is supposed to be logically consistent? The problem of morality is therefore not different from the problem of any belief, and the problem is that we don't know how false beliefs can exist. The solution to this problem—as we have seen previously—requires a shift in thinking about nature; nature should not be viewed as things which are given meanings (because things never become meanings). Rather, nature should be viewed as meanings which become things; all such things are now symbols of meanings. When nature is treated in this way, there is a difference between existence and truth, and the difference is created because there are meanings.

The sensations about objects are now contingent meanings and morals about objects are abstract meanings. We cannot see, hear, taste, touch, or smell morality, but that doesn't mean it doesn't exist. To perceive meanings, we need a method of observation that goes beyond sensation. The problem of morality however is only a progression in the process of perception—senses perceive sensations, the mind perceives concepts, the intellect perceives order and structure, the ego perceives intentions, and, therefore, there must be a "moral sense" that perceives morals, if indeed morals are facts and not merely beliefs. Unless deeper forms of perceptions can be developed, the reality corresponding to such percepts cannot be understood, because the theories that explain such observations themselves cannot be formulated. Morality about facts is a deeper fact, but to even envision deeper facts we must recognize that there is something deeper than sensations; this viewpoint is possible only if objects themselves can be viewed as conceptual entities, because then it becomes possible to understand more abstract concepts.

The problem of morality therefore does not begin in morality itself. It rather begins in the question of truth and why some things that exist may not necessarily be true. If my brain cannot denote sensations, concepts, order, and intentions, then it also cannot denote morality. If the material objects do not denote sensations, concepts, order, and intentions, then morality too cannot be real. However, this isn't necessarily a problem of morality itself; it is rather a question about whether my other perceptions of sensations, concepts, order, and intentions are real. If I see yellow and yellowness is not real, then if I see morality those morals too must be unreal.

In Vedic philosophy, the universe begins in morals as a form of material consciousness called *mahattattva*. This material element represents the good and bad, right and wrong. Judgments of morality are higher than intentions, and only when we consider something good and right, we intend it. From the intentions notions about order and structure develop, from this order concepts emerge, from the concepts sensations emerge, and from the sensations objects emerge. This emergence can be understood in a semantic view of nature where morals are a deep form of material reality. Unless material objects can denote concepts, they cannot denote morals.

We cannot perceive morals when we limit our consciousness to the observation of material objects through sensations. The observer's perception must rise through deeper forms of perceptions to uncover the deeper kinds of material existence. Morality in Vedic philosophy is therefore natural, not transcendental. However, morality is a deeper form of matter. When an observer's consciousness is covered by ignorance—called *māya*—he does not perceive deeper forms of matter. Even though morality exists in all facts of nature, it is a deeper kind of truth than the truth of sensations. An observer whose consciousness is limited to the perception of sensations does not perceive this morality. Such an observer therefore believes that sensations are real but every other deeper form of semantic reality—including morality—is an imagination of the religious mind. He therefore could potentially indulge in immoral experiences.

The immorality begins in a shortfall in experience by which deeper facts about the world are not perceived. The Vedas describe that such incomplete perception creates consequences—called *karma*—which force the living being into naturally determined experiences. The shortfall in perception is therefore followed by *karma*, which is then followed by experiential consequences. This succession of limited experience followed by determined experience constitutes the law of nature. *Karma* is therefore the gap between reality and our theory of nature. If our theory is perfect, and we perceive the entire reality, we would also perceive morality and act morally, freeing us from the consequences of our actions. But, if we perceive limited parts of reality, we don't perceive the morality and therefore misconstrue it, and we are bound by consequences. *Moral Materialism* describes this theory of action and consequence in detail, and the interested reader may refer to it for further discussion about how and why morality is a natural phenomenon and law.

The singular point that I wish to highlight here is that the current debate about morality between religion and atheism is flawed. The religious person believes that morality is transcendental and therefore a commandment of God. The atheist on the other hand supposes that morality is not a fact of nature, or if it were a fact then it would be reducible to the observations of the senses; this view then leads to the idea that morality is simply the greatest amount of sensual pleasure for the greatest number of people, or that a moral judgment for an individual is the greatest pleasure for himself. Both the atheistic and the religious stances are problematic. The religious view is problematic because God must punish the immoral person but how He interacts with matter (and whether that interaction violates material laws) is unexplained in most religious theories. The scientific view is problematic because truths and morals can never be reduced to physical states since such states cannot be interpreted as meanings without also creating logical contradictions.

Effectively, both religion and atheism reduce morality to beliefs which cannot be connected to matter: religion to the belief in God's commandments which cannot be connected to natural causality and atheism to personal beliefs which cannot be reduced to material states. Both viewpoints are false; if morality is real, it should be a question of truth. However, even before it can be about truth, there should be room in science to describe meanings within matter.

The Problem of Theodicy

The failure to connect morality to matter leads to the problem of theodicy: Why do bad things happen to good people? The problem exists only for religion because God is supposed to be good and if He is good then why does He create suffering? Why was I born poor? Why was I born to parents with congenital diseases? Why was I born into a society or culture that preempted my chances of success in life? Why was I born handicapped, ugly, or less intelligent?

There can never be any explanation for these questions in science because the questions themselves assume the ability to define what we mean by suffering, poverty, disease, handicap, ugliness, or intelligence, which in turn requires the ability to associate certain meanings with material states, and such meanings cannot be associated in a physical theory without creating logical contradictions, as we saw above. The problem is simply this: if the same laws of nature can produce two distinct states which we would call poverty and richness, and these two states are semantically opposite, then the laws would seem to produce mutually contradictory propositions. Any system that produces such contradictions is logically inconsistent. A single instance of such a contradiction would invalidate the entire theory and the fact that the universe comprises many such contradictions would entail that it is not a logically consistent system. If the universe is logically inconsistent, we cannot use logic to describe it, which in turn entails the impossibility of science.

Note how this problem begins when we label some physical states as poverty and richness, health and disease, beautiful and ugly, etc. The question of morality cannot be dealt with in current science because we cannot deal in meanings without creating contradictions. The problem of theodicy assumes that we can speak about poverty and richness, health and disease, beautiful and ugly, etc. And if we assume these meanings, then we must reject science. This means that even before we can speak about the problem of theodicy, we must first find an explanation of why nature contains opposites without creating a logical contradiction. That in turn requires a dramatic shift in terms of our thinking about matter.

Of course, materialists may insist that poverty and richness are not scientific concepts, and therefore don't need to be explained. We only need to explain the succession of material states, but how these states are interpreted as poverty or richness has no role in science. But it is here that the problems of indeterminism in science become very important. All scientific theories—even the most deterministic ones—are indeterministic with regard to initial and boundary conditions. For instance, the laws of classical physics explain the motion of objects after these objects have been set into a particular initial and boundary condition, but they don't explain why matter is in fact set into a particular initial or boundary condition. The initial and boundary conditions represent the information which must be added to the theory to make it predictively useful, but this information has no causal explanation within that theory. To solve this problem, we might add another theory, which would also be similarly indeterministic, leading to an infinite cascade of incomplete theories.

The problem gets much worse when we recognize that even the most deterministic theories are deterministic only because of an assumption about object immutability which is not in fact true[50]. For instance, classical physics presents a deterministic picture only so long as particle identities are immutable; the theory becomes indeterministic when particles can split and coalesce while keeping the total amount of energy, mass, momentum, etc., conserved. As the particles split or coalesce, the total number of particles in the system changes, which in turn alters the number of simultaneous equations that have to be solved to determine system behavior, which in turn makes the system as a whole indeterministic. The laws of classical physics permit such indeterminism and the resulting explanatory gaps preempt even a complete causal account of nature.

As we have seen above, the problems of indeterminism can only be solved when the objects are given a semantic interpretation: a bottle of ink can be spread on paper in many ways, subject to the total amount of ink remaining conserved; the only way to understand that spread is to associate it with meanings. In short, the problem of theodicy begins in the meanings of physical states. But if we associate meanings with physical states, it leads to logical contradictions. If we avoid associating meanings with physical states, the theories are incomplete anyway. Thus, if there is a problem of suffering, the current physical model of nature is logically *inconsistent*. Without the problem of suffering (and meanings in general), the current scientific model is *incomplete*. We can choose between inconsistency and incompleteness, and either way, we would have to recognize that the problem cannot be solved. The problem, however, has little to do with God or religion; the problem is simply unsolvable even within current models of scientific description.

The problem has a solution in the semantic view of nature, but that view changes the causal model of nature. Objects are now symbols of meanings, and theories of nature are real material entities. Morality is the gap between reality and its theory, and this gap produces a consequence which determines the subsequent experiences. The point of this view is rather straightforward—if your theory of nature is incorrect, then nature will arrange an encounter with phenomena using which the theory can be corrected. As we saw in the previous chapter, the scientific method is incomplete[51] because its termination cannot be known. We also saw earlier (in the discussion of Turing's Halting problem) that a procedure that does not terminate (or whose termination cannot be predicted) is semantically incorrect, even though the steps in the procedure may be syntactically correct. The crux of the problem in the scientific method is that a false theory can be corrected only if the falsifying phenomena are encountered but there is no way to determine if and when these phenomena would be encountered, or if the theory is indeed perfect and no such phenomena would ever be encountered in the future. The semantic view of morality addresses this problem in the scientific method; it ensures that if the theory is incorrect, the falsifying phenomena would be encountered, and their encounter can be predicted. However, if the theory is indeed correct, then the theoretician would be freed from the control of the natural laws because the gap between theory and reality has already been dissolved.

The semantic view therefore gives the test for both the theory's correctness and incorrectness, and that test is not the empirical validity of the theory's predictions; the test is whether the theory would be falsified in the future, or whether the theory is correct because its awareness frees the observer from the laws themselves.

Rewards and punishments are, however, in this view, naturally determined rather than through God's intervention into nature. If the theory has improved, then there will be more phenomena that fit the theory and this greater fit between theory and phenomena appears as a reward. If, however, there are still gaps between the theory and reality, then these gaps appear as punishments, which force a revision to the theory. The fact is that both rewards and punishments are relative to the observer; whether you treat some phenomena as a reward or as a punishment depends on the theory you hold. The same phenomena would be considered a reward if it fits the theory's predictions, because you would anticipate the outcome of your actions, and therefore act according to those predictions, engaging only in those actions whose outcomes you intend. The phenomena become a punishment only when they differ from the predictions of the theory, because you predicted something else.

For instance, if your theory of nature says that putting hands in the fire would burn the hand, then you put your hand in the fire only if you wish to burn it. The burn itself is not reward or punishment; if you wanted to burn the hand and the fire did not burn it, then that outcome would be considered a punishment. If, on the other hand, your theory does not predict that fire burns the hand, then the burnt hand after you have put it into the fire would be a punishment. Rewards and punishments are therefore only relative to your theory. As the theory comes closer to reality, more and more phenomena are perceived as being rewards; as the theory moves away from reality, ever more experiences are interpreted as punishments. If the theory of nature has been perfected, everything is a reward.

The morality of nature is therefore a generalization of the scientific method by which each observer understands and models reality. Each observer has the ability to know the nature of truth, because the entire truth (from root to leaf in the semantic tree) is available in each phenomenon. The question is only whether we perceive this entire truth, or only limited parts of it. The acknowledgement of this reality depends on our ability to perceive it, which in turn depends on the extent to which we acknowledge the existence of deeper forms of existence and practice their perception.

The problem of theodicy exists primarily in Abrahamic religions because in Eastern thought—e.g., in Buddhism, Jainism, Sikhism, and Hinduism—both suffering and pleasure are consequences of previous actions of the living being, not caused by God. The living being is responsible for understanding the nature of reality, and thereby of the morality underlying the sensations, concepts, order and intentions, and the extent to which a person understands the nature of reality leads to suffering or enjoyment. The gap between theory and reality represents the consequences of an action called *karma* and it represents not just suffering, but also enjoyment. The goal of life in Eastern religions is to become free of both enjoyment and suffering, although different religions construe that state devoid of material happiness and enjoyment differently. The impersonalist and voidistic views, for instance, dissolve the living being's individuality and free will itself in the quest for freedom from enjoyment and suffering. The personalist views instead state that the perfect understanding of nature frees one from the laws of nature, and create the ability to choose any phenomena, since all these phenomena are consistent with the truth theory of nature. Such an enlightened person treats the so-called enjoyment and suffering with equal detachment, rather than as a punishment or reward given by God.

The theory of nature in Vedic philosophy is called *guna*[52] and the consequences of this theory are called *karma*. Every living being's life experiences are constructed from *guna* and *karma*. *Guna* determines the kind of body and mind available to a living being and can be called the living being's *nature*[53]. *Karma* determines the actual events encountered in life, and they can be called the living being's *nurture*. Nature determines how the nurture is interpreted as happiness or suffering. For instance, certain species that feed on decaying matter would consider its consumption enjoyment, while wholesome fresh food would be considered suffering. There is no absolute interpretation of an event into suffering or enjoyment; the interpretation rather depends on your own nature or *guna*. The laws of nature are never about enjoyment or suffering; they are only about nature and nurture. The combination of the two produces enjoyment or suffering. In effect, by changing one's *guna* or nature, the same experiences can be converted from enjoyment to suffering or vice versa. A common paraphrasing of this fact is that we cannot change what happens to us, although we can change how we react to it. Essentially, the nurture is fixed as the consequence of previous actions, but by changing our nature, we can alter our happiness.

The living being controls his *guna* or nature, but not *karma* or the consequences of nature. As the living being undergoes the *karma* caused by previous *guna*, his present *guna* creates more *karma*. The living being is thus set into a cyclic evolution into the universe, and this evolution is called the *transmigration* of the soul. Different *guna* represent different theories of nature and they produce different species of life. The consequences of these theories represent the events that a living being must undergo in successive lives. The combination of the two produces the life experiences of an individual—i.e. the experience of events in a type of body and mind. The transmigration of the soul is arrested only when the living being becomes free of *guna* because then he perceives nature as it is, and the difference between theory and reality is dissolved. The goal of life in Vedic philosophy is to correct our understanding of nature. The goal is not to enjoy or suffer, but to transcend both enjoyment and suffering as subjective interpretations of an event that arises through a limited theory of nature. As the understanding of nature is perfected, the soul is freed from enjoyment and suffering.

The problem of theodicy never arises in Vedic philosophy because the living being is responsible for his view of nature, and the consequences of that view. God does not create a world of suffering; however, he creates a world in which the living being can choose his view of nature. These views are theories which exist materially and interact with material reality. Nature is therefore a single reality and many possible theories. The conceptual *ingredients* of reality and theory are the same (otherwise the theory could not accurately model the reality) and hence they are often described by the same words—*guna*, *prakṛti*, *māya*, etc. However, the theory is personal while the reality is impersonal; even though the theory exists materially, it effects only the specific person who accepts it as true, rather than the rest of the universe (it is notable that matter in science acts universally on all other material objects in the universe). We can call this theory our deepest beliefs about the world we live in, which condition and cause our evolution in the universe. The theory is a choice, and that choice is not enforced by God. Therefore, the outcomes of those choices are not caused by God; they are simply outcomes of natural laws that take these choices into account.

5

Religion vs. Dharma

In the age of Satya [truthfulness] your four legs were established by the four principles of austerity, cleanliness, mercy, and truthfulness. But it appears that three of your legs are broken due to rampant irreligion in the form of pride, lust for women, and intoxication.

—*Śrimad Bhāgavatām*

What Is Dharma?

While the term 'religion' has been attributed to Vedic theories in recent times, there are some fundamental differences between what the West understands as 'religion' and what the Vedas themselves consider *dharma*. The term *dharma* denotes a few different things, which are worth noting here. First, the term *dharma* means the law of nature, and has often been denoted by the *dharma-chakra* or the wheel of time which denoted the view that nature evolves in a cyclic manner. Second, the term *dharma* is derived from the root *dhri* which means the ground or platform on which other things stand, and that which holds the diversity of the nature together. Third, the term also means the fundamental properties of a thing—e.g., the *dharma* of fire is to be hot and the *dharma* of water is fluidity. The quest for *dharma* is therefore the quest for the laws of nature, the unity in nature that reconciles its diversities, and the understanding of the fundamental properties of all things, including of the self.

The Vedic doctrine is that the universe is like an inverted tree which springs from a non-dual source that reconciles all oppositions. The source of the universe is the *dharma* of the universe because He is the ground on which the universe stands and He is the unity that ties together the diversity, and creates that diversity. The universe is not permanent (although its source is) and the universe appears and disappears cyclically, and this cyclic appearance and disappearance represents the fundamental law of nature, and it is also *dharma*. Finally, the different things, senses, minds, and experiences cyclically produced from the singular ground under the influence of time are properties of the object from which they were produced and to which they are to be attributed, and they are *dharma* as they describe the nature and behavior of things in the universe.

The term 'religion' and the term *dharma* have very little in common. The closest translation of the term *dharma* in English is perhaps *reality*. Reality is the goal, and therefore *dharma* is the goal. Reality exists, and therefore *dharma* exists. Reality is that which remains unchanged when the world changes and therefore *dharma* is the law of nature which remains unchanged with time (it is the structure of time). Reality is that which binds diverse entities, and *dharma* is therefore the unchanging foundation of appearances. In a semantic universe, there is no difference between the true theory of the universe and the universe itself, because the universe is idea-like. Therefore, there is no time-based origin of the theory of reality because that theory is actually reality. The theory of the universe is time, and this time (or theory) produces the universe and destroys it[54]. The real theory of the universe therefore has no origin; it is as old as time itself, because the theory itself is the timely evolution.

In contrast, the term 'religion' denotes something that originated in time; since religion originates in time, it is a byproduct of the effect of time. Everything that is produced in time would also be destroyed by time, and all such religions are temporary. The property of time is to produce and destroy ideas, and religions are ideological movements produced as an effect of time. The crucial difference between religion and *dharma* is therefore that the former is a byproduct of time (or the theory of nature) while the latter is time itself. All religions are temporary, because they are products of time. Time is, however, itself eternal; it evolves cyclically but this cycle has no beginning and end. In that sense, *dharma* is the wheel that moves cyclically, and its motion represents the changes wrought by time—i.e., the nature of things, the beliefs in right and wrong, the evolution of ideas—but *dharma* is not the changes *in* time, but the theory that describes these changes. The theory governs the changes, but the theory is eternal; the theory is *dharma*—the wheel of time.

Dharma is therefore called *sanātana* or eternal in Vedic philosophy, and most knowledgeable people refer to Vedic philosophy not as Hinduism but as *sanātana-dharma*. Reality is called *sat* or eternal[55], and knowledge of this reality is thus called *sanātana-dharma*. How does reality produce the phenomena? In Vedic philosophy, the reality is the reconciliation of opposites—e.g., 'hot' and 'cold,' 'bitter' and 'sweet,' etc. The phenomena on the other hand are the outcome of splitting this reality into opposite parts. By this splitting, the non-dual is expressed or illustrated through examples. For instance, if we say that the source of the universe is 'non-dual,' most people would not understand it. But if we said that non-dual is that which reconciles 'hot' and 'cold,' 'bitter' and 'sweet,' etc., many people may understand it. The idea here is quite simple: prior to creation, there is a singularity, but during creation time splits it into opposites. Since religions are created as an effect of time, they are going to carry some of these opposites. Each religion will advocate some meanings while denying the truth of the other meanings. The conflict between religions is thus a byproduct of their temporal nature.

Of course, Vedic philosophy is no exception to this; it also describes the worship of demigods and demons, which are opposed in their life preferences. How can a single philosophy advocate adherence to these kinds of opposites? The answer to this is that not everything described in the Vedas is *sanātana-dharma*; some of these descriptions are also called *kaitava-dharma* or cheating religion. The Vedas distinguish between *para* and *apara* knowledge; the former is transcendental and eternal and the latter is mundane and temporary. The mundane knowledge is useful for day-to-day subsistence but it is not eternally true. The mundane knowledge changes with time, as do the notions of good and bad, right and wrong. The ultimate Vedic injunction is therefore not obedience to these mundane principles (although we may use them pragmatically) but detachment from both the good and bad of the material nature.

The key point of this discussion is that the material universe is duality, although it is produced from the non-dual. The cause of this production is time, which selectively produces different kinds of opposites at different times. Different things may be right or wrong for different people at different times, but these temporary notions about goodness also constitute material notions of religion. They are not *sanātana-dharma* because they are not eternal. The eternal truth is that which describes the production of temporary truths, and it constitutes the theory of nature. Religions, on the other hand, are temporary truths, being produced within time; they may appear right or wrong to different people, which is somewhat beside the point here. The key point is that everything that is produced in time will carry the imprints of that time in which it was created. Most Abrahamic religions, for instance, carry the imprint of the sociological circumstances in which they were created. Those times have now changed, but some religions have evolved while others haven't. Many religions, for instance, still suppress the rights of women which was the sociological circumstances in times past. People who criticize religions for these excesses perhaps don't recognize that they are only criticizing the values in the past, and that the values they currently champion would be obsoleted in the future.

It should be recognized that there are two kinds of *dharma*—eternal and temporal. The eternal principles of *dharma* represent the truth that is unchanging while the temporal principles of religion are convenient methods of practicing and understanding the eternal principles. Whether polygamy and polyandry are good or bad, whether democracy or autocracy is better, whether men and women should shave their heads or grow their hair, whether circumcision is right or wrong, whether fasting or feasting is the right way to celebrate, or whether borrowing and lending money are good or bad—are not central questions about the eternal religion. They are sociological, cultural, and practical norms that could and would change with time. The morality of the time is different from the eternal truth. The eternal truth produces the temporal effects. It does not mean that everything is always good; however, it means that everything would be good in some particular situation. Whether it is good in the present situation needs to be determined, and that determination can be made only by one cardinal rule—does this aid in the understanding and development of eternal truth?

The Institutionalization of Religion

Religions become problematic when they take the temporal aspects of religion far more seriously than the eternal truth. The temporal aspects are never completely right or wrong; there are always situations in which they will be certainly right, and there will be always situations in which they will be certainly wrong. This has nothing to do with the eternal aspects of religion, but everything to do with the fact that true and false, right and wrong, good and bad, when they embody the oppositions of duality are also only contextually true. When religion is institutionalized to propagate the contextual and temporal beliefs, it becomes outmoded over time. Even within a period, contextual and temporal beliefs are not necessarily good for everyone, and forcing followers to obey those beliefs not only creates discord in their lives, but also hampers their long-term search for the eternal truth. Institutions are unproblematic when used to propagate the eternal truth, but they become problematic when used to emphasize the temporal. Most religions today practice the canons that were sociologically, culturally, and morally right in the past, but may have questionable value in the present moment.

Many Vedic practices from olden times are no exception to this rule. For instance, the practice of polygamy arose because many men renounced sex, thereby creating an excess of unmarried women and a far fewer eligible men. This problem could only have been solved by polygamy, or by forcing women to renounce material enjoyments, and the path most likely to succeed was chosen. Polygamy has, however, little to do with eternal truth. In fact, in modern times when men are not prepared to renounce sex, this problem is non-existent, and hence polygamy should never be practiced because it was a solution to a practical problem which doesn't exist today.

The *varna-aśrama* system, which is sometimes called the caste system, is another such example. The first thing to note about this system is that it has two parts—*varna* or social orders, and *aśrama* or stages of life. Life, in this system, is divided into four stages, of which only one quarter is spent on earning money, creating a family and material possessions, etc. The other three quarters are spent in education, renunciation, and the search for truth. Similarly, *varna* or the caste system was not supposed to be determined by birth, but rather by the qualities, capabilities, and activities of the person. Over time, people have forgotten about *aśrama* and spend their entire life enjoying family life, rather than only one-fourth of it as specified in the system. They have also forgotten that the *varna* denotes the qualification of a person and is a meritorious system rather than a caste system. There is certainly a need to abolish this degraded system and revive the truly meritorious and eclectic social system.

When religions become institutionalized, and they are designed to emphasize the temporal over the eternal, they become irrelevant over time. When the followers of religion are unable to distinguish between the eternal and temporal aspects of religion, changes in the circumstances and situations of the world appears to create a conflict with their temporal beliefs. People undergoing such conflicts seem to have a sense of being socio-culturally different from the others, based on a confused notion about the religion as the temporal practices that were instituted in times that are now long gone. The real question in such situation is (or should be): If we are not material, then how much of the material socio-cultural differences actually matter to the eventual pursuit of the eternal truth? On the other hand, if you truly believe that all the socio-cultural differences define your sense of what it means to be religious, how can this religion be the pursuit of that eternal truth that transcends matter?

Unfortunately, the institutionalized versions of religions forbid rather than foster critical thinking. From a Vedic viewpoint, they are not actually after the truth that transcends matter, but only after the power, wealth, fame, and material goods, that could be obtained through other more directly materialistic means but have been disguised as religion. When you identify yourself with the material circumstances, and think that you are this specific body and mind, you have fallen victim to the very illusion that binds us to the material world. By identifying with one side of the duality in matter, you have failed to develop a perfect understanding of non-dual reality. And, then, if you happen to confuse this duality-filled worldview with religious canons that were handed down from previous generations and are therefore the unquestioned truth, you have certainly set the stage for conflicts with others who similarly identify with the opposite side of the duality. Under the influence of duality, the person supposes that only one side of this duality must be true. The world is hot or cold, bitter or sweet, red or blue, democratic or republican in reality while the other position must simply be false and illusory. These beliefs were most likely dominant at one time and have been carried on for generations. They were not absolutely true even then, and they could be even less true now, because the truth is non-dual. Truth is that which reconciles the oppositions and transcends them. Truth is from which duality springs forth in time.

The only solution to these problems is institutional reform, which can only begin through an understanding of the distinction between dual and non-dual. Both dual and non-dual have forms, and the only difference between them is that certain forms are created and destroyed in time while others remain unchanged. There is a need to distinguish the forms that are produced as an effect of the laws of nature (i.e. the evolution of time) from the forms that exist unchanged even outside the laws of nature (and time). Unless this distinction can be made, it would be impossible to distinguish between the temporal and transcendental aspects of religion, and thereby of which claims are fundamental or simply pragmatic.

Misconceptions about Altruism

Religions the world over are associated with two things: (1) belief in the existence of God, soul and afterlife, and (2) leading a life of good moral character to obtain a good afterlife through God's benedictions. Atheists wish to separate the above two aspects of religion. Their argument is that it is not necessary to be religious (i.e. have faith in God and the soul) to possess a good character. It is further not guaranteed that a religious person will also have a good character. The atheists argue that they would like people to develop a good character without actually developing faith in God and the soul. For instance, the atheists may argue that it is possible to be altruistic to your community, nation, or race, without a belief in God or soul.

Altruism is a big issue in Abrahamic religions, especially Christianity, and Christian missionaries have used charitable work as a vehicle to spread the teachings of Christ. Altruism has, however, never been an issue in Vedic philosophy because of *karma*—you suffer and enjoy the results of your past activities, and no one (except your own choices) can change the extent of enjoyment or suffering. By being altruistic, you are aggregating good *karma* for yourself, but you are not actually doing anything for others that they would not have received anyway otherwise. Being altruistic therefore only makes your own life better, not the lives of others, contrary to what the altruists often believe. Charitable work is therefore not factual selflessness; instead, it is a more profound form of selfishness under which you do good to others only to get the good back in return. For instance, you may do good to others only to be rewarded a place in heaven, with a much better form of afterlife.

The atheist acknowledges the selfishness embedded in altruism; the goal of altruism is to aid the collective survival and betterment, because the individual benefits from that collectivism. Of course, in some cases, the individual may even sacrifice his own life to make the lives of others better. However, the atheist would argue that this sacrifice is an evolutionary phenomena developed over time by which the species that were not altruistic would be eliminated as a whole. The atheist may argue that selfishness is not merely individual; it can also be collective, and if this collective selfishness helps with the survival of the species then evolution guarantees its appearance as altruism in nature. However, this notion of altruism does not depend on the existence of the soul, morality, and God; it only depends on random mutations for altruism which are then genetically transmitted to offspring, and because they aid the collective survival of the species, they are naturally reinforced.

I surveyed the problems in evolution in the first chapter and have discussed them more fully in *Signs of Life*. The key conclusion from that discussion is that randomness in nature (which is supposed to cause random mutations) is itself a problem and appears as the incompleteness of scientific theories; if there is randomness in nature, then we cannot predict the succession of object states, and hence we also cannot predict evolution. Natural selection does not solve the selection problem because it is merely a fit between pegs and holes, and there are infinitely many ways in which nature can be divided into pegs and holes; which peg and hole is real cannot be predicted. Furthermore, selection requires the ability to determine if a program is well-behaved, but a mechanical procedure that makes that determination cannot exist due to Turing's halting problem. It is possible to construct uber programs that make that assessment, but such programs would forbid random mutations. The evolutionary account for altruism is therefore flawed because evolution itself is flawed; it posits ideas which are intuitive in an everyday sense but they are impossible within a physical theory.

This, however, does not entail the denial of evolution itself. Rather, we have to construe evolution in a new way as the evolution of meanings. Meanings appear in a hierarchy, which leads us to a hierarchical and semantic view of space-time, in which the abstract appears before the contingent, and the contingent is produced from the abstract. The contingent objects are therefore not related to other contingent objects as in current models of causality. Rather, the contingent is related to the abstract. This dramatically shifts the causal model in nature, in ways that needs a detailed discussion.

In current science, objects exert forces on other objects due to their physical properties, and two objects can interact only when they have the same type of properties. In the semantic causal model, all changes are caused by the addition or removal of information, and two interacting objects *must* have different types. For instance, an object can have a yellow color if information about yellowness is added to the concept of color. The interaction here is between yellowness and color, and the latter is necessarily more abstract than the former. We can never speak about the interaction between yellow and red, unless color is already present. And when color is present, the interaction has to be modeled as the interaction between yellow and color rather than as the interaction between yellow and red. The interaction is therefore between abstract and the contingent, not between contingent and contingent. This changes the causal model: the source and destination of a cause have the same type in physical theories, but they must have different types in a semantic theory; specifically, the destination must be more abstract than the source. Every type of entity must interact with the next semantically higher and more abstract type of entity. When yellow is added to red, redness is not modified; rather, color is modified.

This simple illustration of the causal model in a semantic view overturns some widely held ideas about altruism, where one man (or woman) serves other men (or women). All these men and women are supposedly at the same conceptual level, and their interactions of give and take are performed according to a physical theory of transferring matter or energy, which in turn changes the matter or energy in their bodies (which may eventually impact the mind). In the semantic view, every object has to interact with a next higher object, which must interact with the next higher object, etc., until the interaction terminates at the root of the semantic tree. If A supposedly serves B, the causal interaction between them is mediated by a more abstract entity C. In a sense, the cause does not directly flow from A to B. Rather, A changes C, which in turn changes B. Quite simply, the cause from A to B is mediated by C; the cause A rises up the semantic tree to reach C and then comes down to B.

The fact about semantic interactions has important implications for the question: Can we construct altruism without God? The short answer to this question is no, although the issue is not just in altruism but in any form of causality. Any causal interaction always occurs with the next higher abstract entity. For this entity to change, another higher entity must be changed first, and so forth. The cause therefore must rise up the semantic tree and then come down. No causal interaction can occur without the root's involvement and therefore all forms of causality are actually impacting the nodes up the hierarchy and eventually the tree's root. In short, every living being who claims to causally affect another living being, has to actually first affect God (the root of the tree), not just in the case of altruism but even in other situations. In Vedic philosophy, thus, the living beings are always "serving" God whether favorably or unfavorably.

The person who understands this causal model of nature also understands that our actions are always towards God, and not towards other living beings. The nodes in between the root and the leaf are also living beings whose form is conceptually more abstract; they are sometimes called *demigods*. These demigods are also served in the process of serving God, and therefore the Vedas recommend the service of God rather than that of demigods. Altruism is therefore never supposed to be directed towards other living beings, including demigods, because all such notions about altruism are causally incomplete. There must be a root of the tree because the causal action can be completed; if this root does not exist, then the branches and trees cannot be changed. Devotion to God is therefore said to be "watering the root" rather than watering the individual branches, twigs, fruits or leaves; by watering the root, everything else is automatically watered. This is not just a principle of religion, but also that of any causal interaction. The difference between the two is simply that the truly enlightened person understands the causality of nature, and therefore aims his or her service towards the tree's root, while those ignorant about the causality believe they are serving other people, even other demigods.

We might even rephrase this idea of altruism as follows: service to man is not necessarily service to God, although service to God is service to man[56]. The physical notion of altruism cannot be constructed because the physical notion of causality is itself false. The problem is therefore not unique to altruism; after all, even the sun transmitting light to the earth could be thought of as altruistic action, as can any quantum object transmission from a source to destination. If such quantum object transmissions are not altruistic, then the transfer of macroscopic objects also cannot be altruism. The problem of altruism is therefore far deeper—the problem is that the physical causal model of nature is incomplete and needs semantics; however, even the semantic causal model is incomplete unless it involves the root of the semantic tree. True altruism therefore cannot be constructed without God because the complete theory of natural causality itself cannot be defined without God.

Rituals and Worship

The above causal model gives us a simple understanding of the nature of ritual and worship in Vedic philosophy. This understanding can be illustrated through the example of the common practice of offering a river's water into the river, which was prevalent in ancient Indian society, and is still seen in certain places where people gather to worship rivers such as the Ganges, the Yamuna, or others. The devotee takes a dip into the river, cups his hands to collect some of the river's water, lifts the hand out of water and then pours the water back into the river by tilting his hands. The idea here is quite simple: the river is an abstract concept and the water in that river is a contingent instantiation of that abstract concept. By offering the river's water into the river, we are offering an instance of the abstract concept into the abstract. This process can be compared to perception where an instance of color—e.g., yellow—is offered into the eye, which represents the idea of color. Color is an abstract concept, and yellow is an instantiation of that abstract concept. When we perceive color, the instance of color is added to the eye (which represents color), thereby "offering" the instance to the abstract.

The point of this offering is quite simple—everything we can offer is already created by God. So what can we actually offer that is not already created by Him? We offer God's creation to God. God is the abstract entity and all His creations are contingent entities. Like the eye perceives yellowness, in the same way by offering God's creation to God, we are giving back to God what originated in Him. By this offering, we are "satisfying" His senses quite like by offering yellowness into color (the eye) we satisfy the sense of seeing.

When the offering is being made, the target of offering must also be remembered. After all, without knowing the target of offering, how do we know where the offering is supposed to be intended? This target is called out during the offering by the chanting of *mantras*, in which the name of the conceptual entity to which the offering is being made is called out. This chanting of *mantras* is not mumbo-jumbo as is often made out; rather, the sound of the *mantra* calls out the name of the entity being called out. These *mantras* don't have to be explicitly uttered; they can also be vibrated mentally or the target of the offering mentally intended in our thoughts. Vedic ritualistic practices describe the offering of many kinds of conceptual entities—sugar, salt, potatoes, rice, pulses, and many other similar objects. These are often targeted towards specific demigods who represent concepts embodied in these objects (the objects are instances of those concepts). Explicit care must be taken in such offerings to not offer an object to the incompatible concept, and the careful execution of such rituals is practically non-existent in present times. For instance, it is possible that when the ritual is not executed correctly, a wrong instance may be offered to a concept, either creating adverse effects or not having any effect at all.

The worship of God—the Supreme Being—holds special significance in this regard. He is the original concept behind every instance that we can experience. Anything and everything can therefore be offered to Him, and no conceptual discrepancies are expected to arise because He is the creator of every conceptual entity. In contrast, only specific kinds of objects can be offered to specific demigods, and mistakes in this offering can make the ritual harmful or useless. When the mind of the worshipper is not fixed upon the intended concept (the mind, for instance, may be thinking about other things than the object of worship), the objects being offered are not pure representations of the concept (the objects may be contaminated by impurities), or the *mantras* are not chanted accurately (the syllables may be uttered incorrectly), various discrepancies in the rituals arise, and they are not therefore recommended in modern times since the executors of such rituals, the ingredients of the ritual, and the chanting of *mantras* have all have become imperfect.

Only the worship of God—who is the source of everything—is still recommended because He is the origin of everything and anything offered to Him is like a leaf connected to the root although every leaf cannot be correctly connected to every other branch. Of course, it is not necessary to only offer material objects; even *mantras* themselves are also objects, and their chanting also represents worship. Finally, the ultimate offering by any living being is his own existence; the living being is also a portion of God and by offering his self to God, the living being can perform the ultimate ritual.

The Criterion for Spiritual Progress

One of the key differences between *dharma* and religion is that the former views liberation from matter as often a long journey requiring freedom from material desires, while the latter views liberation simply as being baptized into a particular faith. In Christianity, for instance, anyone who has "accepted" Christ as the savior would be "saved" from hell; everyone else would enter hell after death. In *dharma*, the process of accepting God as the master involves freedom from material desires of name, fame, wealth, success, love, and various forms of sense gratification; it doesn't matter which church, temple, mosque or synagogue you go to, which particular scripture you accept, or which religion you are or are not baptized into. The *test* of whatever you are doing in the name of religion is detachment. If you are progressively getting detached from the hankering of material objects, then you are also progressing in *dharma*.

I discussed the three aspects of reality in earlier chapters (and showed how these together form the three parts of a logical system): *sat* or meaning, *chit* or choice, and *ananda* or pleasure. These three aspects of reality become three distinct categories which cover the living being in the material world. First, *ananda* or pleasure manifests in matter as *desire* for pleasure; these desires condition the living being to seek various kinds of pleasures, and they are sometimes also called *guna*, *prakṛti*, or *māya*. Second, *chit* or experience becomes the various capabilities by which we can experience different kinds of knowledge and activity; after all, to know or do something, we must have a particular type of sensual, mental, intellectual, intentional, and moral capacity; these capabilities are produced as the outcome of previous actions, also called *karma*. Third, *sat* becomes the material mind and body of the living being.

Everything in the material world is a combination of these three categories; for instance, the senses of the observer comprise some desires, some capabilities, and some existence. The material body too is the repository of desires, capabilities, and existence. The existence does not bind the living being to the material laws, although the desires do. Depending on the desires[57] the same experience is enjoyed or suffered (the desires are therefore also called *guna* or the living being's tendencies). It is also due to desires which filter parts of the world into our perception that consequences or *karma* are created, which represent what we *deserve*. This deserving appears as the capabilities of senses by which they can acquire different forms of knowledge, and engage in various sensual activities. Finally, everything is also some conceptual entity that exists objectively, and which we might call existence or *meaning*; this meaning is not eternal and it may not necessarily be true; however, it exists.

The material covering of the living being defined as *sat*, *chit*, and *ananda* is therefore *meaning*, *deserving*, and *desiring*. The bodies and minds of the living entities have all three, but the non-living things are only meanings (including abstract meanings, which we might call their 'mind'), although they don't have deserving and desiring. My shirt, for instance, has the property of blueness, color, conceptual type (shirt), relationship to me (it is my shirt), etc. but it has no desiring or deserving. Therefore, we do not apply moral judgments to the shirt, even though we apply them to people. The difference between the living and non-living things is that the non-living things are only manifestations of *sat* or existence while the living things also have *chit* or deserving and *ananda* or desiring. This entails that we can apply the conceptual hierarchy of concepts even to non-living things—and therefore machines can also think—although the machines cannot desire, nor would they be responsible for their actions, or entitled to receive rewards or punishments.

The purpose of *dharma* is to free the living being of two of its coverings—deserving and desiring—while keeping the meaning covering. The freedom from desiring and deserving is called "purification" of the body, senses, mind, intellect, ego, and morality, and if these have been purified then the living being can see the world just at is—i.e. just as it exists—without being filtered by perception. That true knowledge and perception of reality also ceases the production of *karma* and thereby frees one from the laws of material nature. Now the living being has the perfect theory of reality and uninhibited free will over the choice of phenomena it experiences. Choices do not cease when desires are finished; there is hence a difference between desiring and choosing. The difference is that a material desire filters the nature of reality to see only parts of a phenomenon, while a free will chooses to completely perceive some of the possible phenomena. Under material desires, a living being will choose limited parts of whatever is presented to him, but he has no choice for what is presented to him. Under free will, a living being will always see the complete nature of what is presented to him, but he can choose what is presented to him. Therefore, freedom from material desires does not entail the end of free will. Rather, it marks the beginning of the perception of variety within the singular.

Liberation is a consequence of the purification from material desires, and it follows a very scientific and natural process. Liberation is not an outcome of baptizing or institutional membership. A person can be baptized into a religion and never reduce his material desires; such a religious affiliation is a waste of time. On the other hand, a person may not be affiliated to any religious system, but many gradually progress in the reduction of material desires, and such a person is on the path to liberation from the laws of nature. The practice of religion and affiliation to an institution or system is useful only to the extent that it accelerates one's freedom from material desires. It is noteworthy that the recommendation is not to cease the upkeep of the body and mind, the regular performance of duties, etc. The recommendation is to stop doing them for enjoyment. Recall that the living being's body and mind comprise meaning, deserving, and desiring; the meanings don't cease, but the desiring and deserving are gradually reduced, and eventually terminated.

Living and Non-Living

What is life and who is living? Many religions (e.g., Christianity) do not believe that animals, plants, aquatics, or birds have a soul; only humans are supposed to have a soul; therefore, only humans have a religion but the other species of life do not. This coupling between religion and life is false in Vedic *dharma*. Life is defined as the presence of the soul in the material world, and it is signified by the existence of desiring and deserving (*guna* and *karma*), which exist in many forms of life. Even when material desires and entitlements are finished, the living being still has a free will by which it can choose the phenomenal experiences. Therefore, ultimately, the living being is characterized by the presence of a soul; the materially bound living beings have *guna* and *karma* but the liberated soul doesn't.

The difference between humans and other species of life is that higher forms of perception—such as the mind, intellect, ego and morality—are far more developed in humans, which leads to the ability to ask existential questions such as: Who am I? Why am I here? What is the origin of life? Why is there death and suffering? What happens after death? What is the origin of the universe? The animals too have a mind, intellect, ego, and morality, but they are underdeveloped. This means that the other species of life do not desire mental, intellectual, intentional, and moral satisfaction as much as humans do; their consciousness is generally limited to the enjoyment of the body and the senses, although different species may have different levels of mind, intellect, ego, and morality development. Of course, even many humans don't always have a profound sense of the reality of mind, intellect, ego, and morality, and they might believe that these are an epiphenomenon of the material body. This has become particularly prominent in recent times with the development of science; people have become so engrossed in the study and enjoyment of material objects that humans are believed to be yet another kind of animal species. While we can see that humans have several advanced capabilities—such as art, music, literature, science, social institutions, and the rule of law—they are generally believed to be outcomes of material complexities.

Part of the problem for the current predicament regarding life is that the religious alternatives in the Western world have divided the living being into only two parts—body and soul. The body is supposed to be material while the soul is transcendental. Since by definition we cannot measure the soul using material techniques, its existence is suspect. The problem is worsened by the fact that even religions do not recognize deeper forms of perceptions—such as that by the mind, intellect, ego, and the moral sense. Once we divide the living being into body and soul, neglecting the various kinds of subtle sensations and perceptions, and the soul cannot be measured by taste, touch, smell, sound, and sight, the natural conclusion is that that there isn't anything beyond the material body; we might then even discard the idea of the soul and just understand the body.

The Abrahamic religious view is as culpable in this problem as scientific materialism. In the Vedic view, there are two broad realms of subtle material reality between the gross material body and the transcendental soul; they are the senses of observation (senses, mind, intellect, ego, and morality) and our abilities of experience (thinking, feeling, willing, knowing, acting, and being) which create the qualitative experience of the concepts perceived by the senses. As we discussed previously, the Vedas describe four "spaces," each successively more abstract than the previous, which contain objects, concepts, experiences, and the observer. The first three are material while the fourth is transcendental. An understanding of the soul can emerge only after one has been able to understand the subtle material realms, because it is necessary to distinguish between the soul and the various kinds of perceptual and experiential methods.

Both Abrahamic religions and Western philosophy do not adequately distinguish between the various forms of perceptions and experiences that lie between the material object and the soul; the tendency, historically, was to attribute everything that is not extended in space to a transcendental "mind" or "soul". As many aspects of this perception and experience have been reduced to their effects on material objects, the idea of the soul has become increasingly contentious. In Vedic philosophy, sensations, concepts, order, intentions, morality, and various qualia such as thinking, feeling, willing, knowing, acting; and being are not properties of the soul; they are subtle material realms that have to be described in a new way. Specifically, the soul is not producing sensations and concepts, although it is a passive observer and "accepts" their existence. The soul is the passenger in the material vehicle, not its driver. The vehicle is deterministically driven by material laws as the soul is carried in the vehicle. However, the soul can get out of the vehicle and occupy another vehicle by understanding the working of the vehicle.

Humans, birds, aquatics, plants and other animals are different vehicles; they are the combination of body, senses, mind, intellect, ego, morality and the abilities to experience qualities, although many of these subtle material properties may be underdeveloped. The soul is different from all these properties (because it is more abstract than all of them), but it occupies the vehicles (becomes the abstraction underlying the contingent) under the ignorance of natural laws. As the soul understands the nature of material reality, it also understands his difference from matter; he sees that he is not the senses, mind, intellect, ego or morality; even when the experiences and perceptions change, he actually remains unchanged. With a profound understanding of various levels of material reality, the soul becomes free of the determinism of natural laws. Until then, the laws of nature compel the soul to occupy various material vehicles, and this evolution of the soul is sometimes called *transmigration*.

In Vedic *dharma*, we (who presently occupy a human body) have previously occupied other kinds of material bodies. Unless we develop a better understanding of nature, we will again end up in other material species. The other species are different kinds of minds (abstract concepts) and the bodies (contingent concepts) are developed from the abstractions. Thus, it is imperative to change the mind in order to change the body. The birds, aquatics, trees, and other animals are different kinds of minds, before they are different kinds of bodies. This "mind" comprises meaning, deserving, and desiring, and while the meaning is left behind at death, the deserving and desiring (*guna* and *karma*) is carried to the next body. Since the meaning is left behind, often the body appears to work or can be made to work using material apparatus. The body in this case operates quite like an ordinary machine: chemical reactions can continue, the eyes can flutter, the hands and legs can twitch, breathing can take place, and the blood can circulate. However, the soul has already left; there is neither enjoyment, nor desires, nor morality.

The difference between living and non-living is that desiring and deserving exist in living beings but not in non-living things. Meanings are necessary for desiring and deserving, but meanings also exist in non-living things. In that sense, the living being needs a body and mind of meanings to enjoy and suffer, but these meanings are left behind when the living being dies and they are recreated in the new body. For instance, you might have been a great athlete in the past life and you may carry forward your desires and abilities for athletics, but you would not be sprinting right from birth. The mechanical working of the material body represents the meanings, not the desiring, deserving, enjoying, or suffering of the living being. Therefore, the body can continue to work after death, although no desires will be fulfilled and no entitlements would be created.

Materialists examine the dead body and claim that life is destroyed at death because they define life as the body. Even the body is described as physical things, and meanings, desiring, deserving, etc. are illusions created by physical interactions. This is a flawed understanding of matter; death does not mean the end of desires, and it does not mean that the consequences of actions in present life are no more applicable. Rather, your desires and entitlements are carried forward to a new bodily and mental form where meanings are again acquired based on the desiring and deserving of the previous life form(s). This understanding of the nature of life, and how *guna* and *karma* transfer the soul into different bodies can emerge within a semantic theory of matter, as I have previously described. The transmigration of the soul would not be a matter of faith; rather, it would be based on a different understanding of matter.

This understanding will refine our view of the difference between living and non-living. There are many living beings apart from the human life. However, not everything is alive because not everything has desiring and deserving, although everything has meanings. The semantic theory of matter is needed to develop an adequate understanding of non-living things before an understanding of living things can emerge in science. This understanding will help us grasp the nature of the soul and how it remains unchanged through different bodies. That would in turn lead to an understanding of the nature of free will and how the living being is bound by the laws through its own desires, and can be freed by understanding the laws. As this knowledge progresses, it is possible to form a clear conception of the nature of God, and life beyond dualistic logic.

Pantheism and Pandeism

Many *New Age* religions which focus on self-spirituality and self-rationality rather than obedience to a transcendental God or adherence to any specific scripture have come to fore since the 1970s. Many of these ideologies arose in response to the dissatisfaction with traditional faith-based religions, and their inability to deal with problems of human existence rationally. The New Age movement is very complex (as it borrows from many antecedents) and it is therefore difficult to give it a firm characterization; I will not attempt to define what it is or what it is not. However, given the growing popularity of the New Age movement, any book that discusses religion and atheism would be incomplete without some attention to its tenets. I will restrict myself to two dominant ideologies—pantheism and pandeism—which play a significant role in New Age thought.

Pantheism holds that the divinity is identical with the universe and that God is immanent (rather than transcendent) to the universe. Pandeism combines pantheism with deism and postulates that there is a God who became the universe and ceased to exist as a separate entity apart from the universe. Both pantheism and pandeism attack the issue of God's interaction with the universe, which has been problematic in conventional accounts of faith-based religion. How does God intervene in the universe? Does His intervention represent the violation of natural laws? How can we understand this violation within a rational theory of nature where everything works according to deterministic laws? Can we even define God without violating conditions of rationality and logic? Pantheism solves this problem by asserting that God is immanent in the universe and there is no God apart from the universe. Pandeism, on the other hand, claims that God was originally transcendent but transformed into the universe. In both cases, once the universe exists, there is no separate God and since God is not separate from the universe, the problem of their interaction does not arise. In fact, it is now possible to understand God simply by studying the universe.

This view, however, does not truly address the problem of how matter interacts with consciousness—if in fact there are two distinct types of entities. Of course, there are non-dual pantheists who deny the separation of matter and consciousness, and for them nature is just matter or energy, and everything is a mutation of that single reality. For the dualists, however, the problem of matter and consciousness interaction is as problematic as the interaction between matter and God. The dualists are therefore compelled to suppose that the material world must eventually be an illusion; at least the separate individualities of observers must be an illusion. The roots of pantheism and pandeism lie in the *Advaita* interpretation of *Vedanta* and in its predecessor—the voidistic view of Buddhism. In these interpretations, the personality and individuality of the observer—i.e. the soul—is an illusion created by a material covering of the undivided and undifferentiated eternal spiritual existence.

Once you acknowledge the undivided and undifferentiated existence as the ultimate reality, you are faced with the problem of how this reality becomes differentiated and divided. How does the variety in the universe—living and non-living things—emerge? When the universe is created from a singular being, an enormous amount of information must be added to that singularity to create diversity. Similarly, when the universe is dissolved, all the diversifying information must also disappear. From where is the information created and how does this information disappear? The impersonal and voidistic views have existed for nearly two millennia[58] and these questions have never been properly understood or answered.

If, on the other hand, you are a non-dualistic pantheist or pandeist, you still have a problem of understanding how the universe came into existence and how the "nothingness" that existed before transformed into the universe. (After all, if the universe is everything that exists, then before the universe must be nothingness.)

These problems, however, are not unique to impersonalism and voidism; they exist even in modern science, when science tries to explain the origin of space and time and their various modifications[59]. If matter is identical to space and time, then the origin of the universe must require an origin of space and time. What existed prior to space and time that caused its production? Without such an explanation the account of the universe is incomplete. Some New Age approaches therefore suppose that nature is a possibility (e.g., a quantum probability wavefunction) that consciousness collapses into definite states through choices. However, this idea of a cosmic consciousness that has choice is incompatible with oneness; choices imply individuality, and if consciousness can choose, then it must also be an individual. Choices without individuality cannot exist. The idea of cosmic conscious choices thus leads to inconsistency. If, on the other hand, we do not acknowledge a choosing consciousness, then the understanding of the universe would remain incomplete. The impersonalist and voidist views therefore lead to the unavoidable dilemma between inconsistency and incompleteness that we have seen many times earlier. Current science is already inconsistent or incomplete; if the theistic solution suffers from the same problem, then it does not add anything to the materialist view.

We are now compelled to reconsider the personalist schools of theism. In Vedic philosophy, the personalist school is far older than impersonalism, and posits that the source of the universe is a deity with three properties—meanings, choices, and pleasures—from which the variety of the universe is created simply by their combination: the meanings are combined to created variety and this combination is caused by the desire for experience and pleasure. Thus, the One becomes many not because of an external force, but due to His innate need to know and express His Self for pleasure.

However, when the One has become many, He does not cease to be the original One; He does not become identical with the universe nor does He become immanent in the universe. Rather, as the branches, twigs, and leaves emanate from the single root, similarly, the One remains transcendent to the many, although He is also connected to the many as His properties. The many are contingent while the One is abstract. The One therefore becomes the *unity* underlying the diversity of the many, just like the idea of a car is the unity underlying the many parts of a car. God is the original idea of knowledge, beauty, objectivity, wealth, power, and eminence, and from Him are created many individual things that instantiate those ideas. The universe therefore has an inverted tree-like structure with its roots at the top and leaves at the bottom; the leaves are detailed ideas while the twigs and trunks are relatively abstract ideas. The root of the tree is the most abstract and the original ideas.

Pantheism and pandeism were proposed to solve the problem of God's interaction with the world; the idea was that if God intervened in the world, it would violate the natural laws. However, the problems of God's interaction with the world do not arise in the inverted sematic tree because the contingent always interacts with the abstract, even in the material world, and thus the interaction between the contingent and abstract does not pose problems when it is supposed to occur between matter, consciousness, and God.

The semantic hierarchical view of nature is a useful scientific hypothesis because it solves problems of incompleteness and inconsistency in mathematics, computing, physics, biology, and many other areas of modern science. This view also presents a natural understanding of morality as the interaction between reality and theories about it. It provides a new causal model of change in which change is the evolution of ideas rather than the motion of things, which has wide applications in the study of history, the progress of science, the shifts in society, culture, and the evolution of the universe as a whole. The semantic view reinstates a central role for free will in nature. Finally, it reinstates the boldest visions of deism in religion without creating conflicts with the objectivity in nature.

Many centuries of ideological conflicts can be resolved through this approach, so I consider the current conflict between religion and atheism as stemming out of an incorrect understanding of matter, God, and their relation. This understanding is flawed because it is either inconsistent or incomplete. An ideological revolution in thinking can occur if we were to make some simple revisions to our understanding of nature—material objects are ideas, the senses of observation are more abstract ideas, the experiences and the observer underlying those experiences are even more abstract, and God who underlies everything in the creation is the most abstract.

Epilogue

The Oxford dictionary defines religion as "the belief in and worship of a superhuman controlling power, especially a personal God or gods." Conversely, atheism is defined as "disbelief or lack of belief in the existence of God or gods." The operative words here are *belief* and *disbelief*. There is something fundamentally wrong with this dictionary meaning of religion and atheism, because it makes both religion and atheism personal preferences rather than concerns of truth. After all, a belief or disbelief is what we have and it may or may not be true. Why should religion or atheism be about beliefs rather than about the truth? When we define religion (or atheism) as a belief rather than knowledge or truth, we have started on a wrong foot, and everything from that erroneous beginning point just leads to one problem after another. It makes no sense to claim that the existence of God is a matter of personal belief or disbelief; it should be a matter of knowledge and truth. Beliefs can be true or false, and we are interested in the truth rather than the belief.

Once we shift the issue from belief to knowledge, we must also define what we mean by *God*. What do we mean by a superhuman controlling power and how does it differ from the human controlling power? The problem now is that we don't have a good characterization of the human controlling power! Then how can we define what we mean by superhuman? In modern science, humans have no controlling power; the control lies in the natural laws. Therefore, to speak about something superhuman would entail something that lies beyond natural laws, which clearly seems very problematic.

In Vedic philosophy, God is defined as *reality*. This reality comprises three parts—*sat* (meaning), *chit* (choice), and *ananda* (pleasure). Each of these three parts has further six parts which constitute six fundamental meanings, six types of choices (or experiences) and six kinds of pleasures. This reality constitutes the basic apparatus necessary for knowledge to exist, and it is therefore also sometimes simply called absolute knowledge. Of course, this apparatus is inadequate to create the universe without a *generative* system which can produce more things by combining the meanings, interpreting these meanings as experiences, and converting those experiences into various kinds of pleasures. The generative system requires *logic* in addition to meanings, experiences, and pleasures. By the application of logic, three kinds of knowledge—external, internal, and marginal—are produced. The external knowledge employs the logical principles of non-contradiction and mutual exclusion, the internal knowledge rejects both these principles, and the marginal knowledge rejects either one of them. The three forms of knowledge are therefore byproducts of different kinds of logics that are used to produce different kinds of meanings, experiences, and pleasures.

If you are a religious person, you can think of this reality as a Supreme Being who creates His own pleasure by experiencing His own existence through His own choices. If you are a scientific person, you can think of this reality as the Ultimate Theory from which all kinds of entities are produced. The religious question of whether the Supreme Being exists is therefore identical to the scientific question of whether the Ultimate Theory is true. Unlike scientific theories which are Platonic ideas, the Ultimate Theory is a generative system that produces additional conceptual entities. The Supreme Being can therefore be defined as the Ultimate Theory that exists prior to the existence of anything else, and generates everything. The truth of the theory can be confirmed from the nature of the generated products. In that sense, while the truth transcends the universe, it can be known from the study of the manifest creations.

I therefore propose to change the definition of religion as "the *knowledge* of God" and that of atheism as "the *ignorance* about God." This shift in definition is necessary to even understand the nature of religion and its opposite, atheism: they are not about beliefs, but about the confirmation or denial of truth. The term "knowledge of God," however, does not just indicate the existence of an entity—God—whose knowledge we have to acquire, because God itself is defined as knowledge. Rather, the term "knowledge of God" must indicate the conditions that make such knowledge possible. The absolute truth is called knowledge because it is *idea-like*: its existence is the existence of fundamental ideas, its choices constitute the experience of ideas, and its pleasure is derived from these experiences. The pleasure forms the goal of knowledge, the experiences represent the methods of knowledge, and the existence denotes what is being known. Therefore, by knowledge the Vedas don't just mean some things that are being known; rather knowledge denotes the combination of the things to be known, the methods of knowing, and the goals of knowing. It is therefore more appropriate to characterize the absolute reality as *epistemology* which creates knowledge by the use of methods in order to fulfill some goals.

God in Abrahamic religions is someone who stands apart from the universe, so much so that He cannot be understood from the study of His creations. God in Vedic philosophy creates the universe out of His own personality and His nature and existence can be understood from the nature and existence of the universe itself. The question therefore isn't whether God exists. The question is only whether the universe exists and we understand why it exists.

This clarification about the nature of religion and atheism is necessary to shift the focus of the debate from belief to truth. But realizing this truth itself requires the development of new kinds of logics, and new methods of knowledge within the dualistic logic. The development of new methods of knowledge requires the development of new kinds of perceptive abilities, which in turn require a detachment from the previous lower form of perception. The essence of that method of knowing truth is called character development. Science has thus far been disconnected from the character development of the scientist. To be a good scientist, you are expected to master the facts of your field, have good reasoning capabilities, have some creative potential, and need loads of luck. Developing good character with kindness, freedom from desire, truthfulness, and detachment are not expectations of great scientists. This may no longer be true for the future development of science. It may well be that only people with good character would be able to make progress in science, because only they can see what others cannot.

Endnotes

1   M. Hiriyanna, "Outlines of Indian Philosophy," Motilal Banarasidass.

2   Clarified butter is aromatic butter that has been used for ages in Indian cooking, and is widely used today in a raw form for its sheer taste.

3   Lest this claim sound too bold and inaccurate, let me clarify that what I mean by the mathematical and computational analysis here the specific sense in which this book will describe the relation between evolution and the logical incompleteness and inconsistency of mathematics, computing and physics. Previous attempts at mathematical analysis tried to treat biological information physically; this book treats it semantically.

A DEFINITION OF GOD

4   There is also a third response—called nominalism—which is not as popular as the other two—realism and idealism.

5   The property of energy is an outcome of the homogeneity of time, the property of angular momentum is the outcome of the isotropicity of space and the property of momentum is the outcome of the homogeneity of space. Something is considered a physical property if it is conserved. The conservation of momentum, energy, and angular momentum arise from the fundamental properties of homogeneity and isotropicity of space and time. These properties can be applied to all material objects, because the space and time cut across all material objects.

6   This problem is sometimes more formally stated as the circular dependence between ordinal and cardinal notions about numbers. The size of a set is called its cardinality. But to know that there are 5 members in a set, we must first label these objects as 1st, 2nd, 3rd, 4th, and 5th. To label the

numbers in this way, we must have the notion of all these numbers, but the definition is only given through a collection of objects. The cardinal and ordinal numbers therefore have a circular dependence: to define cardinality, we need ordinals and vice versa.

7   Even in classical physics, this notion was problematic. For instance, the mass of an object is defined only by measuring its acceleration in a gravitational field which must be set up by another object's mass. So, it is impossible to define a single object's mass in isolation. The problem concerns the definition of the *first* massive object—the standard against which we can define other object masses. The recursive definition of mass and gravity entails that we cannot define the first such object, and therefore any subsequent objects. Classical physics, however, moved on by supposing that masses are already objective properties of objects, and we are not concerned with defining the *origin* of these properties but only their *measurement*. However, when science shifts its focus from trying to measure properties to understanding their origin—in this case, the origin of mass—the problem would reappear. In the relativistic gravitational theory, for instance, where masses are defined by the curvature of space-time, the question amounts to the origin of space-time curvature itself.

8   In atomic theory, for instance, the positions of the quanta detected depend on the number of slits used in the slit experiment. If the number of slits in the experiment is changed, the positions of the quanta also change. Therefore, the properties detected in measurement cannot be said to exist prior to the measurement, and we cannot assert that the measurement reveals exactly how the world exists prior to its being measured.

9   Bishop George Berkeley—one of the earliest architects of philosophical empiricism—was also an idealist. He believed that we cannot know the nature of reality as it exists prior to being known, because we only have access to our perceptions. Objectifications of these properties, such as those used in science, therefore are derived from perceptual properties. However, this raises a question: If the world is perceptual properties, then what happens when no one is seeing the world? Does the world simply disappear when no one is observing it? Berkeley (the bishop that he was!) asserted that even when no one is watching, God must watch it anyway. The

world therefore exists because God always watches it.

10 Refer to http://en.wikipedia.org/wiki/Burali-Forti_paradox.

11 In classical physics, for instance, all particles are conceptually identical. Similarly, all locations in space are identical because they can be interconverted by the use of coordinate transforms.

12 Quantum states are defined by eigenfunctions, and each eigenfunction has two representations—position and momentum—which carry identical information (since one representation can be constructed from another). The eigenfunction completely defines the quantum's physical properties, and since this eigenfunction can be completely represented by the position representation, the *position state* completely specifies all the quantum's properties. It is worth noting here that the "position state" is different from the classical position because the position state is extended while the position is infinitesimal.

13 Of course, in practice, different ATMs may follow certain fixed rules of delivering currency notes, and if you happen to use the same ATM many times over, you can predict in advance the behavior of that ATM. In that sense, this example is not identical to the quantum problem.

14 Here, P denotes polynomial time and NP denotes non-polynomial time. The P = NP is an unsolved problem in computing theory and it concerns the question whether problems that can be *verified* in polynomial time can also be *solved* in polynomial time. For instance, your computer password can be verified in polynomial time (when you enter your password), but can your password also be *hacked* in the same amount of time? P = NP states the conjecture that if the password can be verified in polynomial time then it should also be possible to hack the password in the same time. However, this conjecture hasn't yet been proven or disproven.

15 I will shortly describe this difference as that between concepts and qualia. The concept yellow and the experience of yellow are different, although the concept yellow must exist before it can be experienced. Attempts to reduce experiences to things are flawed unless things have first

been reduced to concepts. The experience of qualia therefore follows the prior reinstatement of concepts in the material world.

16 These differences can be viewed as the difference between *thinking* yellow and *feeling* yellow. Thinking and feeling are more abstract relative to the content of that thinking or feeling. Subsequent sections discuss the difference, and how content depends on thinking and feeling.

17 This problem has led to efforts in recent times on the development of a *semantic web* which can be understood by machines which don't *per se* understand meanings. The idea is simply that if machines cannot process the semantics, then we might try to define more syntax to reduce meanings to syntax which the machines can process.

18 Damasio, Antonio (1994), Descartes' Error: Emotion, Reason, and the Human Brain, Putnam.

19 Searle, John (1980), 'Minds, Brains and Programs,' Behavioral and Brain Sciences, 3: 417–57.

20 In fact, we can often know whether a person is happy or sad simply by watching their expressions and it seems that even though happiness and sadness are feelings, they are objectively represented in matter. And yet, what exactly in matter qualifies as a feeling is hard to tell.

21 I have discussed this property of consciousness at length in the book *Six Causes*: consciousness is described as the ability and need to know and express itself. Each observer is therefore the creator and consumer of information; information creation reflects the observer's persona while information consumption absorbs the information prior created by the same or another observer.

22 I will later describe how theories can be experienced through their *representations*. Quite like classical physics is the cause of the classical objects, but we can know that theory by representing it, similarly, it is possible to know the soul and God through representation.

23 There is the Renaissance concept in Christianity that God gave us two books, The Bible and The Book of Nature, and that by studying the book of nature we can know God. It is this type of thinking that led to the justification of doing science because otherwise the Church would not have allowed it. It is against this backdrop that the Reformation current of Martin Luther, with his concept of Sola Scriptura – only scripture began, and then, in a competitive rush the Catholic Church began to be against science, for instance burning Galileo Galilei at the stake.

AN INTRODUCTION TO VEDIC PHILOSOPHY

24 This moral sense is also called *mahattattva* in Vedic philosophy.

25 Thomas Nagel in his article "What is it like to be a bat?" speaks about the feeling of *being* something—e.g. a bat. Knowing a bat is conceptual but being a bat is not. Being cannot be reduced to this knowing.

26 It is convenient at this point to speak of material entities as *objects*. I will later argue that they are properties and not objects. These properties refer to deeper properties. For instance, the property of yellowness refers to the property of color. The property of color refers to meanings (which have been elaborated in terms of sensations). In that sense, what we call objects are actually just properties. In Vedic philosophy, there is a hierarchical structure of properties, which originates in God. All these are ultimately properties of God, although for reasons of convenience we can sometimes also speak of them as objects.

27 Rothermich, M. E. Friedrich August Kekulé: A Scientist and Dreamer. Princeton, NJ: Woodrow Wilson Leadership Program in Chemistry.

28 A living being always has free will—either of theory or of phenomena. These are, however, not the only extreme choices; the living being can also exercise his free will of phenomena within a partially correct theory of nature. The free will of theory and phenomena are just two logical extremes, but they do not preclude each other. When your theory of nature is partially correct, you have partial free will. As the theory perfects, the free will of phenomena increases; likewise, as the theory becomes more incorrect, the free will of phenomena decreases.

29 It is worth remembering that context-dependence is not the same as relativism. The latter views meanings as being 'relative' to a perceiver and it arises from the assumption that the 'same' object can be placed in a different collection, resulting in a different interpretation. For instance, I can take a red object and then try to fix the meaning of this object by placing it in relation to other colors. In relation to white, redness denotes danger. In relation to blue, redness denotes passion. And in relation to green, redness denotes stop. This contextualization of meanings assumes that the 'same' object can be moved from one context to another. What if such movement isn't possible? What if in changing the object's context we also change its physical and semantic properties? If this were the case, the object's meaning would still be given in relation to its context, but the context's meaning would in turn be fixed by a higher context, and so forth, until the meanings are fixed in relation to the original root of the tree. Relativism assumes that the boundaries that separate contexts are arbitrary. That I can choose to include or exclude whichever objects I wish to demarcate a context. This entails that boundaries in nature are not real; that we draw these boundaries by cutting up the world in arbitrary ways. What if the boundaries in nature were real? What if the meaning of the objects in these boundaries is fixed by the hierarchy of boundaries? That would also entail that an object's meaning is not arbitrary as it is fixed by the next higher boundary. The semantic hierarchical tree therefore fixes the meanings of each object, and they are not relative. Since these meanings depend on contexts, contextualization is not relativism. Contextualization entails that objects have fixed meanings, but they are given in contexts.

30 This is a deeper point about the material universe that all physical properties are essentially properties of space and time. Being at a certain location in space and time completely defines an object's properties. However, for all physical properties to be reduced to the location in space and time, space and time themselves have to be defined hierarchically rather than linearly.

31 This assertion is used logically as the separation between concepts, although in practice we know that the weather can be warm; the ability to mix concepts leads to what is now called fuzzy logic. The limitations of classical logic in reasoning are known all too well now, and that has led to the

development of various alternative logics such as modal logic which deals in not just true or false but the possibilities, temporal logic which deals in reasoning about time, and epistemic logic which deals in the reasoning about beliefs or knowledge, different from reality.

32 Intuitionism is a philosophy of mathematics that drops the principle of non-contradiction (also called the excluded middle). Mathematicians have often proved theorems by supposing this principle—either a statement must be true or its negation must be true. For instance, if you are trying to prove the existence of X. You have two possible routes: (a) you can construct entities of type X, and (b) you can suppose that X doesn't exist, and show that this assumption leads to a contradiction. Intuitionists reject the use of the second method for proving. This view is therefore also called *constructivism* because it relies on explicit construction rather than a contradiction arising from denial of existence.

33 The term *kuṇṭha* means latent desires and *vaikuṇṭha* therefore means freedom from latent desires. This freedom can be acquired even in matter and the living being then becomes free of material preferences and is said to be liberated from material choices, even though matter still exists. When the living being becomes free of such desires he is said to be present in *vaikuṇṭha* even though he may be living within the material world; the opposites exist, but there is no preference for them.

34 There is however a different kind of existence in which hot and cold exist, but these are not mutually opposed. Both hot and cold are individuals but their existence is not logically contradictory.

35 In current physics, matter is described as particles and anti-particles; the anti-particles can be modeled as entities with negative energy moving in negative time. *Moral Materialism* describes in detail how time produces, destroys, and modifies opposites, and how this process can be understood in terms of quantum objects. Quantum theory cannot predict when a particle and anti-particle pair would be created, modified, or annihilated, because quantum theory is indeterministic about predictions. These predictions are possible when these particles are viewed as meanings, however, we would still need a *causal agency* that drives these changes. That

causal agency is time in Vedic philosophy. *Quantum Meaning* discusses how particle and anti-particle pairs can be understood as representing the opposite sides of a distinction.

36 The periodic behavior of atoms is currently modeled as their wave-like property, in contrast to their individuality which represents their particle-like property. The wave-particle duality in quantum theory is an unsolved problem, but it can be solved if the atom is seen as a symbol of meaning.

37 Dialectical Logic (the ideas were proposed originally by Hegel and then advanced by Marx and Engels) claims that not-X follows X as thesis and anti-thesis, and then they combine to form a new synthesis. In Semantic Logic, X and not-X are created and destroyed simultaneously. The evolution of the meanings is not caused by the nature of the meanings themselves; rather, it is controlled by the cyclic time.

EPISTEMOLOGICAL ISSUES

38 Each of these issues is related to the problem of meaning and *Moral Materialism* discusses these problems and illustrates how they can be solved by a semantic view of nature. It also shows, how the reconciliation of quantum theory, general relativity and thermodynamics—the biggest outstanding problem in physics today—depends on solving this problem. Finally, the book shows the new predictions that will emerge from such a reconciliation using a semantic theory of matter.

39 You might argue that the convergence thesis can be refuted based on observations. E.g., we might say that if the tracks actually converged, the train that runs on these tracks would fall off the tracks. Since the train doesn't fall off the tracks, we can conclude that the tracks don't converge. However, even the train appears to converge as it moves away! The point is not that the train or tracks actually converge. The point is only that obser-vations about these facts are misleading. They exist, but their existence is not an indication of any kind of truth.

40 One example of such a dramatic shift in science lies in the conflict between classical and quantum physics. In classical physics, the same

particle could exist in many locations (in different times) and therefore we could speak about a particle's motion. In quantum physics, a particle at a different location is a different particle, and particles do not move, although one particle disappears and another one appears. If we see the succession of particle states, under classical physics we would have concluded motion, but under quantum theory we conclude appearance and disappearance. Classical physics still seems to work for many macroscopic objects, but fails when physics is widened with more data.

41 Gödel's incompleteness, Turing's Halting Problem, and quantum theory are some prominent examples of such incompleteness vs. inconsistency dilemma. The incompleteness theorem states that all number systems are incomplete, but if they were to be complete, they would be inconsistent. Turing's proof shows that the assumption that the Halting Problem can be solved leads to a logical contradiction. Finally, Bell's Theorem shows that quantum theory is forever incomplete, but if we tried to address this incompleteness by adding some 'hidden variables' then the theory would also be inconsistent.

42 These 'truths' are obviously not absolute truth, but they are 'parts' of a larger truth. Their existence entails that they can be *proved*, and yet they will obviously contradict many other similar 'truths' in the universe, which can also be proved (simply because they are produced according to some natural law). They are what we might call 'relative' truths. They exist, but they are not eternal, and they are not absolute. The root of the semantic tree is both eternal and absolute.

43 It is more accurate to say that the mind, intellect, and consciousness of the elephant are present in the tail and in the leg, even though they transcend it. This leads to a more nuanced point that the elephant is not the body of parts, but actually the mind, intellect, and consciousness. This is related to a deeper issue in biology where species have to be defined by the nature of the mind, rather than the nature of their bodies. However, this will take us away from our present discussion, and so I will not get into it. Readers interested in this area, can refer to *Signs of Life*.

44 Linear time is actually a simplification. In practice, if the password is

encrypted, then the entire password has to be encrypted using some algorithm and checked against a copy of the encrypted password. This comparison is not always linear, but it would be some polynomial function (although the polynomial would not have any exponential factors). I have used linear time to simplify the expression, as some readers may get confused by the use of the technical term 'polynomial'.

45 I'm only speaking about the ease of verification in relative terms here. The comparison is to the time taken in the discovery of the theory rather than trivializing the effort or time goes in verification itself.

46 In Vedic philosophy, experience and reason are flatly rejected as methods of knowledge. This is not because the Vedas don't use experience or reason; it is only because they don't consider them viable to know the absolute truth. The person who goes out in search of truth depending on his own senses and mind can never find the absolute truth, without the grace of a teacher guiding him to succeed.

47 In material knowledge, it is not difficult to understand how an abstract entity can contain more contingent entities; for instance, the set 'color' can contain individual colors like red, blue, and yellow. However, self-knowledge and God-knowledge involve the self-inclusion of a set, and the inclusion of something more abstract than that set respectively. These two kinds of knowledge therefore are harder to understand in terms of material constructs. Nevertheless, this type of knowledge is commonly available even in the material world. For instance, even though yellow is one of the colors, the idea of color exists even in yellow, although we cannot *see* this idea by the eye; we must see it by the mind. Similarly, the understanding of the nature of the self and God exists in the self but it requires a deeper form of consciousness to uncover it.

48 Not all philosophers of science actually agree that science is the discovery of the order in experiences; many *realist* philosophers believe that science is the discovery of the order in nature as it exists independent of observation. This view of science, however, has come under suspicion in 20th century physics (especially in atomic theory) where the attempt to observe reality (and the methods employed in that observation) appear to

have an effect on the outcome of the observation.

PROBLEMS IN ATHEISM

49 *Moral Materialism* discusses these problems at great length, and shows how they appear in atomic theory, general relativity, and thermodynamics. I would refer the interested reader to that discussion.

50 In physical theories, measurable properties likes energy, momentum, angular momentum, mass, charge, etc., are considered real because they are also *conserved*. In contrast, objects that combine these properties into a unified entity are not conserved. The same total amount of energy, momentum, mass, charge, and angular momentum can be combined and divided in many ways, creating a different number of objects. The theories permit all such "matter distributions," which entails that while physical properties are conserved, the "objects" underlying them are not. Thus, we cannot speak about the reality of physical particles.

51 There are two broad approaches to the scientific method of theory formation—verification and falsification. The former states that if we have a theory that makes correct predictions then it is correct. The problem in verification is underdetermination: there can be several good explanations for the same phenomena which explain the phenomena equally well. If a theory explains a phenomenon, then its predictive successes don't rule out the possibility of a better theory that also explains this as well as other phenomena in future. Therefore, falsification suggests that theories cannot be verified; they can only be falsified. However, with falsification we do not know if a theory is indeed correct, because falsifying phenomena could be found in future. We also don't know if the theory is indeed false, because no falsifying phenomena may be found in future. As a method, therefore, both verification and falsification don't tell us whether and when the method terminates.

52 The term *guna* means a "rope" which binds the living being to a limited view of nature. The limited view is also called *māya* ("that which is not") because the theory of nature is defined not by its assertions but by its negations of reality. For instance, refusing to acknowledge the reality of sensations and concepts is a different kind of *guna* or *māya* than the refusal to acknowledge the reality of intentions or morality. When the living being

is freed from the *guna*, he is said to be freed from the consequences of his actions, and thereby of *karma*.

53 The term *guna* is also sometimes translated as "modes of nature" which are different proclivities in the living being to act in various ways.

RELIGION VS. DHARMA

54 Those familiar with Vedic philosophy know that the Vedas draw a subtle distinction between reality and its theory. The theory is said to be the first *representation* of reality. In the *goloka* realm, for instance, Krishna is reality and Balarama is the theory about this reality and Balarama is therefore called the first *representation* of Krishna. From this theory manifests the rest of the creation, as the theory creates more theories or idea-like entities. Balarama is also said to be the original *guru* or teacher of the knowledge of reality, and all teachers (who teach the nature of truth) are said to be representations of Balarama. As the original knower of the perfect truth, all subsequent expansions of Balarama also are knowledge of the perfect truth. Both material and spiritual creations are therefore said to be manifestations of Balarama who is the theory of reality. The creation is therefore not reality itself, but an explanation or expansion of reality. For instance, if we have to explain an esoteric idea, then we provide examples or instances of that idea by which we understand it. In the same way, Krishna is the reality and He is the esoteric truth. Balarama is the conceptual representation of this truth and He expands into examples or instances of this idea to create the universe. In the material creation, Balarama's expansion is called *Saṅkarṣaṇa* or Time which represents the theory of nature; the theory here is simply that nature evolves cyclically and everything is temporary. Creation, dissolution, and sustaining are parts of this cycle. The original esoteric truth is so profound that no matter how many examples and illustrations we provide of this truth, they still don't seem to completely exhaust it. The original truth is therefore also said to inexhaustible or *akshaya*, the term *kshaya* denoting exhaustion.

55 There is an important difference between *reality* and *existence* in Vedic philosophy. The world exists but it is not real, because it is not eternal. Reality is defined as that which is eternal, which is different from existence. The theory of nature (or the working of time) is eternal, but its working

produces temporary things. In that sense, the theory is real but its effect is existence (although not reality).

56 Even though all living beings are interacting with God through the hierarchical tree, and therefore be said to be "serving" Him, Vedas define two forms of God—as He engages in austerity or self-denial and as He engages in self-assertion or pleasure. Both are said to be different forms of knowledge; the former as the knowledge of what God is *not* and the latter as the knowledge of what He *is*. The negative form of knowledge constitutes the material world, and represents the use of dualistic logic; the dualism is created as a conflict of meanings. While living beings in duality are serving the negated form of God, this is not the same as service in the asserted form of God. In that specific sense, materialistic actions are not "service" even though it is "serving."

57 Desires are the mechanism by which we selectively filter parts of reality—the parts that we consider *undesirable*. I called these desires earlier as *theories* of nature, because a theory represents what is filtered from reality to create a limited picture of reality.

58 In Vedic philosophy, Impersonalism (the idea that there is an ultimate being, although that being is formless) arose in the 8th century in the philosophy of the great savant *Sankarāchārya* who produced an interpretation of *Vedanta Sutra* (the summarized conclusions of the Vedas) arguing that *Brahman* is real while this world is an illusion: there is only one observer that is segregated into many observers, and this separation is an illusion. The impersonalism of *Sankarāchārya* was a response to the inroads that Buddhism was making in Indian society around 8th century AD. Buddhism criticized the rampant ritualism prevalent in Indian society at that time, and thereby undermined the authority of the Vedas. *Sankarāchārya* revived Vedic philosophy, although he rejected rituals. His work led to a new interpretation of *Vedanta Sutra*, in which ultimate reality is conceived as being formless and impersonal.

59 Material objects are supposed to be modifications of space and time in modern physics. For instance, in relativity theory, the curvature of space-time creates the property of mass and therefore gravitation.

Acknowledgements

The inspiration behind this book lies in the writings of His Divine Grace A.C. Bhaktivedanta Swami Prabhupāda. He spoke about matter and science with as much ease as he did about soul and God. From his work I first came to believe that there is indeed an alternative way of looking at the material world, different from how it is described in modern science. I am deeply indebted to him in more ways than I can express here in a few words.

The book in the current form would have been impossible without the tireless efforts of Ciprian Begu. He has been my friend and partner in bringing this to life. He read through drafts, edited, did the layout and helped with the cover design. He has tried to teach me the nuances of English grammar, although I haven't been a good student. He figured out all the nits on publishing—something that I did not have the time, energy or the inclination for.

I would like to thank my long-time friend Rukesh Patel. His exuberance, encouragement, patient hearing and drive have helped me in innumerable ways. We have laughed so much together—often at our own stupidity and ignorance— that simply thinking of him makes me smile.

I would like to thank Prof. Pinaki Gupta-Bhaya, my professor and supervisor at IIT Kanpur, who showed me the beauty and excitement of science. From him I learnt that it was not important to know everything, as long as you know where to find it. Looking at his breadth and depth, I came to believe it was possible to step out of the parochial boundaries in science.

My immense gratitude also goes to my parents, who taught me honesty, hard work and simplicity. They gave me the values and upbringing for which I am deeply indebted. My heart also reaches out to my daughter, whose affection and kindness inspires me everyday to become a better person. My wife has been the leveling force in my life. She keeps me grounded to reality, distills complex problems into a succinct bottom-line, and manages the relationships that I would not.

And finally a big thank you to all my readers who have, over the years, written (and continue to write) showing a deep sense of excitement about these books. Their encouragement continues to instill confidence in me that there is a need for these types of books.

My Story

I have always had a great curiosity for the inner workings of nature, the mysteries of the human mind and the origins of the universe. This naturally drew me towards pure sciences. My father, a more practical man, saw this interest as pointless; he was upset when I chose a 5-year program in Chemistry at IIT Kanpur rather than one of the engineering programs, which stood to offer me a better career.

When I started at IIT Kanpur, I believed that my long-held curiosities about the inner workings of nature would be satisfied by an understanding of science. But as I scraped through the coursework and scoured through nearly every section of IIT's extensive library looking for answers, I found that, contrary to my belief, many fundamental and important questions in science remained unanswered. That prompted me to turn towards other departments—since chemistry pointed towards physics which in turn pointed towards mathematics, it seemed that the answers lay elsewhere. However, as I sat through courses offered by other departments—mathematics, physics and philosophy—my worst fears began to materialize: I realized that the problems required discarding many fundamental assumptions in science.

That started me on a journey into the search for alternatives, which has now been spanning 20 years. It was not uncommon in India for students in elite institutions to spend a lot of time discussing philosophy, although often in a tongue-in-cheek manner. My intentions were more serious.

I studied Western philosophy—both classical and modern—as well as Eastern ideas (such as Zen and Taoism) before turning towards Vedic philosophy. I was primarily interested in the nature of matter, the mind and the universe and only Vedic philosophy seemed to offer the kind of synthetic detail I was looking for. I suspected that if the ideas of reincarnation, soul and God in Vedic philosophy were connected to a different view of matter, mind and the universe, then I might actually find an alternative view that could solve the problems in modern science.

At the end of my 5 years at IIT Kanpur, I knew I wanted to pursue the alternative, but I wasn't quite clear how that could work.

I anticipated the pursuit of an alternative in mainstream academia to be very hard. The development of the alternative would frequently run into opposition, and would not fit into the publish-and-tenure practices. A reasonable understanding of ideas often requires longer discussions which may not fit into 3000-word papers. Alternatives often require stepping outside the parochial boundaries of a single field and the journals that accepted such multi-disciplinary articles did not exist at that time—they are more common now.

I therefore faced a difficult choice—pursue a mainstream academic career and defer the search for alternatives until I had established a reputation through conventional means, or pursue a non-academic career to finance my interest in academic alternatives. I chose to separate academics from profession. It was a risky proposition when I started, but in hindsight I think it has worked better than I initially imagined. This and my other books are byproducts of my search for answers to the problems in science, outside mainstream academia.

My career is that of a computer engineer and I have worked for over 17 years in multi-national corporations on telecommunications, wireless and networking technologies. I have co-authored 10 patents and presented at many conferences. I live in Bangalore, India, with my wife and 10-year old daughter.

Connect with Me

Has this book raised your interest? You can connect to my blog or get involved in discussions on www.ashishdalela.com. For any questions or comments please e-mail me at adalela@shabdapress.net.

Other Books by Ashish Dalela

Moral Materialism
A Semantic Theory of Ethical Naturalism

Modern science describes the physical effects of material causes, but not the moral consequences of conscious choices. Is nature merely a rational place, or is it also a moral place? The question of morality has always been important for economists, sociologists, political theorists, and lawmakers. However, it has had almost no impact on the understanding of material nature in science.

This book argues that the questions of morality can be connected to natural law in science when science is revised to describe nature as meaningful symbols rather than as meaningless things. The revision, of course, is entailed not just by issues of morality but also due to profound unsolved problems of incompleteness, indeterminism, irreversibility and incomputability in physics, mathematics, and computing theory. This book shows how the two kinds of problems are deeply connected.

The book argues that the lawfulness in nature is different from that presented in current science. Nature comprises not just *things* but also our *theories* about those things. The world of things is determined but the world of theories is not—our theories represent our free will, and the interaction between free will and matter now has a causal consequence in the evolution of scientific theories.

The moral consequences of free will represent the ideological evolution of the observer, and the correct theory represents the freedom from this evolution. Free will is therefore not the choice of arbitrary and false theories; free will is the choice of the correct theory. Once the correct theory is chosen, the observer is free of natural laws, since all phenomena are consistent with the correct theory.

Signs of Life
A Semantic Critique of Evolutionary Theory

This book challenges the fundamental ideas in the Neo-Darwinian theory of evolution from the perspective of mathematics, physics, computing, game theory, and non-linear dynamics.

It argues that the key ideas underlying evolution—random mutation and natural selection—are based on notions about matter, causality, space-time, and lawfulness, which were supposed true in Darwin's time, but have been unseated through 20th century developments in physics, mathematics, computing, game theory, and complex system theory. Evolution, however, continues in a relative time-warp, disregarding these developments, which, if considered, would alter our view of evolution.

The book illustrates why natural selection and random mutation are logically inconsistent together. Separately, they are incomplete to account for biological complexity. In other words, the theory of evolution is either inconsistent or incomplete.

The book, however, does not deny evolution. It presents a new theory of evolution that is modeled after the evolution of cultures, ideologies, societies, and civilizations. This is called *Semantic Evolution* and the book illustrates how this new model of evolution will emerge from the resolution of fundamental unsolved problems of meaning in mathematics, physics, and computing theory.

Quantum Meaning
A Semantic Interpretation of Quantum Theory

The problems of indeterminism, uncertainty and statistics in quantum theory are legend and have spawned a wide-variety of interpretations none too satisfactory. The key issue of dissatisfaction is the conflict between the microscopic and macroscopic worlds: How does a classically certain world emerge from a world of uncertainty and probability?

This book presents a Semantic Interpretation of Quantum Theory in which atomic objects are treated as symbols of meaning. The book shows that quantum problems of uncertainty, indeterminism and statistics arise when we try to describe meaningful symbols as objects without meaning.

A symbol is also an object, although an object is not necessarily a symbol. The same object can denote many meanings in different contexts, and if we reduce symbols to objects, it naturally results in incompleteness.

This book argues that the current quantum theory is not a final theory of reality. Rather, the theory can be replaced by a better theory in which objects are treated as symbols, because this approach is free of indeterminism and statistics.

The Semantic Interpretation makes it possible to formulate new laws of nature, which can be empirically confirmed. These laws will predict the order amongst symbols, similar to the notes in a musical composition or words in a book.

Gödel's Mistake
The Role of Meaning in Mathematics

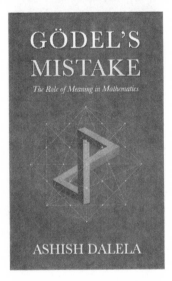

Mathematics is the queen of sciences but problems of incompleteness and incomputability in mathematics have raised serious questions about whether it can indeed be used to describe nature's entire splendor. Proofs that demonstrate the incompleteness and incomputability are respectively called Gödel's Incompleteness and Turing's Halting Problem.

This book connects Gödel's and Turing's theorems to the question of meaning and shows that these proofs rest on what philosophers call category mistakes. Ordinary language contains many categories - such as names, concepts, things, programs, algorithms, problems, etc. but mathematics and computing theory do not. A thing can denote many concepts and vice versa. Similarly, a program can solve many problems, and vice versa. A category mistake arises when we reduce one category to another, and this leads to logical paradoxes because these categories are not mutually reducible.

The book shows that the solution to category mistakes requires a new approach in which numbers are treated as types rather than quantities. This is called Type Number Theory (TNT) in the book. TNT requires a hierarchical theory of space and time, because it is through a hierarchical embedding that objects become symbols of meanings.

Hierarchical notions of space and time are well-known; for instance postal addresses and clock times are hierarchical. A formal theory of hierarchical space-time will also be a theory of symbols and will address problems of incomputability in computing and incompleteness in mathematics.

Sāṅkhya and Science
Applications of Vedic Philosophy to Modern Science

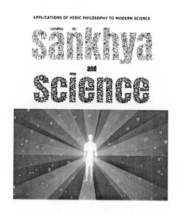

ASHISH DALELA

Since the time of Descartes, science has kept questions of mind and meaning outside science, and in recent times materialists aim to reduce mind and meaning to matter. Both approaches have failed. There are problems of meaning in mathematics, computing, physics, biology and neuroscience. A new view of nature is needed, one that integrates matter and meaning more directly.

The Vedic theory of matter—called Sāṅkhya—shows a path fruitful to the resolution of modern scientific problems. In Sāṅkhya, material objects are created when the mind transfers meanings or information into space-time. These objects are not meaningless things, but symbols with meanings.

The book shows how a symbolic view of nature can be used to solve the problems of incompleteness and indeterminism in atomic theory, chemistry, biology, mathematics and computing. In the process, the book builds a new foundation for science, based on a semantic or symbolic view of nature.

The book will be of interest to both scientists and philosophers, especially those looking to integrate mind and matter without stepping outside the rational-empirical approach to science.

Is the Apple Really Red?
10 Essays on Science and Religion

Conventional wisdom on science and religion says the former is based on experiment and reason, while the latter is based on faith and belief.

Is the Apple Really Red? discusses how the notions of soul, morality and afterlife in religion can be scientific. But for this to be possible, a new science that studies meanings instead of objects is needed.

The clash of ideologies between science and religion—this book argues—is based on an incorrect understanding of matter, disconnected from consciousness, and an incorrect notion of God, disconnected from matter, space and time.

A revision of the current views on religion and science is needed, not only to settle the conflict but also to deepen our understanding of matter (and its relation to consciousness) and God (and His relation to matter, space and time)

Written for the layperson, in 10 essays, the book delineates the Vedic view of matter, God, soul, morality, space and time. The author shows how the existence of the soul and God implies a new view of matter, space and time which is empirical and can be used to form new scientific theories.

Such theories will not only change our understanding of matter but will also change our outlook on religion. Readers interested in the science and religion debate will benefit significantly from the viewpoint described in Is the Apple Really Red?

Six Causes
The Vedic Theory of Creation

In Vedic philosophy, creation is modeled as the creative activity of consciousness. Six Causes shows us how the universe's creation can be understood based on insights about our own everyday creative activities.

The nature of material objects when they are created by consciousness is different than when they are independent of consciousness. Six Causes discusses this difference. Essentially, objects in the Vedic view are symbols of meaning originating in consciousness rather than meaningless things.

Different aspects of conscious experience—and the different roles they play in the creation—are called the six causes.

Presented in lay person's language, and written for those who don't have any background in Vedic philosophy, this book will allow you to truly understand the intricacies in Vedic texts.

In the process, you will also see many common misconceptions about Vedic philosophy being overturned through a deeper understanding of not just soul, God, reincarnation and karma but also matter, senses, mind, intelligence, ego and the unconscious.

Did You Like Uncommon Wisdom?

If you enjoyed this book or found it insightful I would be grateful if you would post a short review on Amazon. Your feedback will allow other readers to discover the book, and can help me improve the future editions. If you'd like to leave a review then go to the website below, click on the customer reviews and then write your own.

http://www.ashishdalela.com/review-amazon-uw

Find Out in Advance When My Next Book Is Out

I'm always working on the next book. You can get a publication alert by signing up to my mailing list on www.ashishdalela.com. Moreover, If you want to receive advance copies of my upcoming books for review, please let me know at adalela@shabdapress.net.

CPSIA information can be obtained at www.ICGtesting.com
Printed in the USA
LVOW08s1527110716

495866LV00004B/374/P